Indiana University Uralic and Altaic Series
Volume 144
Stephen Halkovic, Editor

Rudi Paul Lindner

NOMADS AND OTTOMANS IN MEDIEVAL ANATOLIA

Research Institute for Inner Asian Studies
Indiana University, Bloomington
1983

NOMADS AND OTTOMANS IN MEDIEVAL ANATOLIA

ISBN 0-933070-12-8
Library of Congress Catalog Card Number 82-061287

TO LIFE

Molly and Clare *Frank and Clare*

Contents

Preface

This is a book about pastoral nomads, the ways they met their needs, their threat to settled society, and how that society controlled them in the high Middle Ages. Since the following chapters describe nomad tribesmen whose careers ended almost half a millenium ago, the approach I have felt compelled to follow rests somewhere in the shifting no-man's-land between historical and anthropological studies. The fieldwork of ethnographers among traditional communities, those largely untouched by modernity, provides a framework for an historical interpretation of the activities of nomads in the past. At the same time, I do not think it possible to appreciate the behavior of modern pastoralists without some reference to the historical legacy which supports their inherited values and the patterns of their behavior, a legacy which only highlights the changes they are undergoing. The reader will have to judge the value and success of these assumptions and the resulting methods I have adopted in this book. The alternative method, as I see it, would have been to adopt the sedentary and therefore antagonistic assumptions of the medieval authors who composed many of the sources for this study: such an approach leads to chronicle, not history. One result of my chosen approach is that these chapters outline an essay on method rather than a full, conventional treatise.

The reader has a right to know what to expect from this book and where my treatment of the subject departs from other views of Anatolian society. The body of the book treats four themes. If I am at all successful, the reader should feel that these themes follow each other naturally, the discussion of one motif suggesting an exploration of the next.

We begin at the beginning, with the nomads (and others) who became the first Ottomans. It would be extremely difficult to discuss the impact of nomadism on early Ottoman history without touching upon some widely-discussed problems of the formation of the Ottoman enterprise. Since the family of Osman appeared as nomads on the Byzantine and Seljuk borders, the student might expect a reconstruction of early Ottoman history to reveal a tribal structure. However, the work of the late Paul Wittek, which defined the approaches of more than two generations of able scholars, firmly based all attempts to interpret early Ottoman history on the role of the Muslim "Holy War." The ideology of this Holy War became the keystone of modern history-writing on the subject. Now, some fifty years after Wittek's initial publication of this view, I trust the reader will allow a re-examination of it. I shall argue two points: first, that the actual behavior of the Ottomans does not fit an ideology of religious fervor, and second, that Wittek's texts stem from an *ex post facto* desire to fit the early Ottoman deeds squarely within an Islamic heritage. My approach has been to work from deeds rather than from later words, and I shall conclude that Wittek in fact uncovered an important phase in the intellectual history of the Ottomans, but not the pulse of their history.

Without the Holy War a tribal reconstruction of early Ottoman history becomes easy and is, I submit, demanded by the sources. The framework for such a reconstruction derives from anthropological studies of pastoral nomadic tribes rather than from the looser notions of tribalism that appear in earlier historical studies of medieval hordes or ancient *gentes.* Since shared political interests will be paramount in my study and genealogy almost entirely ignored, the reader who is unversed in recent anthropological literature will find some of my conclusions unexpected. I hope, therefore, that this study of the contribution of nomads to early Ottoman history will alert historians to the contribution which anthropological inquiries can make to a sharper, well-defined history of the growth of a tribe and its transformation into a more complex society.

Once Ottoman society emerged, with its former Byzantine farmers and townspeople, its emigré Muslim scholars, and its concern for the welfare of a settled society, nomads ceased to be a central, prized, element in Ottoman eyes. The nomads were no longer fellow tribesmen of a chief; they had become just a few of the many subjects of a sultan. Their fall in status, moreover, turned them from a military bulwark of the régime into a potential source of trouble. Their mobile, independent, occasionally predatory mode of life rendered them an unpredictable element which the sedentary Ottomans now had to control. Our second theme, therefore, is Ottoman restraint of nomads. I chose to look at Ottoman control first through lists of regulations by which the Ottomans administered their subjects. These regulations enumerate taxes, fines, methods of administration, and like subjects covering the Ottoman domains. This theme forms a chapter on the sections of these regulations that touched Anatolian nomads. Many scholars have worked with these regulations and discussed their genesis, meaning, and impact on settled society. I try to round out these studies with an attempt to estimate their impact on pastoral nomadic society in Anatolia. Studies of Anatolian pastoralism from the pens of anthropologists and studies of pre-modern animal husbandry allow us to draw an interesting outline of herd management, history, and profitability. Applying Ottoman regulations to nomadic herds will yield a good idea of the impact of Ottoman rule on Anatolian nomads: the size of the fiscal burden, the logic behind the regulations, a nomad's chance of bearing the burden, and the role of the regulations in forcing the settlement of nomads. Thus I bring a rough quantitative dimension to the study of medieval nomads. Limitations of time in Turkey, difficulties with research permits, and a refusal to allow me to photograph documents have restricted my coverage to the section of Anatolia supporting the largest population of pastoralists, but these limitations did allow a closer treatment of the materials I was fortunate enough to examine.

From regulations follows my third theme, watching the Ottomans in control of the nomads. My concern is not with occasional police actions or military campaigns to punish or pacify, but with the more gradual impact of Ottoman government over the years. This third chapter is drawn from Ottoman population, land, and tax cadasters. The value of these cadasters for demographic, toponymic, and economic history has been reflected in a growing number of studies. In this one, pastoral society joins the list. The Ottoman cadasters have an enormous potential for students of nomadic societies. In using them to outline the saga of a tribe I wish to bring this source, and some methods of handling it, to wider attention. We shall follow and gauge the Ottomans controlling and settling a large pastoral population. If there is a special advantage to this venture, it lies in the possibility of asking some of the questions that ethnographers ask in the field and in examining data which extend not simply over the year or so available to field workers, but over a generation or more.

Finally, given the Ottoman success in circumscribing tribal activities, we should look at the alternatives open to Anatolian nomads. This is my final theme. Among the alternatives were the Anatolian emirates which opposed the Ottomans. We shall look at the policies of the house of Karaman, which controlled much of central Anatolia until 1467. A local romance of Karaman will show us Ottoman opponents attempting to emulate the Ottomans' sedentary success, offering nomads no true alternative but a mere change of masters. The real alternative for Anatolian nomads was the millenarian revolt of the Safavid religious order in Persia, which roused Anatolian nomads to attempt the overthrow of the Ottomans in the name of a literal pastoral paradise. Thus we shall view the Ottoman-Safavid rivalry of the early sixteenth century from a slightly unconventional perspective, revealing it as a struggle not simply between two uncompromising visions of the true faith, but also as a re-enactment of the ancient contest between steppe and sown, herdsman and farmer, Abel and Cain. I remind the reader at the outset that Cain, the killer of Abel, was a settled farmer; Abel was the nomad.

It is my hope that these pages will provide a new and promising perspective on certain issues in the history of pastoral societies, a different account of the development of the early Ottoman enterprise, and, in the most general terms, a plea for the greater use of anthropological perspectives in the historical study of nomads. Although some of the material in this book will be familiar to specialized scholars, much of it will not be; and I trust that the approach I have taken will cause further discussion of the methods we use in our studies and of the points of view we have inherited.

Acknowledgements

A number of persons and institutions helped me to produce this book, and it is a pleasure to thank them here. Molly McGlannan Lindner, my wife, provided decisive support and wise perspective when they mattered most. Her good humor and inner strength have been my fondest companions for nearly a decade; may my gratitude to her be as constant as her faith in my work. I could not have done as good a book without her.

My parents, Frank Lindner and Clare Kalman Lindner, led an unwilling nomadic existence for much of this century, beginning in the Habsburg domains and ending in Stockton, California. They gave me a cosmopolitan outlook and cultural heritage, Viennese and valley, for which I would not trade anything. I thank my father and bless the memory of my mother.

To my masters at the University of California at Berkeley I owe affectionate thanks for my training as author and historian. John Smith taught me about nomads and gently shepherded me through my dissertation; Paul Alexander taught me to respect texts, and his approval of my work remains a special joy to me; Robert Brentano made me aware of the beauty and danger of the written word, and, perhaps more than any other influence, his seminar formed my view of history as literature. I also learned much from the teachings of Arthur Fisher, Ira Lapidus, and Bill Hickman. While I was in Istanbul the example of Professor Nejat Göyünç, who taught me to read the court scripts and welcomed me to the archives, inspired my work.

A number of scholars have read one or another incarnation of this book, in whole or in part, and I thank them for their comments and helpful suggestions: Professors Jonathan Marwil, Clive Foss, John Fine, Joseph Fletcher, Charles Tilly, Andreas Tietze, Hélène Ahrweiler, Halil Inalcik, and an "anonymous" Byzantinist. Professor V.L. Ménage was particularly helpful at a crucial point in the gestation of the work. None of these fine scholars is responsible, of course, for the defects in this book, which are all of my inspiration and devising.

I am grateful to the ladies and gentlemen of the following agencies who funded my training and research in medieval history: the University of

California, the U.S. Office of Education, the Foreign Area Fellowship Program, the American Research Institute in Turkey, the American Council of Learned Societies, the Social Science Research Council, and the National Endowment for the Humanities. The trustees for Harvard University made it possible for me to spend two years at Dumbarton Oaks, and I remain especially grateful to them for introducing me to my wife.

The University of Michigan Center for Near Eastern and North African Studies brought us to Ann Arbor, and its Directors, William D. Schorger and Ernest Abdel-Massih, as well as its staff, have made us welcome and supported my work. My thanks to them all. I would also like to thank the Horace H. Rackham Graduate School of the University of Michigan for a grant in support of the publication of this book, and Professor Halkovic for accepting it into the Indiana series. Steve Heydemann did a graceful job of editing my text for the printer.

I shall always remain grateful to the numerous librarians, here and abroad, who have cheerfully filled my arcane requests over the years. In particular I recall with affection the gentle treatment I received in Turkey from librarians, archivists, and scholars during times far more trying to them than to us. I worked in Turkey during parts of 1969, 1970, 1971, and briefly in 1978. I would like to thank the Turkish authorities for allowing me to perform research during those visits, although I regret the restrictions and occasional refusals that the authorities felt themselves forced to impose. I shall not soon forget the deterioration that some documents suffered between my 1969 and 1978 visits, and I fervently hope that some way will be found to hasten the preservation of Turkey's historical heritage and to reveal that heritage to a wider audience.

Soon after we returned from Istanbul in 1978, our daughter Clare Joan was born. She also has played a role in the appearance of this volume. Had I not moved from medieval texts to reading her bedtime stories, had I not turned from her toys to my cadasters, I do not think that I should have sufficiently appreciated the complex and shifting nature of the men and women whose long-lost stories I try to recapitulate here. So this is Clare's book too, and I thank her for it.

Abbreviations

Anon. Chron.	*Die altosmanischen anonymen Chroniken, in Text und Übersetzung herausgegeben von Dr. Friedrich Giese. Teil I: Text und Variantenverzeichnis.* Breslau, 1922.
APZ	*Die altosmanische Chronik des Aşikpaşazade, herausgegeben von Friedrich Giese.* Leipzig, 1929.
Arnakis	George G. Arnakis, *Hoi Protoi Othomanoi.* Athens, 1947: Texte und Forschungen zur Byzantinisch-neugriechischen Philologie, 41.
Barkan	Ömer Lutfi Barkan, *XV ve XVI inci asırlarda Osmanlı imparatorluğunda zirai ekonominin hukuki ve mali esasları, I, kanunlar.* Istanbul, 1943.
Barth, *Nomads*	Fredrik Barth, *Nomads of South Persia.* Oslo, 1961.
IBS	Irène Beldiceanu - Steinherr, *Recherches sur les actes des règnes des sultans Osman, Orkhan et Murad I.* Munich, 1967.
Laiou, *Cpl.*	Angeliki E. Laiou, *Constantinople and the Latins: the Foreign Policy of Andronicus II, 1282-1326.* Cambridge, 1972.
Neşri	*Ğihannüma, die altosmanische Chronik des Mevlana Mehemmed Neschri, Band I: Einleitung und Text des Cod. Menzel,* hrsg. von Franz Taeschner. Leipzig, 1951.
Pach.	*Georgii Pachymeris de Michaele et Andronico Palaeologis libri tredecim,* ed. I. Bekker. 2 vols., Bonn, 1835: Corpus scriptorum historiae Byzantinae.

Ruhi	Berlin, Staatsbibliothek. MS Or. Qu. 821.
SHK	M.F. Ugur and M. Koman, eds., *Şikari'nin Karamanoğulları tarihi.* Konya, 1946.
TT	Istanbul, Başvekalet Arşivi, Tapu ve Tahrir collection (followed by cadaster number).
Vryonis, *Decline*	Speros Vryonis, Jr., *The Decline of Medieval Hellenism in Asia Minor and the Process of Islamization from the Eleventh through the Fifteenth Century.* Los Angeles, 1971.

Chapter One:

The Tent of Osman, The House of Osman

Our conventional image of an Ottoman owes much to Gentile Bellini's portrait of Mehmet the Conqueror. In 1479, nearing the end of his reign, Mehmet invited Bellini to paint a European view of the sultan. Adding crowns, Latin inscriptions, an arch, and a jeweled textile, later artists only reinforced Mehmet's purpose. The Conqueror, whose troops were investing Otranto, had come a long way, and he was looking to the future rather than back to the past.

There is little in Bellini's Mehmet to remind the viewer that the earliest Ottomans were pastoral nomads. The distance from the felt tent to Bellini's canvas is too great for a passerby, seeing the one, to catch sight of the other in the same field of view. As, however, the subject of this essay is Anatolian nomadism in old Ottoman times, it is necessary for us to understand how the ruling Ottomans changed from nomadic shepherds to the sedentary rulers of a vast bureaucratic enterprise. The purpose of this chapter is to outline and explain that transformation in the late thirteenth and early fourteenth centuries.

At the outset it will be convenient to describe the path which this chapter's argument follows. The most important element in the argument—the leitmotif of the essay, in fact—has to do with the nature and limits of the tribe as a device for organizing society. Moreover, since the tribe will be defined as an inclusive rather than as an exclusive body, we will have to start with a discussion of the view that an exclusive or adversary ideology—the Holy War (jihad or ghaza) and its warriors (ghazis)—dominated early Ottoman history. After a consideration of this view the following pages will unfold the story of the early Ottomans in their Byzantine, Seljuk, and Mongol environment. I shall not tell all of that story, nor shall I dwell on its parts at equal length. It is my object to place before the reader only those aspects of old Ottoman history which bear directly upon the nomadic, pastoral, and tribal themes of this book. As most Ottoman histories view their subject from the perspective of its later cultural complexity and sophistication, this treatment will shed a different light on our view of Ottoman origins. Having given a selective chronological treatment of this era, we will move to a more analytic review. We will view the early Ottoman transformation through those categories which are most important to a student of nomads: How did the early Ottomans make their living, that is, how did they pass from pastoralism and predation to agriculture and settled commerce? Second, how did they fight—why and how did mounted archery give way to infantry and cavalry tactics? Finally, what was the political import of these developments? What happened to the Ottoman tribe?

Having examined the careers of Osman and his son Orkhan from a nomad's perspective, and having analyzed the transformation of their enterprise from the economic, military, and political point of view, we may conclude with a consideration of the ideology which emerged and became dominant at the Ottoman court in the fifteenth century. Possessed of a romantic view of their nomadic origins, the Ottomans nonetheless kept the nomads of their own day out of the way and well out of their image of the perfect world. While a ceremonial herd of sheep grazed near Bursa as a memento of the past, the Ottoman present and future in cosmopolitan Istanbul was starkly different, as a closing text will demonstrate.[1]

* * * *

There is some significance for the purposes of this essay in the famous theory that zeal for the Holy War powered early Ottoman history. First, in whole or in part, this theory plays a major role in modern treatments of Ottoman history. Scholars have publicly or privately adjusted or altered the theory, added additional factors or redefined the vocabulary, but its simplicity, directness, and elegance render it as attractive today as it was over a generation ago when Professor Paul Wittek first formulated it. No treatment of old Ottoman history can avoid Wittek's theory. There is, in addition, a second reason for an essay on nomadic history to begin with the Holy War. As I shall demonstrate, the tribe was a political organism whose membership was defined by shared interests (and, in medieval Eurasia, subordination to a chief). In thirteenth-century Bithynia the pool from which a tribe could form and grow consisted, for all practical purposes, of Byzantines and Turks, Greek-speaking Christians and Turkish-speaking nomads. If fervor for the Holy War played an important role in this frontier area, then our pool would clearly exclude Byzantines, for they would have become the detested enemy of the faithful. Since this essay will, later on, develop the notion of an early Ottoman tribe embracing both Byzantines and Turks under Osman's leadership, we must begin with an attempt to decide just how important the Holy War was in Osman's time. I shall try to convince the reader that it was unimportant.

Although traces of Wittek's theory appear in his work as early as 1925, it will be most convenient to review his argument on the basis of his English summation, a series of London lectures published in 1938.[2] Wittek began with a demolition of the tribal genealogies of the Ottomans, and we shall return to his discussion of them shortly. He then drew the conclusion that without a proven genealogy there could have been no Ottoman tribe. Hence, tribalism was not a factor in early Ottoman history. How, then, had the Ottomans risen to power? In examining the early Ottoman chronicles, and in particular the rhymed chronicle of Ahmedi (d. 1412-13), he recognized the leitmotif, or in Ahmedi's case the solo strain, of the Holy War. But Ahmedi's treatment of the Ottomans was composed, at the earliest, in 1390; could there be earlier literary evidence for this zeal? Wittek soon came to recognize the significance, for his case, of an Arabic inscription, clearly dated 1337, now in the citadel of Bursa. In part the text reads: "The great and magnificent emir, the warrior of the Holy War, . . . Sultan of the ghazis, ghazi son of ghazi, hero of the world and of the faith . . . Orkhan son of Osman."[3] This precisely dated inscription brought the vocabulary of the Holy War much closer to the foundation of the Ottoman enterprise. Wittek now concluded that this text clinched his argument that the impact of the Holy War caused the Ottoman unity and expansion: "From the first appearance of the Ottomans, the principal factor in this political tradition was the struggle against their Christian neighbors . . . "[4] The ghaza spirit came to have an almost physical reality. Formation of a state on that ideal, which served as "the motive force" of such a state, made the expansion of the emirate "only a necessary consequence and a matter of time."[5] Indeed, one demonstration of the strength of the ghaza as a historical force had occurred in his own lifetime, when the Ottomans abandoned the ghaza by allying themselves with their traditional Habsburg enemies in World War I: "By this alliance both the empire of Austria and Turkey broke with their most essential traditions and thus showed that they had outlived themselves. It is not surprising, that both empires failed the test of the Great War and disappeared for ever."[6]

Before we embark on a discussion of Wittek's thesis and its proof from the medieval sources, let us set it within its own framework: German intellectual life of the Weimar years. Most scholars have glossed over the exuberance of tone and animation of spirit which adorn Wittek's claims for the role of the ghaza (not to mention the penalty for abandoning it), but we may keep in mind that his words accord well with certain popular notions during the interwar years: first, that ideas have a special life of their own, and second, that they are the direct motivation and fuel for action. These assumptions of Wittek's history-writing make plain his debt to *The Protestant Ethic and the Spirit of Capitalism.* Weber's influence on the scholars of the interregnum was great, and the *Geistesgeschichte* which those years spawned must have appealed greatly to a scholar and textual critic of Wittek's caliber.[7] As far as I am able to tell, Wittek never questioned these assumptions about history as the play of ideas.

In contrast to Wittek's emphasis on ideas and the claims of propaganda, I propose to examine the behavior of the early Ottomans. Rather than rely solely upon the summary claims of the authors, let us look at their accounts of early Ottoman acts and then decide whether that story reflects the ideology of the Holy War. It seems to me that only an examination of Ottoman deeds will help us decide whether such a text as the 1337 inscription reflects the Holy War as the true stimulus behind early Ottoman history, or rather a justification which later viewers used to glorify and romanticize the pragmatism of Osman and Orkhan.[8]

We begin with the goal of early Ottoman conquest. More frequently than one might expect of Holy Warriors who strive to expand the lands of Islam and to shrink the influence of the infidel, Ottoman enmity and action was directed against neighboring Muslims. One of the earliest, if not indisputably the first, of Ottoman conquests was the citadel of Karacahisar, which looms above the southwestern suburbs of Eskişehir. The Ottoman chronicles imply that the lord of Karacahisar was Christian, but such a claim is false. Eskişehir, the nearby site of Dorylaeum, Karacahisar, and the southwesterly city of Kütahya/Cotyaeum, all had been in Muslim hands for over a century before the Ottomans arrived on the scene.[9] Since Karacahisar defends the low road from Eskişehir to Kütahya it is reasonable to suppose that the Ottomans captured it from the neighboring Muslim emirs of Germiyan, rulers of Kütahya and pretenders to overlordship of the frontier emirates. There were in any case no Christian frontier lords anywhere near Karacahisar in the last quarter of the thirteenth century.

Such a reconstruction of the story of the fall of Karacahisar helps to explain the long-standing enmity between Germiyan and the Ottomans. Warfare and quarreling between the emirs of the two powers began no later than the youth of Osman and ended only with Ottoman acquisition of the emirate late in the fourteenth century. Ottoman expansion at the expense of Muslims was, however, not limited to Germiyan. During the 1320s and 1330s the Ottomans swallowed up their western neighbor, the emirate of Karası. To the north, the last years of Osman's reign and the first decade of Orkhan's rule saw Ottoman expansion down the Sakarya/Sangarius as far as the Black Sea. These campaigns were against Muslim, not Christian beys.[10] It is important, then, to bear in mind that while the early Ottomans did conquer Byzantine lands and towns, they were also engaged in campaigns of conquest against their Muslim neighbors. It was no accident that the Ottomans spread their rule over Muslim Anatolia in step with their expansion into the Christian Balkans.

In addition to conquering infidel lands, one of the presumed duties of the ghazi was coaxing the inhabitants of those lands to convert to Islam. Neither Osman nor Orkhan, on the other hand, seem to have placed much emphasis on converting their Christian neighbors. At least as late as 1340, Christians could serve as judges in Ottoman Bithynia.[11] In 1354, late in Orkhan's reign, a Byzantine observer commented that there was no persecution of Christians or pressure to convert to Islam in the Ottoman domains. Further, conversion was not a condition for advancement to relatively high office, as the example of two Christians demonstrated. There was considerable Turkish interest in conciliation and mutual adaptability. As one of the Muslims put it, "The time will come when we will be in accord with each other." These are words of moderation, not of zeal.[12]

If fact, early Ottoman conquest seems associated more with cooperation than with coercion. One of our most valuable sources for this period is the chronicle of Aşıkpaşazade, which contains material from mid-fourteenth century Bithynian witnesses.[13] We learn that the young Osman liked to hunt in remote areas. A certain Köse Mihal, the Christian lord of Harman Kaya, always accompanied him. Our source calls Köse Mihal a ghazi and states that "Most of these ghazis' attendants were Christians from Harman Kaya."[14] It is important to note that Köse Mihal did become a Muslim, but much later. Here we must conclude that if Mihal had really been a ghazi, the term must have been a label in no sense describing the character and behavior of a Muslim Holy Warrior. While Mihal is perhaps the most famous "Christian ghazi" his story is only the most dramatic example of Ottoman-Byzantine cooperation in the early days: dramatic because it is ultimately a story of military cooperation. There are other, more common, stories of cooperation: exchanges, trade, and protection against other Muslims, and these will be related in the course of the narrative. The rationale for this co-existence appears in a "conversation" between Osman and his brother Gündüz. Osman inquired of Gündüz the best way to subdue the land and raise an army. In response to his brother's suggestion that they simply lay waste the entire area, Osman pointed out that the villages and towns would cease to prosper. He thought it better for the long run to gain their Christian neighbors' confidence.[15] Although the conversation is probably no more accurate a transcription than the speeches of Thucydides, the supposed dialogue neatly covers the alternatives that were open to the new Turkish immigrants, and it is a sensible gloss explaining the ties with Köse Mihal and the trade between Byzantine and Turk.

The co-existence which Osman urged on his brother may explain a singular fact which defenders of the Holy War ideology must puzzle over: this "motive force" left so little impress on the mind of the enemy that no Byzantine text composed in the early Ottoman period mentions the ghaza or ghazis.[16] Three of the Byzantine Short Chronicles refer to Murad I as Murad Ghazi, but all three belong to a family of chronicles composed after 1512. One chronicle refers to Osman as Osman Ghazi, but it stems from a text of 1540.[17] When chroniclers of the stature of the Byzantines George Pachymeres, John Cantacuzenus, and Nicetas Gregoras know nothing of such a zeal animating their enemies, it is reasonable to doubt its existence.

My final ground for questioning the Wittek ghaza theory here reflects the religious practices of the early Ottomans. It seems reasonable to suppose that religious zeal would find some sort of reflection in religious practice; but if so, the fact that the early Ottomans allowed heterodoxy freedom in their midst argues against their commitment to an untarnished Islam. The Anonymous Chronicles preserve the folk-tale of the conversion, through the magic of a dervish's conjurings, of a village near Yalova, on the south shore of the Marmora.[18] The acts and impact of such a man reveal an atmosphere of tolerance and latitude, of symbiosis rather than separation. Further, there is evidence that the Ottomans (and others) may have practiced ritual human sacrifice and mummification in the fourteenth century.[19]. Osman's nephew Aydoğdu fell in battle at Koyunhisar. Ceremonies at his grave were sure to cure fever-stricken men and colicky horses.[20] Saruyatı, one of Osman's brothers, died in battle. A pine tree grew on the spot where he fell, and from time to time a mysterious flame spouted from its top.[21] The mixture of mystery and magic in these accounts tempts us to see only the first stirrings of Muslim influence upon the warriors of Osman.

At this point the reader may wish to object: must we require Holy Warriors to be observant believers? What of the "folk Islam" which, although more lenient, is still a profoundly religious experience? I would respond that popular folk religious practices are usually marked by syncretism and latitudinarianism, not by single-minded and exclusive zeal. The role of popular religious practices is to accommodate, not to repel, and their appeal is to crowds more than to isolated puritans. If we are to view the Ottomans as missionary zealots in a religious cause, the episodes in the preceding paragraph would seem to mark them as crusaders for Shamanism rather than for Islam.[22]

The constellation of events and evidence in these last few paragraphs should have left the clear impression that the Holy War played no role in early Ottoman history, despite the later claims of Muslim propagandists. Economic and social symbiosis, political cosmopolitanism, and religious syncretism all combined to exclude the ghaza as an effective influence on the early Ottomans. To deny the ghaza a role in this period is, however, simply to raise another question. How, then, did this terminology and titulature come to permeate the Ottoman tradition? Even more to the point, what gave rise to the 1337 inscription? We have a hint to the answer in a passing remark of the Arab chronicler Ibn Hajar al-Asqalani (d. 1449), who states that it was in Orkhan's time that Muslim scholars began to gather in the Ottoman domains.

Şukrullah, an Ottoman chronicler whose source is shared by Ahmedi, makes a parallel statement.[23] Orkhan had need of the expertise of such men, for after the surrender of the towns of Byzantine Bithynia he had to secure the organization of a settled administration. Since, as we shall soon see, the administrative heedlessness and occasional oppression of the Byzantine rulers Michael VIII and Andronicus II had failed to rally the Bithynians of the previous generation, Orkhan had to seek elsewhere for a model and for bureaucratic manpower.[24] As they did elsewhere, the schoolmen provided the basis for the first Ottoman bureaucracy. In the earliest days the most visible representatives of Islam were dervishes, but soon thereafter more orthodox figures emigrated from the east in order to serve, and be well served by, the Ottomans.[25] In order to understand why the schoolmen left the interior of Anatolia for the western frontiers, we must recall that the 1320s and 1330s were decades of insecurity and disquiet on the plateau, as the Mongol governors quarrelled, fought among themselves, and rebelled against the central government.[26] Patronage of religion and its representatives suffered from the diversion of resources to civil war; the scholars sought employment elsewhere, wherever a need for their skills (or at least their administrative skills) appeared. Orkhan afforded protection and power to these men at a time when the Mongol authority was insecure and parsimonious.[27] The arrival of the schoolmen in numbers thus provided the Ottomans with a sedentary tradition and a pool of capable, literate men to staff an administration.

The men of religion had other benefits to bestow on their new benefactors, and to the secure revenues accruing from the settled administration of the Ottoman future they added the gift of an orthodox heroic past. Looking at the frontier life of Osman's youth, they saw not nomad pragmatists but clever Holy Warriors. Religious zeal, to them, was obviously a worthier motivation for the creation of the Ottoman enterprise, an enterprise they were busily fitting into a classical administrative mould. After all, the schoolmen professionally could never be supporters of a declassé pastoralism. Thus, in my mind, the significance of the 1337 inscription lies not in its evidence of an early Ottoman mind but in its revelation of the transformation and encapsulation of that mind in a safe, orthodox setting. The inscription's ideological content, its *ex post facto* purification of early Ottoman deeds, speak more of later propaganda than of early history.[28]

The Bursa inscription of 1337 is our first evidence of an important change in Ottoman society, one of many which spanned the first half of the fourteenth century. The ghaza became a useful convention for interpreting, to orthodox and sedentary audiences, the formative years of the dynasty. The fifteenth-century chronicles, beginning with Ahmedi, did their best to fit the recalled facts of Ottoman history to this ideological justification. It made sense to these later Ottomans to do so; it is, however, not incumbent upon us to continue in that task. The Holy War should, instead, take a rightful and honored place in Ottoman intellectual history.

* * * *

Up to this point, the discussion of Wittek's work has been critical, for the Holy War must be proven a negligible factor in the historical events of early Ottoman history if the tribe is to be given credit as an organizing factor in that history. An exclusive doctrine such as the ghaza, and an inclusive social organization such as the tribe, may not both work and grow in a multi-cultural environment at the same time. I have therefore contended that Wittek placed far too much emphasis on the Holy War as a historical actor. It is only fitting and proper for me to point out here how Wittek also took the decisive step towards demonstrating that the early Ottomans were tribally organized.

Let us recall that Wittek devoted much space to a discussion of the dynastic genealogies contained in almost all the Ottoman chronicles. He was concerned with refuting the notion, which he erroneously ascribed to the dean of Turkish historians, Fuad Köprülü, that because the Ottomans appeared to be descended from the premier Kayı clan of the old Oğuz tribe, their prestige as representatives of this clan rendered them the natural heirs to leadership of the Anatolian Turks. In a precise, restrained manner Wittek demonstrated that the Ottoman "tribal" genealogies are not only incompatible with one another but also that they all stem from the fifteenth century.[29] This analysis led Wittek to the conclusion that tribal links forged in the fifteenth century could not have existed in the thirteenth. In fact, no matter how hard one were to try, the sources simply did not allow the recovery of a family tree linking the antecedents of Osman to the Kayı of the Oğuz tribe. Without a proven genealogy, or even without evidence of sufficient care to produce a single genealogy to be presented by all the court chroniclers, there obviously could be no tribe; thus, the tribe was not a factor in early Ottoman history.

Wittek's demolition of the genealogies was a masterful display of textual criticism, an art in which he was pre-eminent. The conclusions that he drew, however, rested upon an assumption common among scholars of his day (including Köprülü), that a tribe is a patrilineal descent group, a clan whose members all share blood ties. He could not have known that later developments in anthropology would undermine this assumption. Neither actual nomadic tribes nor clans admit of such a neat definition. What is a clan? To begin with, the basic unit of pastoral nomadism is the family, "an autonomous unit of production and consumption." The actual organization of nomadic and pastoral activity requires cooperation in selecting personnel for herding, in composing a herd of optimal size for management, and in the efficient performance of the daily routine. Cooperation and self-protection necessitate the creation of (temporary) residence groups, such as camps, and the perpetuation of lineages composed of real and fictitious relations, clans. Shared membership in a clan removes a potential source of suspicion and makes possible the cooperation which nomadism imposes on the family. The ideology which comfortably expresses this process resides in an idiom of kinship, but the reality is harsher, and ability or shared interest count for as much as blood.[30] As for the tribe itself, clans may contribute to its membership, and its members may claim that they are all related, each to the others, but here membership is actually the result of a political choice to follow, or continue in the next generation to follow, the leadership of a particular chief in response to external pressures. Turkish tribes in the Near East and in Inner Asia were pragmatic, often temporary political groupings around a successful chief. Each tribesman may boast a genealogy demonstrating his connection with the other tribesmen: these genealogies, however, tend to display their common ancestors at some great distance up the genealogical tree. Characteristically, such genealogies contain very vague notions about the generations intervening between the common ancestor at the apex and, say, the great-grandparents of the tribesman in question. This vagueness about the middle generations, which Wittek took to be proof that the early Ottomans were not tribal, is the necessary mechanism allowing new members to graft themselves onto the kinship tree of tribal ideology. In any tribe whose membership waxes and wanes with success or failure in leadership, the hunt, or finding pasture, the tribal genealogy is a necessary fiction, a sort of political charter. In brief, then, the clan results from the nomad's social response to the conditions of a harsh and often insecure life; the tribe is his political response to external pressures. Both ideas find expression in terms of blood lines, but both in practice can and do ignore those constraints. Thus, while Wittek proved that the Ottomans were not a blood-linked clan, his revelation of the inconsistencies in their genealogies was in fact the major step in a demonstration that their social organization was in fact tribal. That the state of anthropological investigation during his early years had not yet reached as far as it later would can in no way be a reproach to Wittek.

* * * *

It is now time to watch the tribal and nomadic aspects of the Ottomans' early days unfold. Let me again remind the reader that what follows is not, nor is it intended to be, a chronological review of early Ottoman history; rather, it is an attempt to highlight certain aspects of that history which bear upon the history of nomadism and of nomadic tribes in their Anatolian setting. We shall look at those aspects of Ottoman history from the time when the

Mongols entered the eastern sections of Anatolia up to the time when, in my opinion, the transformation of the Ottoman enterprise from a tribe to something like a state was a virtual certainty.

The Seljuk victory over the Byzantine army at Manzikert, near Lake Van, in 1071 destroyed the last barrier against a land rush by Turkish nomads. The geography of western Anatolia rendered it an especially inviting destination for nomads over the next few centuries. It is a land of valleys and rivers flowing down to the sea. Separating these river valleys are high ridges, western extensions of the central Anatolian plateau. The river valleys are fertile and offer prosperous opportunities for cultivators. The finger-like ridges channel access to the valleys from the plateau and abound in nutritious summer pastures. To the nomads such a combination was irresistible. The lowland valleys contained rich possibilities for predation as well as snow-free, fertile winter pasture. The highlands and ridges contained excellent summer pasture and their broken terrain made them difficult for the less-mobile Byzantine armies and castle lords to penetrate or to defend.[31]

The Byzantines could not prevent the nomad immigration. In the summer, when their armies went on campaign, the nomads were in the rough terrain of their highland summer pastures. They were difficult to catch, thanks to their light equipment and remount reserve of horses, and they easily avoided the few Byzantine fortresses. In the winter the Byzantine troops did not campaign, and so the river valleys were open to the nomads' descent.[32] The Byzantine emperors complained that the Seljuk sultans were fostering these nomadic movements, and they treated this assumed breach of agreements as grounds for war. The Byzantines did not realize that the Seljuks also could not control the pastoralists' search for pasture, always more suitable below the plateau and across the frontier zone.[33] After the Seljuk victory over Manuel I Comnenus at Myriocephalon in 1176, Byzantine efforts to maintain a foothold on the edge of the plateau were limited to occasional summer forays in the north and south. The hope was to keep the Turks above the river valleys, especially those of the Gediz/Hermus and Menderes/Maeander. To do this, however, winter campaigns would have been necessary. In Bithynia, the approaches to the lower Sakarya/Sangarius and the main road down from the plateau via Bozüyük/Lamunia were poorly defended. Nomads regularly wintered on the Sarı Su/Bathys, a tributary of the Sakarya, and in the spring of 1198 Alexius III Angelus led troops from Iznik/Nicaea and Bursa in a vain attempt to prevent their raiding the upper reaches of the river and descending from the plateau.[34] The plains here average 1000 meters in elevation and were long a favored summer grazing area, or *yaylak,* for pastoral nomads. In the 1830s Hamilton, a careful observer, noted the frequency of their camps on the river banks and throughout the Haymana, the plain southwest of Ankara.[35] When the sons of Kilij Arslan II, the victor of Myriocephalon, partitioned his legacy, Mesud received Eskişehir, Ankara, and points west, along with lands in Paphlagonia and the Pontus. The Turks now had a foothold in Bithynia.[36]

The advance of the nomads and their activities, pastoralism and predation, were based on economic and ecological need. Sheep and goat husbandry in the valleys was much warmer and safer in winter than weathering the uncertain frosts of plateau elevations. In order to maximize grazing opportunities and minimize herd losses, good herding strategy led to the infiltration of the better, if Byzantine, farmland for pasture. As a Greek author put it, "... because of grassy meadows the whole race invades the borders of the Romans."[37] The predation of which the Byzantines complained had little to do with political or religious animosities. Predatory acts are a natural accompaniment to nomadic life. Cereals, manufactures, and the work of skilled artisans, all are difficult for pastoralists to produce by themselves. Pastoralism is not a self-sufficient mode of adaptation. Many commodities must be gotten from settled society through one form of economic exchange or another. Predation is a normal and inexpensive means for nomads to obtain necessities or desired goods which the pastoral round does not produce. It became an exceptionally inexpensive means when Byzantine defenses were weak. As such, predation may be viewed as the logical extension of the hunt.[38]

The Fourth Crusade, the loss of Constantinople, and the foundation of the Latin Empire constrained the Byzantines to devote considerable energy to Anatolia and the eastern extremities of their former state. The Lascarid emperors, first at Nicaea, then (for the remainder of their Anatolian exile) at Nif/Nymphaeum in the southwest, attended to the economic, military, and physical reconstruction of west Anatolia below the plateau in order to finance their European campaigns and threats against Constantinople. They meant to revive Anatolia, but for the sake of Constantinople. They wanted Anatolia to prosper, but only so they could leave it.[39]

The agricultural prosperity achieved during the half-century of Lascarid rule centered in the south, in the valleys of the Gediz and Menderes rivers. The silk production of Nicaea was Bithynia's major contribution.[40] John III Ducas Vatatzes (1222-1254) fostered a more intensive exploitation of farm resources in the lands surrounding Manisa/Magnesia. His egg ranch is perhaps best known for the crown its profits bought. During his reign, the state obtained hard currency by selling commodities to the Seljuk Turks for gold and luxury goods.[41] At the same time, the gold content in the coinage fell to sixteen carats.[42] The revenues in gold were spent on the objects of Lascarid foreign policy rather than for bolstering the fineness of the coinage.

The Lascarid military might rested on the shoulders of two categories of men: holders of *pronoiai* or "fiefs" and border guards, *akritai.* Information concerning the *pronoiai* derives largely from the Lembiotissa monastic documents, which only cover the neighborhood of Izmir. While there is no surviving record of *pronoiai* in Bithynia, although some were presumably granted there, the military organization of the south, around Izmir, is much clearer. Theodore I Lascaris confiscated lands of the Latin-held Constantinopolitan churches and transformed them into *pronoiai* for his high officials. These large holdings were to produce incomes appropriate to the rank and responsibilities of his councillors.[43] Later, John III created *pronoiai* of more modest extent, termed *stratiotikai pronoiai,* whose beneficiaries owed military service. These small holdings supplied manpower for a large army.[44] For example, Vatatzes granted some of these farms in Phrygia to Cumans from Europe.[45] Decentralization and thrift were essential features of this extension of the *pronoiai.* The larger grants, to the aristocracy, bore rights of inheritance. *Pronoiars* dealt directly with the peasants who owed them dues *epiteleia)* and services *(angareia, douleia).* The *pronoiars* appointed managers for their new lands in place of the imperial officials. While imperial revenues diminished, administrative expenses dropped accordingly.[46]

The *akritai* or frontier warriors dotted border stations along the ridges from the south up into Bithynia. Some of their leaders held imperial diplomas and *pronoiai.* The *akritai* were exempt from taxation and enjoyed full disposition of booty won in raids on the plateau. Little is certain about these borderers. They were left to fend for themselves in the expectation that they would keep the Seljuks away, or, at least, occupied defending their own settlements. Unfortunately, the loyalty of the *akritai* was assumed, not earned. Freebooters, they found no difficulty in switching sides when more promising opportunities beckoned.[47]

The Nicene military did a creditable job of preserving order inside the borders. The success of the army against the Latins and other Byzantine competitors in Europe implies that the extension of *pronoia* grants secured its purpose. There were no complaints against the *akritai.* The eastern front calmed down. When the Seljuks campaigned, they chose to annex the routes leading due north and south rather than to contend with the Lascarids for the Aegean littoral. So for much of the Nicene era, Seljuk expansion was limited to the north and south coasts (especially Cilicia), while after the Mongols imposed their protectorate in 1243, the Seljuks were in no condition to expand at all. Taking quick advantage of this weakness, independent tribal turbulence was directed against the Seljuks much more than against the periphery of the plateau. Good examples are the early raids of the house of Karaman on the Seljuk capital, Konya/Iconium. In short, Lascarid Anatolia lived at peace.

Besides undertaking economic and military measures to strengthen their state, the Lascarids were active in monumental reconstruction. Bithynian evidence comes from the reports of the German excavations in Nicaea. Theodore I Lascaris constructed an outer wall for the city just beyond the main walls, and he repaired the broken sections of the main walls. Vatatzes continued work on the outer wall.[48] Within the walls, new buildings included a hospital, an elementary school, the patriarchal residence (although the emperors had moved to Nymphaeum, the patriarchs remained in Nicaea), a church in honor of St. Anthony (a local martyr), and perhaps a church dedicated to the archangel Michael.[49] An inscription also states that Theodore I refortified Bursa. Excavations and literary monuments confirm similar building, as well as artistic, programs elsewhere in the state.[50]

Reduced to western Anatolia, the Lascarid enterprise sought renovation and recovery. It is difficult to judge how deep the broad measures of two generations reached.[51] Certainly most of the monuments bearing Nicene additions preserve little trace of such upkeep during the preceding centuries. From the Persian invasions of the seventh century up to the Lascarids' resuscitation, there were no such building programs in the area.[52] The majority of the monuments restored during those centuries are Roman or late antique.

The point of this excursus on the Lascarid era is to demonstrate that two generations of Anatolian Byzantines had come to expect good government and economic stability from their rulers. For those born in the 1240s and 1250s, every expectation of continuing and improving upon their parents' prosperity seemed justified. The denial of their expectations, of what they considered to be no more than their just due and the traditional order, would damage their loyalties much more than it would the loyalties of those who had lived through harder times. And yet the reigns of Michael VIII and Andronicus II dashed just those comfortable illusions of the generation born during the 1240s. I contend that the Anatolian Byzantine acceptance of Ottoman rule, and indeed occasional cooperation in that enterprise, finds its best explanation in the history not only of Palaeologan misrule, but especially in the history of that misrule framed against the dim memory of Lascarid prosperity.

Michael VIII Palaeologus, who usurped the Byzantine throne in 1258, found himself in possession of a pacific Anatolian domain. Its frontier began on the Black Sea east of Amasra/Amastris, cut west to the Sakarya, followed the line of the plateau, excluding Eskişehir and Kütahya, and then ran south over the Carian highlands to the Dalaman Çay/Indus on the Aegean.[53] On Michael's accession there was peace in the east. After the recovery of Constantinople, however, he neglected and even antagonized his Anatolian subjects at a time when Turkish tribesmen and Seljuk successors were beginning to look west to their fortunes, away from the increasingly threatening Mongols.

Michael was no stranger to the Turks and their capabilities. In 1256 he had fled to the Seljuk court for refuge from Lascarid suspicions and had served Konya as head of the contingent of foreign soldiers. On the way across the frontier zone east of Nicaea nomads had ambushed him. The Byzantine chronicler Acropolites described his captors. The Türkmen, according to him, lie in ambush on the farthest frontiers of the Seljuks. Filled with irreconcilable hatred against the Romans, they take pleasure in looting them and seizing booty. Acropolites notes also that at the time Michael passed they were particularly rapacious, for Mongol pressure had set many tribes in motion.[54]

Such Mongol pressure, exerted a number of times in the years of Michael's youth and adulthood, had a decisive effect on the size of the nomadic population at the western edge of the plateau. In the 1230s the Mongols had assigned four *tümens,* each of which contained ten thousand men, to pasture in Azerbaijan. Their apparition brought some 200,000 people and the equivalent of three or four million sheep and goats, who displaced the nomads already there and pressed them westward. It is no surprise that from 1239-1240 central Anatolia suffered from the series of nomad risings known as the Baba'i revolt. The Seljuks barely managed to put down the nomads before succumbing themselves in defeat to Mongol arms in 1243. Later on in the 1250s the Mongols forced the Seljuks to allow more *tümens* into Anatolia, and these newcomers forced yet another stream of refugees westward.[55] The same Mongol pressure on the Seljuks in 1277 brought still more nomads west. An Arab geographer, writing in mid-century, describes the results: some 30,000 tents of nomads in the mountains of Gerede Bolu, east of the Sakarya, and another 100,000 tents near Kastamonu.[56] Thus, in search of pasture, unsure of their proper niche in their new home on the Bithynian frontier, the Türkmen were even more dependent on predation for survival and well-being.

What Acropolites terms irreconcilable hated was in fact nomadic necessity, cupidity rather than loathing. In any event, the nomads robbed Michael of his belongings and held him until he got a message to Konya. The sultan freed Michael but was unable to recover his possessions.[57] We do not know what Michael made of this experience. After the recovery of Constantinople, however, he saw the main foreign threat as western and his actions reflected this concern. At the moment when pressure on nomads on the plateau was increasing their numbers just east of the Sakarya, Byzantium was ruled by a man who was destined to fulfil the Lascarids' Constantinopolitan dream and ignore their Anatolian successes. The generation of the 1240s paid the price and learned a new lesson.

Anatolian discontent with Michael began with his usurpation, which brought on him opposition from the Arsenite faction in the church, a loose grouping supposed to have been strong in Anatolia. Michael, in turn, sought the support of his fellow aristocrats, in this case at the expense of the small holder and soldier on the land.[58] He recalled troops serving in Anatolia to deploy them in the Balkans.[59] Future Anatolian operations were undertaken by expeditions from Europe, not by local garrisons. To the populace, then, Byzantine military responses were tardy and manned by soldiers sharing no ties with, and perhaps little care for, the land and citizens to be protected. The military forces on the borders, the *akritai,* lost their privileges and many consequently deserted.[60] In 1265 Michael confiscated lands held from the state by some *akritai* and replaced their revenues with a pension of forty *hyperpyra.* He also tried to enrole the *akritai* in the regular army. His brother John persuaded him to reconsider, but the *akritai* were not convinced of their emperor's good intentions.[61]

In dealing with his Anatolian subjects Michael showed less concern for defense and security than for political and personal loyalty, which always came first as long as the Arsenites seemed to pose a threat. In 1261 or 1262 some of the residents of the high ridge northeast of Nicaea, and in particular the keepers of the fort Tricoccia, recognized as their emperor a supposed son of Theodore Lascaris.[62] Michael dispatched troops to return them to obedience. In order to strip the mountaineers of their cover the troops burned the surrounding forests. Those who did not immediately make their peace had to pay heavy fines.The contemporary chronicler Pachymeres claims that the imperial officers wanted to expel the rebels from the country, an action which would have even further denuded the passes to the plateau of defenders.[63] Loyalty, then, bought freedom from imperial persecution, but it was not sufficient to procure from Constantinople an adequate border defense.

The impact of the withdrawal of defense forces from the frontiers was palpable. On 23 February 1265 the unfounded rumor swept through Nicaea that the Mongols were at hand. Panic ensued, and those who were able are said to have fled to Constantinople. This hysterical episode was a manifestation of fears which the chroniclers lamented at length and connected with a slow, steady migration of Byzantine subjects to Europe.[64] The size of this migration cannot be gauged. It would have a depressing effect on the morale and expectations of those who remained.

Mongol pressure on central Anatolia, and a falling-out among the Seljuk princes, increased the danger in the west. Michael took this as an opportunity to enlist Turks in his service. Pachymeres gives a picture of the frontier chaos in the 1260s. According to Pachymeres, some persons called tent-dwellers, who found the idea of government odious, desired independence. They attacked the Byzantine forts. Some, recognizing the danger of an open attack, joined with the emperor. Others waited nights in ambush and plundered Byzantine property. In the end, says Pachymeres, the damage was not so great, since "our own" did the same sort of thing. There was considerable local collaboration with the Turks.[65]

These comments are precious. After the Mongols usurped pastures in the east, numerous nomads shifted west. Some of them found their way to

Bithynia. They sought easy pickings from the Byzantine frontier stations, but, as nomads without mechanical engineers and as pastoralists governed by the necessity of periodic moves to new pastures, they could not undertake siege warfare. Some, ignoring differences of cult and culture, became mercenaries for Byzantium. Others turned to canonical nomad tactics to extract a living from the countryside. They were not alone. Were "our own" the disaffected *akritai?* Loyalties, in Bithynia, were founded increasingly on mutual advantage rather than on competing ideologies. All the ingredients for a tribe were present, save only one—the chief. The results were predictable. By 1269 travelers could no longer reach Pontic Heraclea overland in safety, thanks to the Turkish nests along the Sakarya. The town was accessible by sea alone.[66] The Turkish occupation of the lower Sakarya implies that by ca. 1280 the Turks had broken through the network of castles erected by the later Comneni.

During the last two years of his reign, freed at last by the Sicilian Vespers from fear of an invasion by Charles of Anjou, Michael turned his attention to Asia Minor. Once again the Byzantine goal was to defend the routes down from the plateau. In 1282 Michael's son Andronicus led a force up the Maeander to rebuild and resettle Aydın/Tralles. He planned to create a large and prosperous city, and a friendly estimate of the population of his new foundation endows this "Andronicopolis" with 36,000 residents. When Andronicus departed without engaging the Turks in the surrounding countryside, they cut the water supply and forced the city's prompt capitulation.[67]

Failure also marked Michael's own effort in Bithynia. There, frontier garrisons which had not received their wages left their posts.[68] In early 1282 Turks on the lower Sakarya had already repelled Byzantine troops.[69] Michael's expedition took the field late in the summer.[70] He advanced up the Sakarya east of Nicaea and was soon surrounded by the desolation which his western concerns had crowded out of his mind. He was unable to catch the Turks. There were very few people tilling the soil, and it was difficult to provide even the coarsest of bread for the soldiers. A mute witness, samples of the bread, the brown harvest of Michael's hopes blasted, was sent to Constantinople. The emperor turned back, marched west of Bursa, and fortified the cities of Achyraous and Ulubad/Lopadion.[71] Michael's resolve to protect these cities, far below the plateau, distant from the Sakarya, reveals the collapse of the frontier defenses. After Michael's death late in 1282, many of those still living near the Sakarya and some of the troops enrolled there quit their stations and crossed to Europe.[72] Marino Sanudo summed up Michael's campaigns with the lament that he "... abandoned the custody of one of his provinces, the best and most powerful, which was called Paphlagonia and which was taken by the Turks...."[73]

During the long reign of Andronicus II, Michael's son and successor, the Byzantine chroniclers found more cause to lament lost Anatolia. To their plaints we may add the letters of Athanasius I, Patriarch of Constantinople. Athanasius was concerned about the state of the church in the east, and he described its travails in much the same fashion as the chroniclers Pachymeres, his contemporary, and Gregoras, who was a young adult at the turn of the century.

Andronicus did not dispatch troops to Asia Minor until 1290. However, a letter of 1285 or 1286 from Patriarch Gregory II proves that danger had already touched Bursa. Andronicus had imposed a fine on the city, and the patriarch had received complaints of its severity. He advised Andronicus of the difficulty in raising such a large sum, as the nearby Turks would remain a threat to the city's prosperity and, if there were no resources left locally, might bring about its ruin. Gregory claimed that the proposed fine of 600 *hyperpyra* was excessive: 300 would be quite enough.[74] For the sake of comparison, the proposed pension to be granted the *akritai* of Asia Minor under Michael VIII in the 1260s had been forty *hyperpyra* each. Bursa's commerce and the silk trade must have been languishing indeed, if a single levy of 600 *hyperpyra* was considered a crushing blow.[75] More than sporadic raids themselves, constant fear of raids must have affected planting and the harvests and thus eroded the Bursan economy. A high fine combined with low income could only lead the Bursans to wonder how they might find a protector.

Andronicus spent the years from 1290 to 1293 in Anatolia arranging defenses. He went to Bithynia and examined the fortified keeps near the Sakarya. He then turned west to Nicaea and Lopadion. After lengthy stays in these two cities he moved south to Nymphaeum, where he passed two years in the former Lascarid capital.[76] He concerned himself with the cities and their security, if not with their provisioning. He made no sorties into the countryside, and the chroniclers do not record any encounters with Turkish forces. Aydın/Tralles, his showpiece, had already fallen.

The intimate relationship between rural security and a city's food supply may have become clearer to Andronicus while he traveled in Anatolia, for he took hesitant steps to defend the peasants. In 1277 a certain Lachanes had rebelled without success against Michael VIII. In his turn Andronicus put down the revolt of a man claiming to be Lachanes *redivivus*. This Pseudo-Lachanes, however, seemed able to inspire men, and so in early 1294 Andronicus sent him to the Sakarya frontier to help the peasants. They welcomed him, many abandoning their holdings to join his militia. As this army and the prestige of its leader grew, Andronicus for his part grew concerned about its potential for revolt. He recalled Pseudo-Lachanes and jailed him.[77] While Pseudo-Lachanes was enjoying too much support in the north, in 1293 Andronicus sent Alexius Philanthropenus, a soldier with much experience (but also with Arsenite connections), to the south to secure the Maeander. Philanthropenus successfully protected Miletus from Turkish bands, securing booty in gold, silver, sheep- and donkey-skins. His accomplishments, and his generosity to his enemies in victory, won over some Turks, who formed a separate corps among his men. His soldiers and the populace he was protecting rose in revolt in 1294 under his banner: to the farmers he represented a blow against high taxes, and to the Turks (in my view) he was a successful (tribal?) chief. Andronicus and his advisors had to rely on deceit to put down the revolt and, in late 1295, imprison and blind its leader.[78] These two episodes illustrate the failure of the Byzantine army to meet the threats of the day. It was indeed weak if any appealing field commander, such as Philanthropenus or even Pseudo-Lachanes, could so easily raise a potential threat to the regime. The imperial concern meant that none of the armed forces operating on the frontiers could be allowed such strength. Loyal or not, the peasants had to bear the consequences of their emperor's fears.

Andronicus again marched forth for the east in late May 1296. After a series of earthquakes (1 June - 17 July) which he interpreted as an admonitory omen he gave up the campaign.[79] Two years later, general John Tarchaneiotes went south, and in another attempt to rebuild the local armed forces he equalized the size of soldiers' holdings so that all could afford to serve. Unwilling donors among the larger *pronoiars* and the bishop of Alaşehir/-Philadelphia turned against him and secured his recall in the summer of 1299.[80]

These efforts betray lack of care, resources, and consistency. A piecemeal restructuring of military holdings occurred only once and was soon abandoned. Farming in Bithynia continued, but its comparative advantage over predation was slight, to judge by the farms abandoned in favor of service under Pseudo-Lachanes. Military leaders left behind no replacement. There is no evidence of any imperial policy other than fear of revolt and poorly-financed, badly-managed expediency. Perhaps there was no money left. Perhaps, also, there was no consuming or continuing interest in the east.

In 1301 a mass of "Alan" families from the Balkans estimated at 8,000 men with an equal number of dependents sought refuge on Byzantine soil. In 1302 Andronicus determined to send them to Anatolia.[81] Michael IX, Andronicus' son, led some of the Alans to the south to dislodge Turks from Manisa/Magnesia. This southern prong of the campaign failed, and the Alans were transported back to Thrace.[82] Mouzalon, the commander at Izmit/-Nicomedia, took other Alans in his charge. Once across the Bosphorus, however, they began looting and had to be subdued. Mouzalon had another struggle that summer. In July a Turkish force gathered outside Nicomedia and Mouzalon went forth to confront them. Their chief was a certain Osman.

* * * *

It is now time to cross the frontier and examine the Turkish setting for early Ottoman history. So far, the Byzantine failure to protect Bithynia, and the discontent felt by Anatolian subjects at their emperor's heedlessness, have been the main themes of the exposition. I have been preparing the ground for a claim, which I shall elaborate upon shortly, that some of the Byzantines joined Osman's tribe. Now, however, it is necessary to look at the beginnings of that tribe from the Turkish perspective.

At this point it is no longer possible to ignore the Ottoman chronicles. They display a tempting panorama of personal glory and institutional success extending from the thirteenth century through the era of the Conqueror. To the eye of a medieval historian their smooth, clean surface shines with the light of Einhard's life of Charlemagne. Behind the sheen lie the questioning shadows that cannot be scrubbed away: how much of this is Einhard, Suetonius, Charlemagne? Before us the chronicles play a *karagöz,* a shadow-play. The high quality of the performance ought not to divert us from seeking a glance behind the curtain at the puppeteer and his patron, the puppet-master.

Aware of discrepancies among their sources, realizing that thirteenth century fact did not square with fifteenth century romance, the Ottoman chroniclers hastened to devise a story harmonizing the discordant notes. To be a chronicler at court was also to be an amanuensis, of course. Sometimes a chronicler saw the Ottoman enterprise as an eternal structure, whose fifteenth century institutions had existed in Osman's day. Such cleansing and polishing to reflect the imperial ideology has resulted in the extant texts.

The study of these chronicles is therefore to be conducted with an attitude of suspicion, shunning the smooth and flowing account, embracing the *lectio difficilior.* The incongruous, the unexpected statement, by its very clash, may reveal an older tradition truer to past life than to present ideology. Thus, as a historian of medieval Europe has characterized similar material, "We may take it as an axiom of historiography that in source-materials of this age and kind a good, glaring contradiction is worth a square yard of smooth, question-begging consistency."[83] This does not reflect a perverse love of the outré. It took the entire fifteenth century for the Ottoman orthodoxy to emerge, and the stages of the Ottomans' "recovery" of their past remain in the early chronicles. Passages which conflict with that orthodoxy should *a fortiori* reflect an earlier memory. The following analysis thus explicitly rests in part on material which the received tradition, ungrateful descendant, has denied.[84]

Very little may be advanced with certainty about Osman's ancestors. The Ottomans claimed that they entered Asia Minor as nomads, displaced by the Mongols and seeking new pastures. Their family claimed descent from the

Oğuz Turks through a line which, as we have seen, Ottoman chroniclers had some difficulty clarifying in the fifteenth century. Towards the middle of the thirteenth century they found themselves in the mountains near Ankara. Some decided to turn back east, others to go south towards Cilicia, while yet another group banded together about Ertoğrul, Osman's father. The families with Ertoğrul are generally held to have entered Seljuk service not in the regular army, but as nomad raiders. The chronicle of Karamani Mehmet Paşa, composed in the sultanate of Mehmet II, claims that Ertoğrul's father had already fought independently against the Byzantines.[85] Ertoğrul received pasture rights in return for his services.

All the chroniclers are agreed about the ancestral pastures of the Ottomans, and a brief discussion of their geographical setting will place some of our later conclusions upon a firmer footing. The winter pastures *(kışlak)* lay in the vale of Söğüt, a fertile glen lying on the most direct route linking Bilecik/Belocome and Eskişehir.[86] Summer pasture *(yaylak)* lay in the mountains of Ermeni Beli ("Armenian" Pass) and Domaniç, southeast of the Bithynian Olympus and west of Eskişehir.[87] The route up country from winter to summer pastures passed by Bilecik, Yarhisar, and Inegöl on the way to Domaniç. The heights range from 1500 to 2000 meters, and the vertical range between winter and summer pastures was therefore some 1000 to 1500 meters.[88] The migration was relatively short: from the Sakarya below Söğüt to the slopes southwest of Bozüyük is perhaps fifty kilometers, and from the same departure point to Domaniç no more than one hundred. The herds probably took no more than ten days to cover this distance.[89] Thus the Ottoman tradition here makes geographical and pastoral sense. We will return to this geographical setting later and analyze its economic import, for later developments demonstrated that this land was simply too good for pastoralism.

Not all the Ottoman traditions involving Ertoğrul inspire such confidence. He is said to have impressed the Seljuk Sultan with his performance at the siege of Karacahisar. His men were assigned the southern watch over against the walls. An invasion of central Anatolia by the Mongols, however, called away the Seljuks, who entrusted Ertoğrul with the siege. He took the fort by storm and proceeded to other raids against Byzantine holdings in the area.[90] The difficulty with this inspiring tale is that, as we noted earlier, Eskişehir had been in Muslim hands since the beginning of the thirteenth century, and Karacahisar lies a few kilometers southwest. Thus, the story appears to be a fabrication. Either it was devised from whole cloth to advance Ertoğrul at the expense of the Seljuks, or it is a post-dated, revised version of the story of the fall of Dorylaeum and its environs to the Turks nearly a century before. Again, if Karacahisar was in fact the proto-Ottomans' first conquest, it must have been achieved at the expense of the Muslim Germiyan.

The sources then mention that Ertoğrul died soon thereafter. The traveler may see a tomb assigned to him at Söğüt.

No source provides a firm and factual recounting of the deeds of Osman's father. The figure of Ertoğrul, however, served the chroniclers well. They had him bring the family to the Byzantine borders, and they made him careful enough to find a Seljuk sanction for his presence. This sanction did not lead to dependence, for Ertoğrul's success was attained outside the shadow of the Sultan, who left the field for Ertoğrul to celebrate the victory. All of this is smooth and attractive; none of it, unfortunately, allows of proof at the moment, but it would be surprising if Ertoğrul were to be as significant in Ottoman history as he was useful in Ottoman historiography. The simple matter of dynastic attribution reinforces the suspicions about Osman's father, since the dynasty is not his but Osman's, as the term "Ottoman" tells us. The Ottomans impressed enemies, as well as enemy chroniclers, and gained followers in Osman's time and in his name, so it is with him that Ottoman history begins.

While Osman's father remains a shadowy figure, who left so few traces that later Ottoman ideologists could freely enlarge his deeds to fit the magnitude of their preconceptions, Osman is real and palpable. Orkhan, his son and successor, referred to him on inscriptions and coins, and the contemporary Byzantine chronicler Pachymeres wrote of him. Nonetheless, his own dates and the sequence of his deeds remain to be clarified. It would, for instance, be very helpful to know just how Osman came to power.

The late fifteenth-century Anonymous Chronicles claimed that Osman "took Ertoğrul's place" and became deputy *(kaymakam)* for his father's lands.[91] A number of questions immediately arise from this statement. Who appointed Osman as deputy? And whose deputy was he? Our source is silent, for good reason; it attributes to the thirteenth century an Ottoman administrative organization which did not arise for another century. Neither the Seljuks, nor the Bithynians, nor the nomads had such an office. In the age of the Anonymous, however, the past was perceived as embryo of the present, and events had to fit a recognizable, legitimized and eternal framework.[92] The Anonymous knew, then, that something had lifted Osman out of obscurity, but he was less interested in reporting the past than foreseeing the present in it.

The chronicle of Karamani Mehmet Paşa gave a fuller, more studied account. Here Ertoğrul, having performed many feats of war against the Byzantines, died at the advanced age of 93. Osman succeeded his father and became Sultan in 699/1299-1300. The Seljuk Sultan, his neighbor to the southeast, sent him worthy gifts, symbols of authority, and exhorted Osman to persevere in the Holy War.[93] When it is not in obvious error, this account is as anachronistic as it is picturesque. The symbols of authority became a feature of Ottoman ceremonial only much later. As for their donor, no Seljuk Sultan could authorize a ruler's accession at the turn of the fourteenth century, as the Seljuks were themselves under notice of eviction. Not a late Seljuk but his Mongol overlord should have granted Osman his license. To pardonable errors of history Mehmet Paşa added slips of sense. Involving another dynasty granted the Ottomans a legitimate succession, but terming Osman Sultan to avoid the implication of dependence strains the reader's credence. Sultans may be pleased to appoint emirs, but they do not create rival Sultans. Şukrullah, writing in the 1450s, recounted the same story, but the copyist of the Vienna manuscript could not resist setting down his, and our own, reservations at the end, "God knows best."[94]

Other sources, however, cast clearer light on the problem of Osman's accession. Commenting on the traditional date of 1299-1300, Mahmud Beyati's short essay on Ottoman genealogy remarks that by then the fall of the house of Seljuk had been accomplished. The death of the last Seljuk, Ala ed-Din Keyqubad III, had brought confusion to the affairs of the sultanate, and so the frontier ghazis chose Osman as their Sultan.[95] One element at least of Mahmud's tale is faulty, for Ala ed-Din died sometime after 1300.[96] What then of his claim that Osman came to power by election? It is significant that Mahmud composed his work in 1481, the year of Mehmet II's death.[97] A struggle for the throne ensued between Mehmet's sons, Cem and Bayezid II, and this contest was in the wind as Mahmud wrote. His work is dedicated to Cem, who lost the protracted struggle. Mahmud may have presented Osman's election to the sultanate by frontier ghazis as a historical parallel to and sanction for the support of Cem by his partisans and thus opposed it to that of Bayezid II, the choice of bureaucrats and janissaries. Osman's election, then, would be merely a historiographical calque on the present.

Yet Mahmud's account finds independent corroboration in Aşıkpaşazade, who writes that at Söğüt "they" (the pronoun has no referent) found Osman suited to succeed his father.[98] Now, the choice of events to recount in Aşıkpaşazade, their order, and also their dates, are sufficiently unlike those in Mahmud's essay to preclude borrowing or a common source. On the other hand, it is true that Aşıkpaşazade used his chronicle, as did Joinville, to direct barbs at Bayezid II's tax collectors. But this particular passage is not contaminated by Aşıkpaşazade's preferences, and it is also true that he had no stake in the Cem-Bayezid war, which had ended as he was writing. Further, this episode in Aşıkpaşazade has no parallel in the text of the Anonymous Chronicles. Passages which are not shared by the Anonymous are probably derived from Aşıkpaşazade's early source, the tales of Yahşi Fakih, which he read in 1413.[99] These tales themselves go back to Orkhan's reign, so they represent a layer of the Ottoman historiographical onion considerably closer to the core than the other versions.

We have further evidence for an elective chieftaincy among the early Ottomans. In the 1420s Yazıcıoğlu Ali reworked the Persian chronicle of the

Seljuks by Ibn Bibi into Turkish, and in the process he added certain items about Osman's early days. One is a passage describing the nomads' election of Osman as their chief.[100] Although laden with romantic verbiage, the essence of the tale, that Osman was elected chief, is worth serious consideration. There is, finally, another independent version of Osman's election. Occasionally the chronicle of Neşri provides material from Bursan sources whose memories have not found their way into other chronicles.[101] One of Neşri's independent Bursan sources related the aftermath of Ertoğrul's death: some of the nomad tents wanted to make Osman their chief, while others preferred his uncle Dündar. But his own family preferred Osman: they informed him in secret and they all consulted. When Dündar came before the people and saw their preference for Osman, he gave up his hopes for the chieftaincy and swore allegiance to Osman.[102] There are, then, grounds for belief that at the end of the thirteenth century the chieftainship of the Ottomans was elective. Not necessarily the eldest or youngest son but the son best equipped for leadership in the eyes of the community received its support.[103]

None of this should seem strange or anachronistically "democratic," for an elected chieftaincy is standard among the nomads of Inner Asian and Turkish history. The ablest candidate gathers followers by his deeds; if none of the close relatives of the deceased chief seem able to protect and further the interests of the tribesmen, an outside candidate may emerge, or the tribesmen may choose to join another tribe. The tribesmen vote in the most basic manner, with their feet. On the other hand, they may gravitate to that pretender, be he Osman or Dündar, whose effective exercise of authority makes him a successful candidate. As tribesmen themselves put it, "the horse feels the rider's thigh."[104] The chronicles' evidence for Osman's election as leader is, in this light, excellent evidence for viewing the earliest Ottoman institution as a tribe.

The chronology of Osman's activities until 1302 cannot be accurately determined. He and his men were in a geographical position to carry out the raids attributed by Byzantine authors to Turks in Bithynia. The Turkish chronicles recount sufficient numbers of tales, and folk tales, of ambush and combat to satisfy the Byzantine moralists and fulfil the need for a heroic Ottoman past. But the Turkish sources also contain hints and allusions about the processes afoot in frontier society which help to define the nature of Osman's support and clarify his relations with his neighbors.[105]

These hints and allusions about Osman and his nomads deal more with predation than with pastoralism. Both of these activities have been staples of nomadic life in the past. The mix of the two has varied in response to the changing comparative strengths of sedentary and nomadic societies. When sedentary society is weak, nomads may prefer to extort, rather than pay for, agricultural products and luxury manufactures. When, as in modern times, the military resources of settled governments predominate, nomads are forced to rely on pastoralism and the patrolled marketplace for their livelihoods. The questions facing Osman were therefore the perennial ones for nomads on the move: on what options would they rely, and in what proportions? Or should they settle?

Others, of course, saw predation in a different light. Such raids might seem to some heroic, or to others inspired by zeal for the true faith, or to yet others grounded in sheer malevolence, but the acts themselves were identical. Only the labels changed, to protect the historians, not the nomads. The point is worth elaborating because, as we have seen earlier, the later Ottoman authors term Osman and his followers ghazis, raiders in the Holy War. I have already suggested that this was not the nomenclature of Osman's time. Ibn Battuta and al-Umari, whose information derives from the early 1330s, used the term neither for Osman nor for his son Orkhan. On the other hand, some of Osman's comrades bore the title "alp," for example Gündüz Alp, Hasan Alp, Turgud Alp.[106] The alp or alp-eren was the heroic figure of old Turkic saga, the warrior-adventurer whose exploits alone justified his way of life. For men who thought themselves cast in such a mold, predation had an appeal, not for a religious justification but for booty and the exhilaration of combat.[107] Since the predation would be largely directed against Byzantines, the actions of a nomad would easily be transmuted by some into the heroics of an alp and by others into the religious feats of the ghazi. Only the label would change. This view makes it easier to understand some of the texts. For example, according to Aşıkpaşazade, after succeeding Ertoğrul Osman began to hunt in remote and far-away places.[108] Köse Mihal, the Byzantine lord of Harman Kaya, always accompanied him. Osman was not the only Ottoman with Christian allies and friends, for his colleague Samsa Çavuş also had friendly relations with Byzantines in his neighborhood.[109] I think it clear that Osman's own entourage was, from a religious point of view, heterogeneous. The common interests of these "strangers" bound them together and allowed Köse Mihal to join the tribe. It is important to keep in mind that such a "multi-ethnic" phenomenon is not the exception in tribal formation and growth, as the quick accretion of disparate elements to the Huns or the Mongols shows. Common interest, be it in politics, predation, pasture, or simple survival, was at the heart of the Ottoman (and every other) tribe.[110]

How did Osman stand with his Christian neighbors when he was neither hunting nor campaigning? Aşıkpaşazade calls the relationship one of friendship or, with fifteenth-century hindsight, feigned friendship *(müdara)*.[111] Popular Byzantine response determined the extent of the friendship. Even were this unfavorable, the Turkish reprisals were modest. On one occasion the Turks are said to have taken booty but no prisoners in order to earn respect.[112] When the farmers submitted to Osman's chieftaincy, he left them in their former tenures and status.[113] Symbiosis followed. We learn that the Byzantine lord of Inegöl was harassing Osman's movements from winter to summer pastures. To ease the journey and increase his mobility, Osman arranged to leave heavy goods with the Byzantine lord of Bilecik for safekeeping when his families were on the march. The women loaded their belongings on oxen and placed them in the citadel of Bilecik. When they returned in the fall, they offered cheese, carpeting, rugs and sheep as payment. This became a routine arrangement.[114] Köse Mihal became a close and trusted friend to Osman.[115] We learn that Osman set up a market place in Eskişehir near a bath, and Christians from Bilecik came there to sell water glasses, for which Bilecik was known. Even when these Christians had complaints against Muslims, Osman gave them justice.[116] We may say that as a tribal chief, Osman acted as a fulcrum or mediator, protecting the rights of "ethnically and ecologically diverse groups."[117] Acting to keep the peace and to help his tribesmen prosper, the chief renders himself indispensable; and if he succeeds, his tribe grows.

While Osman and his Byzantine neighbors were beginning to perceive their common interests, hostility arose between Osman and his Muslim neighbors to the southwest, the emirs of Germiyan, whose headquarters were at Kütahya.[118] Except for an episode in the last half of the 1280s the emirs of Germiyan had been Seljuk allies,[119] and they seem to have inherited some of the Seljuk pretensions to authority, weak though it may have been, over the marches.[120] It is my belief that the enmity between the Ottomans and Germiyan goes back to the Ottoman seizure of Karacahisar, to which I have already alluded. It also seems that Germiyan favored harsher treatment of the Byzantines than did Osman.[121] Under these conditions, living with hostile neighbors to the south and threatening Mongols to the east, Osman's interest in co-existence with the relatively weak Byzantines makes sense. Some of these Byzantines found him a promising leader and they joined the tribe, becoming his followers, or Osmanlıs.[122]

* * * *

We may now rejoin Mouzalon and his troops at Bapheus, outside Izmit, on 27 July 1302. The positions of the Byzantines and Ottomans at this moment were not to be envied. Mouzalon needed to clear the Ottomans away so that the harvest could proceed, while the Byzantines within the city walls were becoming more and more restive, for without the benefit of the harvest their lives would hang in the balance during the coming winter. Mouzalon may also have been worried about the possibility of the city's population going over to Osman in order to obtain peace.[123] On the other hand, the Ottoman campaign in the coastal lowlands was also a matter of necessity. Spring flooding of the Sakarya and its tributaries, thanks to a series of violent storms, had devastated the higher valleys and washed away much vegetation: such a spring deluge had ruined the crops in 1282 and remains a problem for the Bithynian peasant in our own day.[124] Thus, a wet spring had ruined the crops in the vale of Söğüt and the high valleys near Bilecik. The same rains and floods also wrought havoc on the pastoral base of Osman's nomads, for the bad weather coincided with the lambing season, decimating the newborn.[125] In the summer of 1302, then, pastoralism could not support the Ottomans, so they took to predation. Domaniç may have been denuded, but Izmit was fruitful. It appears from the account of Pachymeres that the Alan mercenaries with Mouzalon decided the battle in Osman's favor: first, because they stood apart and seemed to misunderstand Mouzalon's plans in the early part of the encounter, and last, when Alan reinforcements covered the Byzantine retreat from an Ottoman cavalry charge.[126] Bapheus proved that Osman could and did look out for the interests of his followers, while it cast doubt once again on Constantinople's ability to reward the loyalty of its subjects.[127]

Thus, both northern and southern prongs of the Byzantine campaign of 1302 had failed of their purpose. The immediate effect in Bithynia was the capitulation of many leaders to Osman, who became their lord and allowed them to retain their lands and perquisites. Bilecik became Osman's within two years.[128] The larger cities held out: their high, heavy walls, which the Lascarids had prudently repaired, could easily withstand the light arms of the Ottoman forces. A flow of refugees from the countryside into the cities and across the straits to Constantinople grew in 1302-1303.[129]

Andronicus did not raise an army for further campaigning.[130] He turned to diplomacy. Sometime before May 1304, he attempted to bring Mongol pressure to bear on the Anatolian emirs through an embassy to Ghazan Khan in Tabriz and, after Ghazan's death, to his successor Uljaytu. The Ilkhans, recent converts to Islam, did not accept the offer of a marriage alliance as inducement sufficient for a Mongol attack against the west.[131] Andronicus also made arrangements with a certain Kocabahşı, a former official of the Mongol Golden Horde, who was to win the emir of Kastamonu in Paphlagonia over to the Byzantines through a marriage alliance. Kocabahşı was then to replace Mouzalon at Nicomedia. None of these strategems bore fruit.[132] Diplomatic pressure brought no respite from the Ottomans.

The military sequel indicates that Andronicus was concerned more with the south than with the advance of Osman. In 1303 Andronicus hired the Catalan Company under its famous leader, Roger de Flor. The Catalans were retained to cross over to Anatolia and drive out the Turks "who, at that place, had taken from the emperor land to the extent of more than thirty days' journeys, covered with good cities and towns and castles which they subdued and which paid tribute to them."[133] In the fall of 1303 the Catalans established a base at Erdek/Artace north of Cyzicus. After wintering at Erdek they skirmished with the Turks and then marched south in early April 1304. Advancing rapidly, the Catalans defeated a Germiyanid army in Phrygia and then freed Philadelphia and Ephesus. Soon, however, great friction arose between the local Byzantines and their new masters, who exacted limitless tribute in preference to regular (but lower) taxation from those whom they had liberated. In the fall and winter of 1304-1305 the Catalans sailed away from the south coast to Thrace, eager to obtain redress of some recent grievances against the emperor. They never returned. The Catalan Company had not campaigned in Bithynia, nor had it left behind agents or deputies to preserve the advantages it had gained at Cyzicus.[134]

The desperation of the emperor is manifest in his reaction to events that followed the departure of the Catalans. A young monk named Hilarion, of the monastery of Peribleptos in Constantinople, managed its lands situated at Kurşunlu/Elegmoi, near Cius, on the Marmora. In retaliation for Turkish raiding in the fields he formed a militia which drove off the Turks and also kept the land under cultivation. Patriarch Athanasius ordered Hilarion, as a monk, to desist from physical combat, and the monk appealed to the emperor. Noting that the Turks had been able to slip past the forts and imperial garrisons, Andronicus encouraged Hilarion to return to his militia as long as the Turkish peril lasted.[135] Andronicus' willingness to foster self-help, even at the expense of monastic vows, demonstrates the gravity of his dilemma. It is even more revealing to realize that Hilarion's amateur host is the only local example of resistance of which the chronicles feel able to boast.

Support for the Byzantine regime and resistance to Osman dwindled as the power of the Bithynian cities to continue in either of these declined. A symptom of this process was the continuing presence of the Anatolian bishops in the capital rather than at their sees. From 1303 to 1305 Athanasius addressed numerous unheeded letters to the emperor, imploring him to force the bishops to return to their posts in order to preserve the faith as well as to win the goodwill of their flocks.[136] One reason why the bishops might have preferred the capital was the severe grain shortage in Bithynia in 1305. Crops were so poor that the government received no tax revenues from the province.[137] Garrisons suffered famine because they could not gather crops in distant areas now lost to their control. To feed them Andronicus requisitioned surplus grain wherever he could from the larger monasteries and sent it east. The shipments were inadequate and there followed risings against the tax collectors. Athanasius complained that even Osman was more generous with grain for his subjects.[138]

Between 1305 and the fall of Bithynia's major cities a generation later, there is little precise information to guide the historian. The small forts fell before the cities: in 1306 Kite/Katoikia, a small keep west of Bursa, surrendered to a surprise attack which befell the garrison as it was being mustered.[139] A year or so later, the garrison of Gübekler/Koubouklia, a small fort near Ulubad, betrayed their post to the Ottomans. The Bursans, now isolated, had to pay tribute to Osman.[140] By 1318 the remaining inhabitants of Bursa were too few or too poor to provide their bishop with the necessities of life, and so the partriarchal synod granted him as a supplement the revenues of the see of Apameia in Phrygia and a monastery in Bursa which had been in patriarchal hands.[141] For a time in 1321 Andronicus contemplated a campaign in Asia Minor with an army of one thousand horse, a force (and an ambition) considerably less than Mouzalon's of not quite twenty years before.[142] The death of Osman in 1324 and the election of Orkhan brought no relief.[143] The Byzantine chroniclers ignore the surrender of Bursa on 6 April 1326, after a lengthy blockade. Ulubad fell on 13 May 1327, Nicaea on 2 March 1331.Two years later Emperor Andronicus III agreed to pay Orkhan tribute; Andronicus purchased the books, relics, and ecclesiastical finery of Nicaea and took them to Constantinople.[144]

Two Arab authors provide a glimpse of Orkhan's enterprise at this moment. The traveler Ibn Battuta arrived in Nicaea in October 1331, seven months after its surrender. He found the city "... in a mouldering condition and uninhabited except for a few men in the sultan's service." Inside the city walls there were orchards, farms, and cultivated fields.[145] In contrast Bursa, taken half a decade earlier, was a thriving city. Its connection with the hinterland established once again without the necessity of paying tribute to a besieger, and having resumed its traditional character as market and silk town, Bursa had prospered to the point that it was the Ottoman mint, producing silver coins and supporting the early Ottoman bureaucracy.[146] Orkhan spent his time making the rounds of his fortresses and keeping them in good order; he kept the Byzantines under blockade in Nicomedia.[147] The geographer al-Umari, whose sources provide information on the Ottoman domains ca. 1331, presents a more critical assessment of Orkhan's strength. According to his informants, Orkhan had 25,000 or 40,000 mediocre horse and an almost innumerable infantry, more warlike in appearance than in reality.[148]

It might seem that the rise of Osman and the conquest of Bithynia simply recast in miniature an eternal battle between steppe and sown familiar to historians, in the first instance, as seen from the Great Wall of China:

> In the new pattern of war, therefore, the great Chinese victories were won when the state was vigorous enough to plan and mobilize carefully and to send out expeditions that moved quickly and won at the first shock. When they could not do this, and frontier warfare was desultory and chronic, the Chinese frontier provinces were slowly drained and exhausted and the prestige of the state eroded, while the nomads profited economically, grew stronger every year, and in the rivalry between chieftains eventually produced one of the Chingis Khan stamp who could not only lead a band of warriors but impose a control of imperial sweep over a conglomerate of tribes.[149]

The transformation of Byzantine into Ottoman loyalties was, however, not so simple.

We have already discussed the processes, and alluded to the events, that would turn many Byzantines in Bithynia into accepting, and even willing, Ottomans. The implication of the preceding summary of the earliest Ottoman decades has been that Byzantines could and, in some numbers, did join the Ottoman tribe. That tribe, however, also included the nomads who had originally elected Osman chief. We must now look at the impact of the transformation of Bithynia into Ottoman territory upon the original Ottomans, the nomad Turks. As indicated at the beginning of this chapter, I intend to simplify the discussion by focusing in turn upon three aspects of the process of transformation: domestic economy, military resources and practices, and political organization. In each of these areas the nomads saw a complete change in their familiar world, a change which turned them from willing comrades to untrustworthy subjects.

First, let us look at the Bithynian repercussions for the pastoral side of Ottoman nomadic life. At the outset we must understand that the introduction of nomadic pastoralism into the area was a historically, not ecologically, determined event. No geographic or climatic feature predisposed any Bithynian to live as a pastoralist. Only their previous custom, not a rational economic choice, had led the Turks in western Anatolia to prefer pastoralism to cultivating crops.[150] The Bithynian soil, even the high ground above Söğüt, was rich and better suited to tillage than to pasture. There, and in all directions downstream towards the Marmora, the environment favored the raising of crops.[151] The potential agricultural earnings from cultivation were steadier and involved less hazard than the livelihood of a pastoralist. From predation and herding the nomads could do well; as landlords and proprietors they might do even better. The distance between Osman's winter and summer pastures was short, and increasing material wealth, in booty if not in sheep, combined with the shortness of the route to create a transhumant routine, in which at least one of the seasonal dwellings was fixed and permanent. A fixed dwelling would soon be encumbered with the sorts of goods which earlier had been eschewed or deposited with, say, the lord of Bilecik while on the march up country. Such transhumance preserves the pastoral routine at the expense of nomadic life. It is a stage of settlement. The lands into which the Turks descended from the plateau had been under cultivation and there is no reason to suppose that agriculture ceased completely during the occasional raids. If the agricultural population dwindled, larger and richer holdings resulted. Osman granted lands to his followers both inside and outside of the cities and villages. He confirmed the Byzantine farmers in their tenures. The slow settlement of Osman's comrades followed as they perceived the advantages and wealth guaranteed thereby.[152]

There is some evidence to help trace the stages of this transition. In a description of the early Ottoman arrival in Bithynia, Aşıkpaşazade has the Byzantines complain that Osman and his followers were not the sort to settle and irrigate land, the sort with whom the Byzantines might reach an understanding.[153] In short, they were nomads. His lightly-armed and agile horsemen at Bapheus may imply that Osman's armed forces retained at least a nomadic element in 1302. In late 1303 the Catalans surprised nomads raiding in the neighborhood of Cyzicus. These Turks traveled with their families, and their horse were by far more numerous than their footsoldiers.[154] At this stage, these nomads all seem able to have lived the boast of the Yomut tribesmen of Iran: "I do not have a mill with willow trees. I have a horse and a whip. I will kill you and go."[155] Soon, however, many must have settled. The large loads kept in storage at Bilecik during the migration provided attractive and weighty grounds for settlement.

Bapheus was won on horseback, but it did not prevent Osman himself from settlement. He founded Yenişehir ("New Town") and settled some of his troops there.[156] The Yenişehir plain, an eastern broadening of the lowland north of Bursa, is a breadbasket of the Marmora region. Rather little animal husbandry was practiced there, for the pastures were scattered; on the other hand, the region was wealthy in crops, gardens, and olive orchards.[157] The foundation of Yenişehir marked, in my opinion, a decisive step in the settlement of the Ottomans.

The assumption behind the preceding few paragraphs is that the pastoral Ottomans followed their own economic self-interest, that is, they settled because they made a much better and more secure living as landlords or cultivators in Bithynia. Stronger than the Byzantines, with little need to field a mobile cavalry against the slow Byzantine infantry, it was unnecessary to preserve their capital in movable form. There is, however, a second argument which I would present to buttress my contention that the Bithynian landscape caused the Ottomans to jettison pastoral animal husbandry as their major economic support. A given area used for cultivation, if it is as fertile as Bithynia, can support a much larger population than it can if used as pasture alone. The yield, in calories, of a plot of good land used for crops is much higher than the ultimate yield if that land is merely grazed. Thus, the manpower available to Osman depended to some extent on the method of land utilization which he supported and fostered. Even among nomads, total military manpower is a quantity to be maximized, and it was glaringly clear that Bithynia would support more farmers than it would nomadic herdsmen.[158] Early Ottoman settlement, then, made excellent sense.

So pastoralism, the economic aspect of nomadism, ceased to be a factor in the early Ottoman tribe. Let us now turn to the military aspect of nomadism and see how, in Osman and Orkhan's time, the Ottoman army was transformed from a tribe of archers into a sedentary source of infantry. It will be useful first to summarize some of the relevant characteristics of steppe warfare.[159] Nomadic warfare depends on speed, mobility, surprise, and the use of archery to avoid the uncertainties of pitched battles. It follows from this that the nomad warrior of Inner Asian history is an archer on horseback. His tactics rest on ambush, the feigned retreat, the shower of arrows loosed from a distance, and the confusion and consequent disruption of his enemy's marching order. These procedures work well in the steppe, when problems of supply prevent determined pursuit by a sedentary power, or in mountainous areas. They can lead to the conquest of settled areas, forts, and cities only when there is sufficient manpower or imported sedentary labor and talent to undertake siege warfare. While the huge Mongol forces were able to conscript such manpower from all of Inner Asia, such reserves were not available in Bithynia.

Thus, early Ottoman military history is, as is its economic parallel, a story of sedentarization for military advantage. To reduce the Bithynian cities, patient negotiations and long sieges were necessary. The levying of troops for blockades and sieges, however, required a settled population, for the necessity of locating fresh pasture prevents the prolonged concentration of nomads in a small area. Thus, early Ottoman siege warfare reflects the sedentarization of the Ottoman military point of view. In the earliest days, forts were taken by ambushing the defenders when they sallied forth, not by the use of engines.[160] Tricoccia was the only fort which Osman stormed. He did this not by the use of engines but by the laborious process of constructing a ramp of rubble up the walls.[161] All this must have impressed on him the importance of a strong infantry.[162] He began to use sedentary armies' siege techniques, and set up stockades to guard the approaches to Bursa; it is instructive that siege engines, which other emirates used in the 1320s, do not appear in the Ottoman sources until later in Orkhan's reign.[163]

Orkhan brought about the sedentarization of the Ottoman army. We have already seen that he was concerned for the maintenance of his forts; let us see what caused him to intensify the growth of his infantry.[164] In my view, the decisive action was the battle of Pelekanon in June 1329.[165] Orkhan's force consisted of nomad archers. A series of brief encounters was indecisive, but the Byzantines were able to repulse two larger Turkish attacks. It would seem as though the two armies had fought to a draw, although the Byzantines began to return to camp as victors. It was only during the undisciplined retirement of the Byzantine infantry that the Turks were able to sow panic and turn an indecisive encounter into a rout. It was the aftermath of the battle, not the direct encounter itself, which furnished Orkhan with victory.

We cannot look over Orkhan's shoulder as he analyzed the lessons of Pelekanon; but we do know the sequel and it may be possible to reconstruct one plausible line of argument connecting it with the battle. A larger nomadic force might well have overcome the Byzantines, but a larger nomadic force of cavalrymen, horses, and remounts could not flourish on the limited Bithynian pastures. And as Orkhan's nomads had failed to force the issue during the battle, the perpetuation of the status quo made little sense. The realistic, possible and sensible alternative was to base a larger army not on expensive horsemen but on infantry. We know that Orkhan did just this, and the creation of the *yaya* infantry corps at this time reflects the Ottoman leaders' resolution that the successful military future of their enterprise demanded the creation of a sedentary army. The mounted archer became an anachronism in Ottoman history, and with its fall from prestige another step in the movement away from nomadism, and respect for nomads' needs, was firmly taken.[166] The success of Orkhan's sieges indicates that his army was founded on settled recruits. Al-Umari's statement that Orkhan had a large infantry and a second-rate cavalry shows how far the sedentarization had gone. One source of the manpower for infantry and siege warfare may still have been nomadic, since nomads who had poor flocks, i.e., under-capitalized nomads, would be available for service on foot or for a longer term. It would, therefore, be an exaggeration to see the settlement of the Ottomans as complete by the 1330s. After all, Orkhan did assign one of his sons to the herding of sheep.[167] If Ibn Khaldun is correct, Orkhan adopted Bursa as his capital but occasionally lived in a tent on the outskirts of the city.[168] The emirate of Orkhan was hardly a nomadic enterprise, even if Orkhan may have seemed somehow still attracted to nomads' ways. A nomadic host did not bring the Ottomans to power, and the Ottomans remembered this.

We have now seen that both economic and military motives acted to settle the Ottomans and to decrease their concern for the welfare of those who remained nomads. Let us now turn to the third aspect of nomadism which is at issue here, that political manifestation of nomadism that we call the tribe. We may begin from the comparative perspective of another frontier area:

> As the Chinese pithily expressed it long ago, an empire could be conquered on horseback, but not ruled from horseback; civil servants more sophisticated than barbarian warriors were needed to extract a regular flow of taxes and tribute from the civilized part of the empire, they could be recruited only among the upper classes of the conquered civilized people, and they and their families had to be protected and allowed to perpetuate themselves.[169]

Osman's role in this process was that of a chief elected by his tribesmen. As the tribe's representative he successfully organized and directed the semi-annual migrations. He helped the tribe cope with outside pressures such as the lords and fortifications of Bilecik and Inegöl. He was the leader in the nomadic enterprises of hunting and predation. As a successful chief, he saw his tribe grow and prosper. As non-pastoralists joined, however, his success brought its own problems.

Osman did not stem from a sedentary, farming family. He was, or was soon to be, an ex-nomad. His concerns: the freedom of the marketplace at Eskişehir, the welfare of his foundation of Yenişehir, the transformation of predation to siege and blockade, all are aspects of sedentary statecraft, and the bureaucratic trappings of sedentary administration are alien to the steppe pastoralist. In anarchic Bithynia, where rumors of Mongols aroused and emptied cities, where such government representatives as Pseudo-Lachanes and Hilarion could raise and support their own establishments, and where the tax collectors were enemies to be abused, how was the untutored Osman to organize his nomads, ex-nomads, and Byzantine allies? We have seen that the Byzantine governmental paradigm was inappropriate if not completely unwelcome. What else did Osman have at his disposal? He had the tribe. Bithynian tribalism, the early Ottoman enterprise, was simply the political legacy of the Turks' former pastoral nomadic society. Tribalism, or the chiefdom,[170] is the political aspect of nomadism, and as such was the sensible way for Osman to organize his followers. As their practice of pastoralism gave way to settled revenue sharing Osman's fellow ex-nomads remained Osman's fellow tribesmen. Osman was that successful Bithynian about whom a multi-confessional, polyglot group crystallized.[171] Historians call this group the Osmanlıs, the tribe of Osman. It is high time to take *that* label seriously.

The tribe was a useful device for pulling together such seemingly disparate groups as Turkish pastoralists and Byzantine settlers.[172] Modern anthropologists' field studies show that tribal, clan, and even camp membership are more open than tribal idiom or ideology might indicate. For instance, the camp consists ideally of a small group of consanguineous members. In fact, however, many camps have members without blood ties to their campmates. These "sharers of the same shade" belong because they can share and serve well, not because they belong to the family: "the camp is, simply, an economically cooperative unit, containing a mixed labor pool, each segment of which is reliant on the others."[173] To the extent that blood ties seemed essential for those who joined the enterprise, clan genealogies were "recalled" which forged distant relationships among lineages much as the Turkmen do today. Wittek discovered this phenomenon when he destroyed the literary clan genealogies of the Ottomans: his hazy area and gaps between generations were just those fertile spots where, in conversation, two men could discover a link between their houses. The idiom of tribal ideology was one of kinship, but the tribal reality was formed of shared interest, advantage, and service.[174]

The tribe was, then, a useful political institution. Kinship, in fact, neither necessarily nor sufficiently defined it. While external dangers may promote the rise of a chief, other criteria help to promote the shared interests that define the tribesmen: "There is no larger group who, besides recognizing themselves as a distinct local community, affirms their obligation to combine in warfare against outsiders and acknowledge the rights of their members to compensation for injury."[175] Membership in the tribe allows groups from varied backgrounds to live in close proximity and carry on their independent affairs in peace, and some Byzantines found this a means of survival and success in Bithynia.[176]

How did Osman manage to lead this tribe? Pehrson's study of the Marri of Baluchistan provides a clue:

> What defines and delimits the Marri as a social unit is thus, not common origin and descent, but political identity as an organized tuman, or politically independent tribes. The critical office in this tribal organization is that of the central chief, the tumandar or sardar.... At its inception, Marri tribal organization may have been primarily an organization of fighting men for military expeditions and the division of spoils.[177]

The most successful leader at predation, at the hunt, at finding pasture or water for survival, and, in Bithynia, at governance, may form his own tribe: "It [was] the fact of political unity under the Basseri chief which in the eyes of the tribesmen and outsiders alike constitute[d] them into a single tribe in the Persian sense."[178] Such was the achievement of Osman.[179]

That achievement reverberated over the next two centuries of Near Eastern history. When the Safavid Persians fought the Ottoman Turks in the early sixteenth century, the "Persian" forces were largely Turkish and the "Turkish" soldiers largely Balkan peoples. It was not only the conscription of children which turned Serbs or Albanians into Ottomans. The Bithynian Byzantines were hardly the only non-Turks who became Ottomans, they were merely the first.[180]

Since, in recruiting members, the tribe may disregard family, language, and religion, it fitted the settled Byzantine Bithynians as well as the nomads. Since the tribe was called the Osmanlıs, we know its development was due to Osman himself. Not only his own blood descendants but also the families of Köse Mihal, Evrenos, and their descendants, became Ottomans.[181] Many Greeks were not happy under their new master and his ways, of course. Some who embraced Islam in the hope of advancement through religious conformity alone later returned to their former faith. Others did not. Byzantine sources affirm that Christians served as Ottoman officials in the 1340s and 1350s. An author who had every reason to hate the Ottomans filled his account with evidence of the tolerant *modus vivendi* established in Bithynia.[182] Descent, faith, occupation were all secondary to the shared political concerns which united men under Osman. This *ad hoc* element in the early development of a tribe is not uncommon in areas of near anarchy. In Afghanistan, an elderly informant described the nineteenth century growth of the Marri Baluch in the following way: "In those days there was war and anarchy. Nobody asked who is your father, brother. You joined in the fighting force, moved and conquered and moved again. Later only did it become fixed and settled like now."[183]

Osman's first success as a tribal chief was due to his ability to protect the few, strong, common interests of his tribesmen: pasture, the hunt, and survival. His authority grew because he served as a fulcrum between tribal and external interests, between his followers and their former Byzantine masters or their Mongol overlords. He gained new tribesmen as he demonstrated success in representing the tribe to those forces threatening Bithynians.[184] His success brought new opportunities and new problems in the form of non-nomad and non-Turkish recruits, such as Köse Mihal.[185]

The tribe, however, is not fitted to serve the needs of a more complex society with disparate and ramifying goals and institutions. The Ottoman foundations at Yenişehir and later at Bursa complicated Osman and Orkhan's role as nomadic chief with the necessities of urban administration and settled agricultural economies. The interests of the Osmanlıs were no longer so simple nor were they wholly nomadic. In a more complex environment a more complex government was necessary. And here we see that our third, political, aspect of nomadism gave way to sedentary models. As the Ottoman chiefs dropped their last ties to nomads' ways, nomads' needs no longer drove them—and in fact no longer concerned them. They now had different aspirations and a different clientele, and if differences occurred, it was now the nomads' interests which suffered and became minimal to the chief—or should we now call him sultan? The settled institutions and ideology for such a bureaucratic enterprise were ready, in the hands of the men of the Muslim schools. They already appear in a pious foundation deed composed for Orkhan in 1324.[186] The schoolmen also, as we have seen, had a ready-made ideology for the next stage of growth in Ottoman government. As the Holy War, the jihad, was invoked for the initial bedouin operations in early Islam, so was the early Ottoman nomad predation justified by the ghaza. The 1337 inscription, then, is a commentary on the state of Ottoman bureaucratic development and not the key to Ottoman origins.

There is another measure of the administrative transformation which Ottomans felt to have occurred as Orkhan's rule achieved its mature form. At the conclusion of many of his tales, the chronicler Aşıkpaşazade sums up his feelings with a short poem. After discussing Orkhan's conquest of the neighboring emirate of Karası (1334-1336), Aşıkpaşazade's concluding poem remarks that a cadaster *(defter)* was drawn up: the warriors' conquest was complete only when the land was written up.[187] Thus, in later eyes, administration was a keynote of Orkhan's rule - but nomads do not have secretaries. There is no extant evidence that Orkhan did in fact have Karası surveyed and registered; nonetheless, the later view saw in his rule the final transformation of Ottoman society to a settled polity and society.

The ghaza became the creed of the Ottomans in their histories and on their buildings. In the early days, however, the need to ward off Germiyan, the slow penetration of the soldiers by Islam and the slower transformation of heroes with powerful graves into martyrs of the faith, all rendered it unlikely that a religious sanction drove Osman on his hunt for power. His descendants were right to boast, in the words of Namık Kemal, "We raised a world-conquering state from a tribe."

Osman made a tribe, the Osmanlıs, of his nomad followers. The political program supporting this tribalization was regular predation that overburdened the supportive capacities of Bithynian nomadism, with its limited pastures and manpower. Both Osman and Orkhan, therefore, opened their tribe and its enterprise to others, especially to the ex-nomads and ex-farmers ruined by other Turkish competition and Byzantine severity. The tribe grew with these new recruits, but it was no longer a nomadic tribe. Successes forced changes in its very nature. Voluntary association was inadequate to raise the numbers and maintain the impetus required in Balkan campaigning. Osman and Orkhan's successors separated themselves entirely from tribal powers and obligations. They were no longer the chiefs of tribesmen. They became the lords over subjects both settled and nomadic. Nomads did not appreciate the transition from chosen chief to distant lord. The Ottomans soon tried to enforce the status of subject upon the nomads through taxation and registration procedures no different from those applied to peasants. The next chapters examine this process.

* * * *

It is time to recapitulate the stages of our journey. The first task we set ourselves was to examine the theory which holds that the spirit of the Holy War promoted the Ottomans to power. It was a necessary task, since any contribution which nomadic tribalism might make to old Ottoman history would be vitiated by the presence of as exclusive a feeling as enthusiastic religious zeal.The result of our preliminary excursion into Ottoman historiography was that the Wittek theory of the Holy War no longer finds support in the evidence. This result allowed us to turn to the history of thirteenth-century Bithynia with an eye to following the traces of pastoral nomads and their impact upon settled Byzantines. Here there were two main strands defining the outlines of the tapestry. Discontent spreading among the Byzantines after their leaders forsook Anatolia for Constantinople, and exchanged investment in the welfare of the East for a concern in its taxes and loyalty: this set of processes colored the first strand. The second, setting off the first, was the growth of Osman's leadership based upon his chieftaincy of Turkish pastoralists and his appeal as leader and protector to some of the discontented Byzantines. We then moved from a more or less chronological resumé of Bithynia's late medieval nomadic history to a threefold analysis of the legacy of nomadism to the early Ottoman enterprise. All three aspects of this analysis, economic, military, and political, pointed the way to nomadism's demise and growing disrepute in the last years of Osman's life and the flowering of the career of his son Orkhan. Ecological considerations dictated the settlement of Osman's pastoralists. Military necessity pointed to the increase of an Ottoman infantry and the decline of mounted archery. And the complexity of administering farms, markets, religious institutions, cities, and secretaries all led to the transformation of a chief into a sultan.

The Ottoman enterprise's settlement, in short, was the story of this chapter. With that sedentarization came the appropriation of sedentary values. These values grew to be so important that it became unthinkable to presume that Osman had ever embraced other notions. Old Ottoman historiography had now to demonstrate that the founder of their greatness reflected the same social views as his descendants. The chroniclers found a simple device with which to express this firm conviction, the dream of future power, and this dream's spurning of nomadic values provides a fitting end to our story.

The dream or portent of future power and grandeur is common in historical literature. Herodotus told of Astyages, ruler of the Medes, and his dream of Cyrus' empire. Later legend held that the grandfather of Muhammad dreamed of his descendant's powerful destiny.[188] Similar dreams adorn the chronicles of such later Turkish dynasties as the Ghaznavids and Seljuks.[189] None of these accounts, however, evidences as much detail and careful revision as the Ottoman version.[190] Let us read the story of Osman's dream:

> Osman Ghazi prayed (for new raids against the Christians) and briefly wept (for fallen comrades). Then sleep won him over, so he lay down and rested. He saw that among (his acquaintances) was a highly-esteemed sheykh, whose many miracles were well-known and whom all the people followed. They called him a dervish, but his dervish qualities were deep within him. He possessed much in the way of worldly goods, comforts, and sheep. He also had both students and knowledge. His guest house was never vacant and Osman Ghazi himself used to come from time to time and be a guest of this holy man. As Osman Ghazi slept he saw that a moon arose from the holy man's breast and came to sink in Osman Ghazi's breast. A tree then sprouted from his navel, and its shade compassed the world. Beneath this shade there were mountains, and streams flowed forth from the foot of each mountain. Some people drank from these running waters, others watered gardens, while yet others caused fountains to flow. (When Osman awoke he went and) told the story to the sheykh, who said, "Osman, my son, congratulations, for God has given the imperial office to you and your descendants, and my daughter Malkhun shall be your wife."[191] He married them forthwith and gave his daughter to Osman Ghazi.[192]

Here Vergil's Aeneas and Bonaventure's Francis find a worthy cousin in the fifteenth century's official Osman. The arboreal image with its firm roots and branches protecting fountains and gardens reflects the purpose of the Ottoman enterprise. The Ottomans represented peace and plenty for settled agriculture, a bucolic promise made explicit in the dream. The Ottoman dream was for farmers and merchants, not for nomads.

Not only were the nomads deprived of a place in the shade, they were now potentially a source of trouble. As the sequel will show, the Ottomans soon went to some trouble to settle the "problem" of the nomads. The nomads, who had been present as partners at the creation of the Ottoman enterprise, became its unwilling and unwanted subjects. Ultimately, they sought for a leader and a dream of their own, and we shall see how they found theirs. Harrassed by their sultan, they created a shah. To the Ottoman dream of peace, they brought the vision of a sword. Let us now see how the Ottoman vision in Anatolia became the Safavi nightmare.

Notes to Chapter One

1. APZ, p. 34.
2. Paul Wittek, *The Rise of the Ottoman Empire* (London, 1938).
3. Robert Mantran, "Les inscriptions arabes de Brousse," *Bulletin d'études orientales* 14 (1952-4), p. 89.
4. Wittek, *Rise,* p. 2.
5. *Ibid.,* p. 4.
6. *Ibid.,* p. 3. For a brief glance at Wittek's attitudes and ambivalent feelings, see the remarks of Professor V.L. Ménage in *International Journal of Middle East Studies* 12 (1980), p. 373.
7. The reader may obtain a fuller vision of Wittek's cultural and philosophical assumptions in this period from a careful reading of his "Türkentum und Islam," *Archiv für Sozialwissenschaft und Sozialpolitik* 59 (1928), pp. 489-525.
8. For some notes on the difference between *ex post facto* justification and actual practice, see W.M. Watt, "Islamic Conceptions of the Holy War," in T.P. Murphy, ed., *The Holy War* (Columbus, 1976), pp. 141-56. For ghazis as a source of unrest within Muslim lands see C.E. Bosworth, *The Ghaznavids* (Edinburgh, 1963), p. 167. On the ambivalence of their "spiritual impulses" see V.V. Barthold, *Turkestan Down to the Mongol Invasion,* third ed. (London, 1968), pp. 215-17, 239, 287.
9. P. Wittek, "Von der byzantinischen zur türkischen Toponymie," *Byzantion* 10 (1935), p. 37.
10. IBS, p. 70.
11. J. Darrouzès, ed., *Les regestes des actes du Patriarcat de Constantinople* 1:5 (Paris, 1977), no. 2198.
12. A. Philippides-Braat, "La captivité de Palamas chez les Turcs: dossier et commentaire," *Travaux et mémoires* 7 (1979), pp. 161, 203-5. These passages provide incidental proof that the introduction of the devşirme must be placed after 1354.
13. The safest guide to this material is V.L. Ménage, "The Menaqib of Yakhshi Faqih," *Bulletin of the School of Oriental and African Studies* 26 (1963), pp. 50-54.
14. APZ, pp. 8, 15.
15. APZ, p. 14.
16. G. Moravcsik, *Byzantinoturcica,* second ed. (Berlin, 1958), vol. 2, s.v. *gaze, gazes.* Contemporary Arabic sources such as Ibn Battuta and al-Umari do not term Osman or Orkhan a ghazi.

17. Peter Schreiner, *Studien zu den Brachea Chronika* (Munich, 1967), pp. 67, 70, 78, 100.

18. Anon. Chron., p. 11. The later tale of Geyikli Baba further illustrates the heterodox ways of the most popular early Ottoman religious leaders. For a harmless, entrepreneurial continuation of the tradition of Geyikli Baba, see *Turkish Letters of Ogier Ghiselin de Busbecq*, trans. by E.S. Forster (Oxford, 1927), pp. 99-100.

19. S. Vryonis, "Evidence on Human Sacrifice among the Early Ottoman Turks," *Journal of Asian History* 5 (1971), pp. 140-46; Vryonis, *Decline*, pp. 273 n. 765, 433; Vryonis, "The Byzantine Legacy and Ottoman Forms," *Dumbarton Oaks Papers* 23-24 (1969-70), p. 260; *The Travels of Ibn Battuta, A.D. 1325-1354*, trans. by H.A.R. Gibb (Cambridge, 1962), vol. 2, p. 447. On mummification see the Ottoman recipes in A. Süheyl Ünver, "Eski Mısırda, Islam dünyasında ve bizde tahnit maddeleri hakkında," *Fuad Köprülü armağanı*, (Istanbul, 1953), pp. 581-87. Professor V.L. Ménage kindly provided this reference and points out that such treatment may have been simply a sanitary measure in those cases when burial had to be delayed (e.g., Murad I).

20. Anon. Chron., p. 12; APZ, p. 22.

21. APZ, pp. 11-12.

22. An extension of this line of argument appears under the title "Stimulus and Justification in Early Ottoman History," in N.M. Vaporis, ed., *Byzantium and Islam* (Boston, in press).

23. Franz Taeschner, "Beiträge zur frühosmanische Epigraphik und Archäologie," *Der Islam* 20 (1932), pp. 114-15; 22 (1934), p. 69; T. Seif, "Der Abschnitt über die Osmanen in Şukrullah's persischer Universalgeschichte," *Mitteilungen zur Osmanischen Geschichte* 2 (1923-26), pp. 82-3; Ibn Battuta, p. 451, noted ulema from Konya and Egypt in western Anatolia.

24. Some ideas and practices were, however, transferred when the Ottoman ulema could find no Muslim parallel or before one came to mind. See the remarks of Professor Ménage in *Bulletin of the School of Oriental and African Studies* 36 (1973), p. 661.

25. I. Beldiceanu-Steinherr, "Le règne de Selim Ier: tournant dans la vie politique et réligieuse de l'empire ottoman," *Turcica* 6 (1975), pp. 36-7. One possible way for Osman or Orkhan to have fallen in with the designs of the ulema appears in the anachronistic tale of the first imposition of an Ottoman market tax: APZ, p. 21.

26. Claude Cahen, *Pre-Ottoman Turkey* (London, 1968), pp. 301-2; Osman Turan, *Selçuklular zamanında Türkiye* (Istanbul, 1971), pp. 645-50.

27. A close study of the architectural history of fourteenth-century Anatolia would show that more foundations (and therefore employment) were due to patronage outside rather than inside the Mongol orbit. For a general and attractive survey see Oktay Aslanapa, ed., *Yüzyıllar boyunca Türk sanatı: ondördüncü yüzyıl* (Istanbul, 1977), with a good photograph of the 1337 inscription on p. 15.

28. For an excellent discussion of the purpose and audience of such inscriptions see Richard Ettinghausen, "Arabic Epigraphy: Communication or Symbolic Affirmation," *Near Eastern Numismatics, Iconography, Epigraphy and History: Studies in Honor of George C. Miles* (Beirut, 1974), pp. 297-317.

29. Wittek, "Der Stammbaum der Osmanen," *Der Islam* 14 (1925), pp. 94-100; Wittek, *Rise*, pp. 7-12; Köprülü's rejoinder is in his "Osmanlı imparatorluğu'nun etnik menşei meselesi," *Belleten* 7 (1943), pp. 285-86, 297-300, 303. For a recent display of the possible uses of such tribal genealogies see J. Woods, *The Aqquyunlu* (Chicago, 1976), pp. 186-96.

30. W.W. Swidler, "Adaptive Processes Regulating Nomad-Sedentary Interaction in the Middle East," in Cynthia Nelson, ed., *The Desert and the Sown: Nomads in the Wider Society* (Berkeley, 1973), p. 30. See also the general essay of Professor John M. Smith, Jr., to appear in the forthcoming *Cambridge History of Inner Asia.*

31. For the major features of the region see J.C. Dewdney, *Turkey, an Introductory Geography* (London, 1971), pp. 151-54, 160-65.

32. Vryonis, *Decline,* pp. 184-94. In an episode narrated by the Byzantine chronicler John Cinnamus (ed. Bonn, pp. 59-60), Manuel I appears to drive off a mass of booty-laden nomads (Vryonis, *Decline,* p. 121); in fact the imperial horsemen were unable to catch the swifter nomads, even though on this occasion the Byzantines had remounts available.

33. The nomads' threat was compounded by the seasonal nature of their migrations. During winter and early spring, when the Byzantine armies did not campaign, the Turkish pastoralists were seeking pasture (or plunder) in the warmer, snow-free lowlands. When summer (and the Byzantine soldiers) came, the nomads sought the greener grazing and cooler weather atop the ridges and plateau; this made it more difficult for the Byzantines to find, chase, and destroy them. By the same token the protection of the heights allowed the nomads ample opportunity to ambush their foes.

34. Nicetas Choniates, *Historia,* ed. by J.-L. van Dieten (Berlin, 1975), pp. 496-97; in general, Vryonis, *Decline,* pp. 127-30. In October 1147 a German contingent of crusaders crossed the watershed of the Sarı Su and noted the large herds of sheep grazing the plains around Eskişehir; Odo of Deuil, *De profectione Ludovici VII in orientem,* ed. by H. Waquet (Paris, 1949), p. 56; W. Tomaschek, "Zur historischen Topographie von Kleinasien im Mittelalter," *SB Wien* 124: 8 (1891), p. 90. The fortifications erected by the Comneni did not hinder the Turks: H. Ahrweiler, "Les forteresses construites en Asie Mineure face à l'invasion Seldjoucide," *Akten des XI. Internationalen Byzantinistenkongresses, München, 1958* (Munich, 1960), pp. 182-89, and also her "Choma-Aggélokastron," *Revue des études byzantines* 24 (1966), pp. 278-83.

35. William J. Hamilton, *Researches in Asia Minor, Pontus, and Armenia* (London, 1842), vol. 1, p. 74n, vol. 2, p. 186.

36. Wittek, "Toponymie," pp. 12-16, 38.

37. Vryonis, *Decline,* p. 189.

38. For a general treatment of this opportunism see Marshall D. Sahlins, *Tribesmen* (Englewood Cliffs, 1968), p. 36.

39. H. Ahrweiler, "L'expérience nicéenne," *Dumbarton Oaks Papers* 29 (1975), pp. 21-40.

40. Alfons Maria Schneider, *Die römischen und byzantinischen Denkmäler von Iznik-Nicaea* (Berlin, 1943), p. 5. On the southern portion of the Nicene state see H. Ahrweiler, "L'histoire et la géographie de la région de Smyrne entre les deux occupations turques (1081-1317), particulièrement au XIIIe siècle," *Travaux et memoires* 1 (1965), pp. 1-204. For a broader study, M. Angold, *A Byzantine Government in Exile: Government and Society under the Laskarids of Nicaea (1204-1261)* (Oxford, 1974).

41. Theodore Scutariotes in George Acropolites, ed. by A. Heisenberg, vol. 1, pp. 284-88; Pach., vol. 1, pp. 68, 70, 71; Nicephorus Gregoras, ed. Bonn, vol. 1, pp. 41-44; in general, Angold, pp. 116-17.

42. During the reign of Michael VIII, the content was fifteen carats. Andronicus II's coinage sank to eleven carats. In all probability there were no mints in Bithynia. M.F. Hendy,

Coinage and Money in the Byzantine Empire, 1081-1261 (Washington, D.C., 1969), pp. 231, 320-21. Angold, pp. 117-19.

43. H. Ahrweiler, "La politique agraire des empereurs de Nicée," *Byzantion* 28 (1958), p. 57. Angold, ch. 7.

44. Ahrweiler, "Politique agraire," p. 57.

45. Gregoras, vol. 1, p. 37; Acropolites, vol. 1, p. 65.

46. Ahrweiler, "Politique agraire," pp. 61, 64; Ahrweiler, "L'épitéleia dans le cartulaire de la Lembiotissa," *Byzantion* 24 (1954), pp. 71-93; "A propos de l'épitéleia," *Byzantion* 25-26 (1955-57), pp. 369-72; Angold, p. 101.

47. Pach., vol. 1, pp. 16-18, 222; Wittek, *Das Fürstentum Mentesche* (Istanbul, 1934), p. 9.

48. A.M. Schneider and W. Karnapp, *Die Stadtmauer von Iznik (Nicaea)* (Berlin, 1938), p. 6, and inscriptions 37-39; Schneider, *Denkmäler*, p. 4; S. Şahin, *Katalog der antiken Inschriften des Museums von Iznik (Nikaia)* (Bonn, 1979), nos. 480-82.

49. Schneider, *Denkmäler*, p. 4; Semavi Eyice, "Iznikde bir Bizans kilisesi," *Belleten* 13 (1949), pp. 37-51; Hans Buchwald, "Lascarid Architecture," *Jahrbuch der Österreichischen Byzantinistik* 28 (1979), p. 263.

50. Nicole Thierry, "L'art monumental byzantin en Asie Mineure du XIe siècle au XIVe," *Dumbarton Oaks Papers* 29 (1975), pp. 73-111; for Bursa, *CIG* no. 8744.

51. For a general appreciation see Clive Foss, *Ephesus after Antiquity* (Cambridge, 1979), p. 131.

52. This topic forms the subject of a forthcoming work by Clive Foss, to whom I am indebted for many conversations on Byzantine archaeology. See for the moment his *Byzantine and Turkish Sardis* (Cambridge, 1976), pp. 66-76, and his "Archaeology and the Twenty Cities of Byzantine Asia," *American Journal of Archaeology* 81 (1977), pp. 469-86. A comparative study of building programs in Anatolia and the Balkans might throw interesting light on the widely-held assumption that Asia Minor was the "heartland" of Byzantium in the ninth and tenth centuries.

53. George G. Arnakis, "Byzantium's Anatolian Provinces during the Reign of Michael Palaeologus," *Actes du XIIe congrès international d'études byzantines, Ochrid 1961* (Belgrade, 1964), vol. 2, p. 37.

54. Acropolites, vol. 1, p. 136.

55. M.F. Brosset, *Histoire de la Géorgie* (St. Petersburg, 1850), vol. 1, pt. 2, pp. 511, 539.

56. C. Cahen, "Ibn Sa'id sur l'Asie Mineure seldjouqide," *Tarih araştırmaları dergisi* 6:10-11 (1968), pp. 44, 48. For the identification of Gerede Bolu, see Alessio Bombaci, "The Army of the Saljuqs of Rum," *Istituto orientale di Napoli, Annali* 38 (1978), p. 364. Ibn Sa'id's numbers give, of course, only the order of magnitude of the nomadic population.

57. Acropolites, vol. 1, p. 137; Pach., vol. 1, p. 25.

58. Ahrweiler, "Politique agraire," p. 66; I.E. Troitskij, *Arsenij i arsenity* (reprint, London, 1973); I. Sykoutres, "Peri to schisma ton arseniaton," *Hellenika* 2 (1929), pp. 267-332, 3 (1930), pp. 15-44.

59. Pach., vol. 1, p. 310.

60. Gregoras, vol. 1, p. 138; Arnakis, p. 41.

61. Pach., vol. 1, pp. 221-23, 243-44; C. Chapman, *Michel Paléologue* (Paris, 1926), p. 157; Arnakis, pp. 40-41.

62. For the date see M. Treu, "Manuel Holobolos," *Byzantinische Zeitschrift* 5 (1896), pp. 541-44; for the site see Tomaschek, p. 8; Pach., vol. 1, pp. 193-94, 201, vol. 2, pp. 637-38. The identification of Tricoccia with Hocahisar, first made by Hammer, is unsure. The text mentioning Tricoccia in the testament of Patriarch Arsenius (*PG* 140, col. 948) provides no further information; at col. 956 Arsenius decides to remain silent concerning the events. He does admit to having baptized the children of Turkish emirs (who were, one presumes, no ghazis).

63. Pach., vol. 1, pp. 193-201; Arnakis, p. 43.

64. Pach., vol. 1, pp. 249-50; Albert Failler, "Chronologie et composition dans l'histoire de Georges Pachymère," *Revue des études byzantines* 39 (1981), pp. 170-71; R. Janin, "Nicée, étude historique et topographique," *Echos d'orient* 24 (1925), p. 487; Janin, "La Bithynie sous l'empire byzantin," *Echos d'orient* 20 (1921), p. 313. Another measure of insecurity was the peasants' lack of coin with which to pay taxes. Without safe routes to market, they could not obtain money and so could pay only in kind. Pach., vol. 1, p. 222.

65. Pach., vol. 1, pp. 133, 222-23; Arnakis, pp. 50, 58. It seems to me that the necessity for stealth, as well as the willingness to serve the Byzantines, argues for the conclusion that these were particularly poor nomads, i.e., pastoralists without adequate herds.

66. Pach., vol. 1, pp. 311-12.

67. Pach., vol. 1, p. 474; Gregoras, vol. 1, p. 142; P. Charanis, "A Note on the Population and Cities of the Byzantine Empire in the Thirteenth Century," *The Joshua Starr Memorial Volume* (New York, 1953), p. 136.

68. Pach., vol. 1, pp. 243-44; Gregoras, vol. 1, pp. 137-38; Laiou, *Cpl.*, p. 22.

69. D.J. Geanakoplos, *The Emperor Michael Palaeologus and the West, 1258-1282* (Cambridge, Mass., 1959), p. 343.

70. Laiou, *Cpl.*, p. 23 n. 38.

71. Pach., vol. 1, pp. 502-5; Failler, "Chronologie et composition," pp. 244-47; Laiou, *Cpl.*, p. 23. The desolation was not all the work of the Turks, for torrential spring rains (as later in 1302) had washed away much of the cover and silted up some of the streams. The fertility of such eroded soil would fall accordingly.

72. Charanis, "Note on Population," p. 137.

73. Quoted by Laiou, *Cpl.*, p. 25.

74. V. Laurent, *Regestes*, 1:4 (Paris, 1971), no. 1492. An imperial grant (ca. 1315) provides another comparison: a village in Paphlagonia and a village in the Optimate theme, yielding rents of 200 and 202 *hyperpyra* each. F. Dölger, *Regesten der Kaiserurkunden des oströmischen Reiches* (Munich, 1924-65), no. 2357.

75. J. Sölch, "Historisch-geographische Studien über bithynische Siedlungen: Nikomedia, Nikaea, Prusa," *Byzantinische-neugriechische Jahrbücher* 1 (1920), pp. 281-82.

76. Laiou, *Cpl.*, pp. 76, 79.

77. *Ibid.*, p. 80; Arnakis, p. 47.

78. Pach., vol. 2, pp. 210-29; Arnakis, pp. 42-43; Vryonis, *Decline*, pp. 136-37; Laiou, *Cpl.*, pp. 80-82; Laiou, "Some Observations on Alexios Philanthropenos and Maximos Planoudes,"

Byzantine and Modern Greek Studies 4 (1978), pp. 89-98. The inhabitants of Philadelphia retained such a strong affection for Philanthropenus that when troops of Aydın and Germiyan besieged the city in 1322-24, Andronicus sent Alexius to rally them and treat with the Turks (who may also have held fond memories of him): P. Schreiner, "Zur Geschichte Philadelpheias im 14. Jahrhundert (1293-1390)," *Orientalia christiana periodica* 35 (1969), pp. 390-92.

79. Arnakis, pp. 47-48; Laiou, *Cpl.*, p. 86.

80. Pach., vol. 2, p. 259; Laurent, *Regestes*, no. 1573; Laiou, *Cpl.*, pp. 87-89.

81. Dölger, *Regesten*, no. 2241.

82. Laiou, *Cpl.*, p. 90.

83. J. Kelleher, quoted in P.H. Sawyer and I.N. Wood, eds., *Early Medieval Kingship* (Leeds, 1977), p. 95.

84. I also rely heavily on the fourteenth-century source which, refracted through APZ's text, contains much good material on old Ottoman Bithynia. On that source see Professor Ménage's "Yakhshi Faqih."

85. Professors Ménage and Inalcik have demonstrated that Karamani Mehmet Paşa's chronicle derives from the same source, now lost, used by Ahmedi and Şukrullah. Here I use the translation of I.H. Konyalı, "Tevarih es-selatin al-osmaniye," in Ç. N. Atsız, ed., *Osmanlı tarihleri* (Istanbul, 1947), p. 343.

86. On the identification of Söğüt with Sagoudaous, see IBS, p. 60.

87. Anon. Chron., p. 5; APZ, pp. 7-8; see also *Cam-i Cem ayin*, in *Osmanlı tarihleri*, p. 394, implying that all the tribesmen soon settled at Söğüt and gave up nomadism.

88. Wittek, *Mentesche*, p. 37, locates Ermeni Beli; see also F. Taeschner, "Anatolische Forschungen," *Zeitschrift der Deutschen Morgenländischen Gesellschaft* 82 (1928), map opposite p. 114. Armenians settled near Nicaea aided the soldiers of the Latin Empire against the Lascarids. To locate them exactly there is no information besides the place names Ermeni Beli, Ermeni Derbend, Ermeni Dağı. It is noteworthy that their memory lived on into the fifteenth century. For Armenians elsewhere in the Lascarid realms, see Ahrweiler, "Smyrne," p. 20.

89. See the chart in F. Barth, *Nomads*, pp. 150-51.

90. Wittek, "Toponymie," p. 37; Karamani Mehmet Paşa, p. 344; "Şukrullah," p. 79; APZ has Osman conquer Karacahisar, while the Anon. Chron. does not discuss the conquest.

91. Anon. Chron., p. 6.

92. The chroniclers use the term "martolos" for similar reasons: Robert Anhegger, "Martoloslar hakkında," *Türkiyat mecmuası* 7-8 (1940-42), pp. 282-320; H. Inalcik, *Fatih devri üzerinde tetkikler ve vesikalar* (Ankara, 1954), pp. 179-81.

93. Karamani Mehmet Paşa, pp. 344-45; for the later Ottoman forgeries based on this "event" see IBS, pp. 59-77.

94. "Şukrullah," pp. 78-79.

95. *Cam-i Cem ayin*, p. 395.

96. Cahen, *Turkey*, pp. 300-1, and Turan, *Türkiye*, pp. 634-35.

97. F. Babinger, *Die Geschichtsschreiber der Osmanen und ihre Werke* (Leipzig, 1927), p. 31.

98. APZ, p. 8.

99. Ménage, "Yakhshi Faqih," pp. 50-54.

100. A.S. Levend, *Türk dilinde gelişme ve sadeleşme evreleri* (Ankara, 1972), p. 18; IBS, p. 67.

101. V.L. Ménage, *Neshri's History of the Ottomans* (London, 1964), pp. 2, 18.

102. Neşri, p. 25.

103. IBS, pp. 45-46, 87, presents a slightly different view based on later evidence. For the growth of Osman's support among the tribesmen, see Anon. Chron., p. 6, lines 8-9. On the election of Orkhan, APZ, p. 34; on the election of Murad I, Ruhi, f.28v. In general, see Joseph Fletcher, "Turco-Mongolian Monarchic Tradition in the Ottoman Empire," *Harvard Ukrainian Studies* 3-4 (1979-80), pp. 236-51.

104. Barth, *Nomads,* p. 84; John Masson Smith, Jr., "Turanian Nomadism and Iranian Politics," *Iranian Studies* 11 (1978), pp. 63-64.

105. On the early raids see F. Tinnefeld, "Pachymeres und Philes als Zeugen für ein frühes Unternehmen gegen die Osmanen," *Byzantinische Zeitschrift* 64 (1971), pp. 46-54. For another example consider the thorny question of the date of the capture of Bilecik. The early Ottoman sources agree on 1299 as the date but give two versions, one a folktale which entered the main stream of Ottoman historiography, the other considerably more sensible: it may be found in Neşri, pp. 28-29. The contemporary Byzantine chronicler Pachymeres, on the other hand, dates the conquest only after the battle of Bapheus in 1302; but Pachymeres' chronology is often doubtful. The traditions concerning Bilecik deserve closer study. For a start, see Arnakis, p. 142 n. 31. But Arnakis did not consider the geography, which demands that Bilecik be neutralized before the environs of Nicomedia could safely be raided.

106. Anon. Chron., p. 7.

107. For the definition of an alp see H. Inalcik, "L'empire ottoman," *Actes du Premier Congrès international des études balkaniques et sud-est européennes, Sofia, 1966,* (Sofia, 1969), vol. 3, p. 75. Professor Inalcik contends that the alp had a Muslim sanction but cites no evidence for this statement.

108. APZ, p. 8.

109. APZ, pp. 15, 16, 25.

110. Barth, *Nomads,* p. 132. For a like practice, but in an ecological setting less conducive to settlement, see E.E. Evans-Pritchard, *The Sanusi of Cyrenaica* (Oxford, 1949), pp. 66-67. Shared interest had, in the past, linked Turks to the Byzantines. The nomads who served under Philanthropenus are a case in point. More central to Byzantine history, John Comnenus Axouch, a pretender to the throne in 1201, was the grandson of a Turk whom John II Comnenus had captured and won over: A. Bryer, "Cultural Relations between East and West in the Twelfth Century," in Derek Baker, ed., *Relations between East and West in the Middle Ages* (Edinburgh, 1973), p. 84. For three centuries members of the Gabras family served Byzantine or Seljuk regimes as their interests moved them: Bryer, "A Byzantine Family: the Gabrades, c.979-c.1653," *University of Birmingham Historical Journal* 12:2 (1970), pp. 164-87.

111. APZ, pp. 8-9, 12-14.

112. APZ, p. 16.

113. APZ, p. 22.

114. APZ, pp. 8-9, 14. That the tribe now disposed of immovable goods (and relatively immobile animals such as oxen) indicates a growth of interest in the trappings of settled life. This acquisitiveness would, in time, tie them to the land. As for Bilecik, according to APZ, Osman was once asked why he got on well with its Christians. He replied, "They are our neighbors. We came as strangers to this land, and they received us well. We must respect them." APZ, p. 16.

115. APZ, p. 14. E. Frances, "La féodalité byzantine et la conquête turque," *Studia et acta orientalia* 4 (1962), p. 70, claims that the Byzantine aristocracy, opposed by the mass of the people, treasonably joined the Turks. But what of the lord of Inegöl?

116. APZ, pp. 14-15. For markets as points of contact or neutral zones between contrasting groups, see K.G. Itzkowitz in F. Barth, ed., *Ethnic Groups and Boundaries* (Oslo, 1969), pp. 137, 144.

117. N. Swidler, "The Political Context of Brahui Sedentarization," *Ethnology* 12 (1973), p. 307.

118. APZ, p. 14.

119. I am influenced here by Don R. Bowen, "Guerilla War in Western Missouri, 1862-1865: Historical Extensions of the Relative Deprivation Hypothesis," *Comparative Studies in Society and History* 19 (1977), pp. 30-51. I thank Professor Mills Thornton for guiding me to this article. M.Ç. Varlık, *Germiyan-oğulları tarihi* (Ankara, 1974), pp. 27-32.

120. C. Cahen, "Notes pour l'histoire des turcomans d'Asie Mineure au XIIIe siècle," *Journal asiatique* 239 (1951), pp. 351-54. See also al-Umari, trans. by E. Quatremère, in *Notices et extraits des manuscrits de la bibliothèque du roi* 13 (1838), p. 375.

121. APZ, pp. 8, 12, 14-15.

122. The suffix -lı simply means "follower of" and normally denotes a tribal context when attached to a personal name in medieval sources. Parallels to Osmanlı are such groups as the Karamanlıs, Evrenoslu, and the Köse Mihallıs in the Balkans.

123. Arnakis, pp. 128-29, presents a good review of the possibilities and threats which entered into Mouzalon's calculations.

124. S. Erinç and N. Tunçdilek, "The Agricultural Regions of Turkey," *Geographical Review* 42 (1952), pp. 193, 199.

125. Pach., vol. 2, pp. 330-31; I hope to deal with the pastoral necessity underlying Osman's campaign at greater length elsewhere. For the impact of wet weather on herds of various animals, see A. Hjort and G. Dahl, *Having Herds* (Stockholm, 1976).

126. Pach., vol. 2, pp. 333-35; Arnakis, p. 129. The exact location of the encounter will be the object of a special study by Clive Foss and H. Inalcik, who also will discuss the possible bearing of Turkish sources on the battle's events. For the moment see Inalcik, "The Rise of Ottoman Historiography," in B. Lewis and P.M. Holt, eds. *Historians of the Middle East* (London, 1962), pp. 152-53.

127. This was, incidentally, Mouzalon's second disastrous brush with the Ottomans. He had almost been captured in an ambush earlier in the spring: Pach., vol. 2, p. 332; Arnakis, p. 128.

128. See n.105 supra and APZ, pp. 22-25; Janin, "La Bithynie," pp. 315-16; on the fall of Tricoccia in 1308 or shortly thereafter, Pach., vol. 2, pp. 637-38. I would tentatively harmonize the Ottoman and Byzantine traditions concerning Bilecik by having the Ottomans hold suzerainty over it in 1299, sovereignty only after Bapheus. Pachymeres,

however, occasionally sacrificed chronological to literary considerations, and it is possible that full control over Bilecik occurred in 1299.

129. Pach., vol. 2, p. 335; Arnakis, p. 133; Laiou, *Cpl.*, pp. 91, 120, 122. How many actually left? For a contrasting view see Laiou, *Peasant Society in the Late Byzantine Empire* (Princeton, 1977), pp. 129-30.

130. See E. Fisher, "A Note on Pachymeres' De Andronico Palaeologo," *Byzantion* 40 (1971), pp. 230-35.

131. Pach., vol. 2, p. 588; Dölger, *Regesten*, nos. 2265, 2280.

132. Pach., vol. 2, p. 345; Dölger, *Regesten*, nos. 2244, 2286; E. Zachariadou, "Observations on Some Turcica of Pachymeres," *Revue des études byzantines* 36 (1978), pp. 262-64.

133. Ramon Muntaner, *The Chronicle of Muntaner*, trans. by Lady Goodenough (London, 1921), vol. 2, p. 488.

134. Muntaner, pp. 203-5; Pach., vol. 2, pp. 398-99, 436-37; Laurent, *Regestes*, no. 1608, summarizes a letter of Patriarch Athanasius I written in the fall of 1304 decrying Roger de Flor's excesses against the Anatolian Byzantines.

135. Pach., vol. 2, pp. 596-97; Laurent, *Regestes*, no. 1645.

136. Laurent, *Regestes*, nos. 1598-1600.

137. Pach., vol. 2, pp. 492-93.

138. Pach., vol. 2, p. 588; Laurent, *Regestes*, no. 1606; Laiou, *Cpl.*, p. 187; Laiou, "The Provisioning of Constantinople during the Winter of 1306-1307," *Byzantion* 37 (1967), p. 95.

139. Pach., vol. 2, p. 414; Arnakis, p. 142.

140. Pach., vol. 2, p. 597; Arnakis, pp. 143-48; F.W. Hasluck, "Bithynica," *Annual of the British School at Athens* 13 (1906-7), p. 301.

141. Laiou, *Cpl.*, p. 248; Vryonis, *Decline*, pp. 300-1; Albert Waechter, *Der Verfall des Griechentums in Kleinasien im XIV. Jahrhundert* (Leipzig, 1902), p. 54.

142. Laiou, *Cpl.*, p. 121.

143. IBS, p. 86.

144. V. Laurent, "La chronique anonyme Cod. Mosquensis gr. 426 et la pénétration turque en Bithynie au début du XIVe siècle," *Revue des études byzantines* 7 (1949), pp. 207-12; Schneider and Karnapp, *Stadtmauer*, p. 6. We do not know what the ex-Byzantine but still Christian residents of Nicaea thought of Andronicus' removal of their religious objects. Andronicus had by these acts clearly made the Ottoman task of governance and reconciliation easier!

145. Ibn Battuta, p. 453.

146. In a separate study Stephen Album, Adon A. Gordus, and the author will discuss the possibility that Ottoman coinage was struck before the fall of Bursa.

147. Ibn Battuta, pp. 451-52.

148. Professor Inalcik reminds me, however, that one of al-Umari's informants was from Germiyan. For the date of al-Umari's information see IBS, pp. 72, 91 n. 9; *Al-Umari's Bericht über Kleinasien*, ed. by F. Taeschner (Leipzig, 1929), pp. 41-42.

149. Owen Lattimore, *Studies in Frontier History* (Oxford, 1962), p. 485.

150. Here I follow X. de Planhol, "Geography, Politics and Nomadism in Anatolia," *International Social Science Journal* 11 (1959), pp. 525-31.

151. Friedrich Dernburg, *Auf deutscher Bahn in Kleinasien* (Berlin, 1892), p. 136, noting also on p. 137 that Bilecik was the market town serving Söğüt, just a two or three hours' ride away; J. Mellaart, "Some Prehistoric Sites in North-Western Anatolia," *Istanbuler Mitteilungen* 6 (1955), p. 55; *Bilecik Il Yıllığı 1967* (Istanbul, 1968), pp. 89-93, 191-92.

152. The reader should recall that wealth in animals, the chief form of pastoral prosperity, was considerably more endangered by the vagaries of rainfall and illness than in the modern world of the *Farm Journal.* The wealthier a nomad became, the more likely was his transformation into a settled rentier. See also Lattimore, *Studies,* p. 541: "... if the frontier feudal noble could collect more revenue from farming than from a pastoral economy, he never resisted either the conversion of his own subjects from herdsmen into farmers or the settlement of Chinese farmers in his domains."

153. APZ, p. 11; the edition of Ali Bey is clearly corrupt at this point, because the copyist did not understand the idiom. My interpretation is based on a parallel passage in Barkan, p. 3. I wish to thank Professors V.L. Ménage and Andreas Tietze for their thoughts about this passage.

154. Muntaner, pp. 490-91.

155. William Irons, *The Yomut Turkmen* (Ann Arbor, 1975), pp. 70-71.

156. Anon. Chron., p. 7; APZ, p. 22; Arnakis, p. 86, saw the creation of a state in the Ottoman settlement of Yenişehir.

157. C.L. Stotz, "The Bursa Region of Turkey," *Geographical Review* 29 (1939), pp. 87-88, 91-96; see also the treatment of the neighboring coastal region in Louis Robert, "Un voyage d'Antiphilos de Byzance," *Journal des savants* (1979), pp. 257-94.

158. On nomadic attempts to field the largest possible force see John M. Smith, Jr., "Mongol Manpower and Persian Population," *Journal of the Economic and Social History of the Orient* 18 (1975), pp. 276, 280, and also his forthcoming study of the battle of Ayn Jalut.

159. For more detail see "Nomadism, Horses and Huns," *Past and Present* 92 (1981), pp. 3-19, and Professor Smith's "Turanian Nomadism."

160. See n. 140 supra; Ruhi, f.23v (ambush at Geyve); APZ, pp. 31-33 (Aydos); APZ, p. 26, and Ruhi, f.23r (Kara Çepiş); and see also Professor Ménage's dissertation, pp. 252-53.

161. Supra n. 128; Pach., vol. 2, p. 638; Arnakis, p. 149.

162. For his earliest use of infantry (in an ambush), APZ, p. 9; IBS, p. 60 n. 7.

163. The emirs of Germiyan and Aydın used six siege engines for their investment of Philadelphia during the years 1322-24; Schreiner, "Zur Geschichte Philadelpheias," pp. 390-92.

164. Ibn Battuta, p. 452.

165. The best treatment of the battle and its sources is by R.-J. Loenertz, "La chronique brève de 1352," *Orientalia christiana periodica* 30 (1964), pp. 45-47.

166. On the *yaya* see IBS, pp. 203-8; APZ, p. 37, emphasizes the fact that the adoption of a strong infantry arm allowed a noticeable increase in the size of the army.

167. APZ, p. 19.

168. C. Huart, "Les origines de l'empire ottoman," *Journal des savants* (1917), p. 163; Ibn Khaldun did not refer to Osman or Orkhan as a ghazi.

169. Lattimore, *Studies,* p. 508.

170. For the contrast between "chiefdoms" and "segmentary tribes," see Sahlins, *Tribesmen,* pp. 20-24. Arnakis, pp. 42-43, saw a certain localist spirit as the cement uniting Christians and Turks in Bithynia, and he developed this concept by referring to what he felt was traditional Bithynian autonomy. His evidence for this autonomy is from Roman sources; he cited no source demonstrating the persistence of such sentiments after the third century. Arnakis later sought other ways of describing the amalgam of peoples (pp. 51, 58), but he did not consider a tribal analysis of the problem. In fairness to him, we must note that when he wrote there was little relevant ethnographic literature, and the whole area of tribal studies was still laden with assumptions that tribesmen were one or another sort of primitive.

171. The struggle for survival against the Byzantine government and neighboring emirs was of paramount importance in forging the tribal identity: "War-bands are tribes in the making." J.M. Wallace-Hadrill, *Early Germanic Kingship in England and on the Continent* (Oxford, 1971), p. 11. Arnakis, p. 66, assumed that there is no political dimension to nomadism and thus found it easy to conclude that nomads and their ways played no role in the development of the Ottoman enterprise. Again, given the literature available to him, his assumption was defensible at the time.

172. For the tribe as an organism uniting settled and nomadic groups, see W.W. Swidler, "Adaptive Processes," pp. 29-30.

173. Stephen Pastner, "Ideological Aspects of Nomad-Sedentary Contact: a Case from Southern Baluchistan," *Anthropological Quarterly* 44:3 (1971), p. 175.

174. Processes of tribal growth parallel to the Ottoman example have occurred in circumstances observed by anthropologists. In Baluchistan, success in obtaining land increased the military manpower and cohesiveness of the Brahui confederacy as new members joined; Swidler, "Adaptive Processes," pp. 24-25. For an example of a shared genealogy linking the Ottomans to a Byzantine origin, see Wittek, *Rise,* p. 9. For other examples of tribal genealogies as political charters, see N. Swidler, "Political Context," pp. 304, 306, and D. A. Bradburd, "Never Give a Shepherd an Even Break: Class and Labor among the Komachi," *American Ethnologist* 7 (1980), p. 604.

175. Evans-Pritchard, *The Nuer* (Oxford, 1940), p. 5. The Nuer share few characteristics with the Ottomans, but Evans-Pritchard's classic remarks about tribalism deserve mention in our context. Put another way to reflect Bithynian realities, "A tribe is the largest group the members of which consider it their duty to combine for raiding and for defensive action." *The Nuer,* p. 120.

176. *The Nuer,* pp. 113, 118. Of course, unlike the Ottomans, the Nuer had no powerful chief. But just as Osman's rise occurred in an age of anarchy in an area threatened by Byzantine tax exactions and Seljuk or Mongol pretensions, so did "proto-chieftains" begin to rise among the Nuer as an adaptation to pressure from European and Arab expansion: *The Nuer,* pp. 188-89. See also Rada and Neville Dyson-Hudson, "Nomadic Pastoralism," *Annual Review of Anthropology 1980,* p. 48.

177. Robert N. Pehrson, *The Social Organization of the Marri Baluch* (Chicago, 1966), p. 3. Pehrson died in the field while preparing his notes for publication. Barth arranged for, and edited, the final publication of this superb study.

178. Barth, *Nomads,* p. 71.

179. The notion of Byzantines becoming Ottomans should not be peculiar. We know that Romans became members of the tribe of Huns; see the report of Priscus in C.D. Gordon, *The*

Age of Attila (Ann Arbor, 1960), pp. 85-88. The man whom Priscus met may have changed his manners and habits, or not. His political allegiance, however, had changed, and he no longer considered himself a Roman subject. Rather, his new political allegiance made him a member of the tribe. See the analysis of this text by Lattimore, *Studies,* p. 481 n. 9.

180. I owe this paragraph to the inspiration of Professor Ménage, who also notes that the word "Turk" eventually came to mean "nomad" in the Ottoman sources, and bore with it pejorative connotations (as in the phrase "Etrak-i bi-idrak").

181. Even the Byzantines had used Turks to rule Greek Christian subjects in Bithynia: Dölger, *Regesten,* no. 2291. Note that the tribe need not be restricted to pastoralists or nomads. Tribes boasting settled and nomad members are attested among Turks, for example, as far back as the age of the Orkhon inscriptions: T. Tekin, *A Grammar of Orkhon Turkic* (Bloomington, 1968), pp. 233, 265, line E12 of the Kül-Tigin inscription.

182. See note 11 supra; Philippides-Braat, "Palamas," pp. 204-5, and the remark by one of Palamas' captors that "the time will come when we will be in accord with each other" (p. 161).

183. Pehrson, *Marri Baluch,* p. 19.

184. For a fascinating study of the role of external pressure in raising a chief's prestige, see Irons, "Variation in Political Stratification among the Yomut Turkmen," *Anthropological Quarterly* 44:3 (1971), pp. 143-56; also Sahlins, *Tribesmen,* pp. 17, 38, 55.

185. For a parallel situation see N. Swidler, "The Development of the Kalat Khanate," in Nelson, ed., *Desert and Sown,* pp. 116-17.

186. I.H. Uzunçarşılı, "Gazi Orhan Bey vakfiyesi," *Belleten* 5 (1971), pp. 277-88.

187. APZ, p. 42.

188. T. Andrae, *Mohammed, the Man and his Faith* (New York, 1936), pp. 33-34.

189. Minhaj al-Din Juzjani, *Tabakat-i Nasiri,* trans. by H.G. Raverty (London, 1881), p. 76; Anonymous, *Histoire des Seldjoukides d'Asie Mineure,* ed. by F.N. Uzluk (Ankara, 1952), p. 2; F. Köprülü, *Les origines de l'empire ottoman* (Paris, 1935), pp. 12-24.

190. For the chronology of the texts and their implications for the historiography of the fifteenth century, see V.L. Ménage, "On the Recensions of Uruj's 'History of the Ottomans'," *Bulletin of the School of Oriental and African Studies* 30 (1967), pp. 314-22.

191. "Benim kızım Malkhun senin helalın oldu." The sheykh's play on words with hilal, moon, and helal, wife, is a stroke of genius confirming his interpretation.

192. APZ, pp. 9-11.

Chapter Two:

Ottoman Regulations and Nomad Custom

Osman was a self-made man. He created a promising enterprise by protecting the interests of nomads on the frontiers of the Mongol domain as well as the interests of the settled (if insecure) farmers of Byzantine Bithynia. His technique, the only one familiar to him, was to create a new tribe, but the tribal aspect of the Ottoman enterprise did not long outlive him.[1] Already in Orkhan's early years such developments as the first Ottoman coinage, the changing composition of the army, and the spread of urban architectural patronage all illustrate the process transforming and elevating an available chief into a distant sultan. This was not a reversible process.

The fourteenth-century rulers Murad I and Bayezid I accelerated the process. The creation of the Janissaries and the imposition of the *devshirme* imply a declining need for nomads in the army, while the beginnings of a land and census registry suggest a concern that all the Ottoman subjects be settled, easily located, and thus easily taxable.[2] Unfortunately, the later history of the fourteenth century is unclear. As further research is done it seems to prove that we know less than we once thought we did.[3] There is, then, a gap in our knowledge of the declining status of nomads in the Ottoman enterprise. The Ottoman decision to accept the imperial tradition offered them by the schoolmen could only end, however, in a stratification of society which placed heterodox nomads at the bottom.

By the fifteenth century, the Ottoman administration viewed the members of their enterprise as divided into two camps, rulers and subjects, as unequal in power as they were in numbers. The administrators decided to treat the nomads of Asia Minor as subjects, almost peasants. They thought little of the nomads' past contributions as they planned for their future obedience. In my opinion, they found many ways to enforce the subject status of the nomads. In this chapter let us explore the Ottoman regulations under which nomads lived. I contend that the purpose, as well as the effect, of these regulations was to settle the nomads, either to sedentarize them or to circumscribe their migrations within a predictable, "settled" routine.

The administrators of the Ottoman enterprise, the "men of the pen," claimed to act within the constraints of formal Islamic law. Large areas of public and private behavior lay within the scope of this law, which the Ottoman courts applied. At the same time, however, changing governmental and administrative needs forced the rulers to supplement the eternal law of God with a series of pragmatic, official regulations, termed *kanun* in their Ottoman manifestation. The *kanun* was an *ad hoc* solution to a particular problem of the moment.[4] The fiction was maintained, of course, that all the *ad hoc* regulations accorded with Islamic law; and in this way the Ottoman jurists were "reduced to being the agents of a hard-headed *Realpolitik.*"[5]

The origin of *kanun* law lies in Mongol legacy and tribal practice. The success of Chinggis Khan caused others to emulate many principles of his rule, among them the elaboration of a supreme dynastic law. Such law was "more than the decrees of a given ruler, it was the sum of such decrees and was to stay in force as long as the family bore rule; it was binding on succeeding sovereigns, at least till explicitly abrogated by them."[6] This independent dynastic law was expressed in decisions of the Sultan in a manner developed from, but still evocative of, the tribal court:

> The chief is not bound by custom or precedent in his decision . . . nor is he expected to give judgment according to [Islamic law] . . . . Quite explicitly, he is expected to make the decision which he feels is 'best for the tribe'—he is expected to exercise his privileged arbitrary authority within a very wide area of free grace, unhampered by consideration of individual justice as derived from rules . . . . Any direction by the chief is an order, any definite statement is a decision, whether expressed as an aside in a conversation, or while washing his hands or taking his meal.[7]

The force of the Ottoman *kanun* derived from the power of its promulgator, the sultan. Before the sixteenth century there was no theological justification for, or attempt to urge, obedience. The phrase "I have ordered that . . ." in imperial documents became, once the documents were arranged in model collections, "What follows is the law."[8]

Ottoman officialdom collected and organized the *kanuns* and the resulting compilations are termed *kanunnames.*[9] Each *kanun* laid down rules in one or many areas neglected or anachronistically treated in Islamic law. These *kanunnames* have survived in a variety of forms.[10]

First are the so-called general compilations containing regulations enforced throughout the Ottoman domains. Mehmet II issued one such compilation, perhaps in the 1450s, and, quite late in his life, may have issued another.[11] His successors added some regulations and altered others, but neither Bayezid II nor Selim I promulgated a wholly recast code.[12]

Second come provincial compilations. These contained regulations valid and confirmed for a particular province, especially regarding taxation. When the provincial collection was gathered together, its model in organization and layout was the general code as amended and in effect. In addition, many provincial customs were allowed to stand. Some provisions found in Ottoman regulations thus simply restate the practice of earlier regimes, such as the emirates of Uzun Hasan of the Ak Koyunlu, the emirate of Karaman, or even the financial practices of the Seljuks.[13]

The provincial compilations, as guides to fiscal and administrative practice current in each province, appear at the beginning of the provincial cadasters. Alterations in provincial practice seem to have been frequent, and large numbers of such compilations survive, either in the original cadasters or in later copies.[14] They were also preserved in manuscript form for ready administrative reference. From revision to revision the order of chapters was often changed and rarely rationalized, so as legal thought these compilations remind the reader more of Lombard or perhaps Anglo-Saxon legislation than of Roman jurisprudence or Islamic legal treatises. Comparing contemporaneous codes from different provinces with differing histories produces a crazy-quilt of customs and procedures.

Finally, excerpts gathered from various compilations on special topics such as criminal penalties are available in manuscript form. It appears that most of these manuscripts, which are now found in libraries rather than in official archives, were prepared to assist bureaucrats, judges, and secretaries. These collections, so diverse in content and order, do not seem to have become fashionable before the time of Bayezid II.[15] Such collections are really "private," prepared by officials for guidance and instruction. It is a short step from these works to the later Ottoman treatises on administration.

Unfortunately, many of the extant codes do not preserve their dates of promulgation or even of later copying. Even within a given collection there may be little uniformity of date, since recent revisions to a regulation often appear only as an appendage to a restatement of the former practice. Dates are often expressed in terms of a particular bureaucrat's term in office, or in a reference to the cadaster prepared by a certain secretary. Such a reference would enable the Ottoman official consulting the code or the cadaster to know just when the *kanun* appeared. Modern scholarship, however has yet to work out a trustworthy concordance between the names of Ottoman officials and the exact dates during which they held specified offices in the fifteenth or sixteenth centuries.[16] Luckily, there remain a large number of provincial codes whose dating is reasonably secure, and thus we may argue that many regulations preserve not only present rule but also give us a *terminus ante quem* for past administrative practice.

How can the codes help us to learn about Anatolian nomads? The extant regulations tell of taxes, fines, and other obligations which touched pastoralists. Even though the clipped prose framing each *kanun* is too elliptical for a reader's immediate comprehension, the texts do provide valuable glimpses into pastoral activities as the Ottomans understood them. The texts also outline Ottoman intent and bureaucratic purpose: how to increase revenues from the nomads, how to fit their lives into a settled model, how to make them pay for their transgressions against settled society. The Ottoman fiscal regulations reveal a government in the process of defining a satisfactory society and using bureaucratic pressure to mould recalcitrant groups into a predictable shape.[17]

The Ottoman regulations set out, first, to describe the nomad, to define and set him apart from the other subjects of the sultan. For this definition the secretaries picked out those facets of nomadic life which struck them as important—or threatening. The *kanuns* generally call the nomads *yürük,* from the verb *yürümek,* to walk or wander.[18] Seeking an explicit definition for administrative purposes, they contrast nomads with the sedentary bureaucrat's model subject, the settled farmer. Here is the preface to a *kanun* from the province of Karaman, ca. 1525: "The *yürük* living near Kayseri have long been nomads: they have neither worked the lands nor possessed vineyards or gardens. Since they tend sheep, the revenues from the sheep tax, taxes due from each group, were assigned to the *sipahis,* and these taxes amounted to a great revenue. The nomads paid neither *çift resmi, bennak,* nor *caba.*"[19] In the compilation of cadasters, chancery officials registered nomads by tribe and not, as with settled subjects, by place of residence.[20] Secretaries then arranged the register by tribe and, within the tribe, by group. This was natural: each tribe, after all, was a political organization easily identifiable with its chief, the intermediary betwen the tribesmen and the outside world. Within the tribe, the registrars proceeded by *cemaat,* each a named group lacking a political chief. An eighteenth-century regulation of Sultan Ahmet III further defined the distance between nomad and Ottoman: "As for the *yürüks* leading a nomadic life, they are not the subjects of any man. Wherever they may go, they pay their dues to the *sipahi* of the village in whose name they and their group are enregistered."[21]

The internal governance of nomad tribes was also alien to the experience and expectations of Ottoman bureaucrats: "The class of *yürüks* is a wandering one. They have no fixed homes nor special relations with the provincial governors. Their own chiefs are their own police. If a *yürük* commits a crime, after the judges have established this they leave punishment to the *yürük's* own police, and this is the imperial order."[22] The tribal chiefs were the point of contact between the Ottoman government and nomadic tribesmen. Not even the local headmen could step in. The chief acted on behalf of the government as a punitive officer, but to tribesmen it would still seem that the only real power, and the power to whom their primary loyalties tended, remained the chief. The government, for its part, came to the conclusion that such an *imperium in imperio* was unacceptable.

In short, to the Ottoman bureaucrat the essence of nomadism lay in the nomad's motion; his "wandering" made him a nomad, made him separate, and also, unfortunately, indistinct: the nomads had no fixed abode where they could be found (and taxed); they would simply camp and then move on.[23] This made them difficult to govern. Their mobility also made them a potential threat, for they might appear suddenly in a distant location and cause trouble by grazing their sheep on cultivated land or raiding villagers. Further, their mode of organization, emphasizing the internal authority of the chief, did not encourage the tribe's dependence on the apparatus of Ottoman government. If their own chiefs were also their own policemen, could they not argue that the central government had no claim on them? The Ottoman *kanuns* emphasize these two aspects of nomadism, movement and independence, because they made the nomads difficult to rule. The Ottoman definition of nomadism rested on political potential and military threat. The nomads, then, were very special subjects, subjects not so easily brought into the smooth ordering of government routine as the immobile farmer or townsman.

The Ottomans knew, however, that settlement would solve that problem. By the time of Süleyman the Magnificent the Kayseri nomads had permanently settled and new taxes, assessed on crops and land holdings, were imposed on them. In principle, a nomad during Süleyman's reign incurred the obligations of a settled subject only after he had forsaken nomadic activity (the long marches), cultivated a parcel of land, and settled in a village, all for at least ten years.[24] According to a later *kanun* from the province of Çankırı, some nomads "preferred repose and settlement," and had by then been settled for some thirty or forty years. Since they now cultivated the lands on which they had previously wintered their herds, they became subject to the normal taxes on agricultural products.[25] The chancery clerks then removed the ex-nomad from the cadaster of nomads and inscribed his name in the cadaster under the locality where he had settled. He was not, however, automatically "saved" or "delivered" from nomadism. A regulation of 20 October 1572 stated that if one or two nomads were to settle one spot even for ten or more years, their former tribal chief could insist on their continued classification as *yürük*. Once, however, the ex-nomad paid agricultural taxes and the cadaster claimed him as a peasant, reversion or recidivism was difficult. He became *reaya* or *yerli,* subject or settled, not *yürük*.[26] He had dissolved his flocks and his raiding parties, and his family had struck its tent.[27]

So the Ottomans saw nomads as a potential threat to the sedentary dream, a threat enforced by both mobility and independence. It was better for nomads to "prefer repose and settlement'" so that they, or rather the Ottomans, could be delivered from such an uncivilized existence.

In the meantime, even though the nomads constituted a sector separate from settled society, they had nonetheless to be fitted into that structure. The decisive means of conforming the nomads to that model lay in taxation. A nomad may be taxed in three ways: on his herd, the product of his herd, or his manpower. Following nomad custom, the early Ottomans taxed the nomads' manpower. Groups of nomads were artificially divided into units of twenty-four men (an *ocak,* "hearth"), of whom one would go on campaign when called, three would be his aides (literally *çatal,* "forks"), while the remaining twenty were helpers, who would pay the nomad soldier's expenses and take up his burdens in his absence. The soldier who went on campaign was freed from forage or other taxes for that year. Every group of ten such soldiers had to bring pack-horse and tent. The soldier's equipment: the iron of his lance, the feather of his arrow, bow, sword, shield, all were to be ready.[28] This form of taxation, the muster of a nomad's military potential, was in reasonable accord with tradition. The nomad used his own military technology, his comrades looked after his herd in his absence, preserving his capital investment in pastoralism, and his fellows underwrote his extraordinary expenses. But as the Ottomans entered the gunpowder era and warfare came to include siege techniques and artillery placement, mounted nomads became militarily obsolete. Their potential for financing the new warfare, on the other hand, was keenly appreciated. Thus the *ocak* system evolved into a monetary rather than a human offering even though the nomads retained the legal status of soldiers. Thirty men now comprised a unit, and in wartime each owed the service of five men plus the payment—to the government, not the soldiers—of 50 *akçes* from each of the twenty-five remaining helpers. Additionally, in peacetime each *ocak* owed an annual sum of 600 *akçes.*[29] The Ottomans saw the nomads now as a financial support for warfare, rather than an active, warring body. The actual services which the former nomad soldiers performed also dwindled in importance, and, as we shall see, later nomad "services" to the enterprise were felt as less than honorable employments for hunters and pastoralists.

The Ottoman flirtation with nomad manpower conscription was but one manner of taxing nomads and speeding their subjection. A much more significant imposition was the tax on sheep, called the *resm-i ganem.* An irregular tax on herds is quite familiar to nomads and was a staple of early Mongol taxation, where it had been one percent of the herd from herds of more than 100 animals, with smaller herds owing no sheep tax.[30] The initial Ottoman sheep tax appears to have been steeper: it was imposed on all herds and it may have been as high as one sheep in every ten. The Ottomans converted it to a payment reckoned in *akçes.*[31] Early in the reign of Mehmet the Conqueror the tax rate was one *akçe* for three sheep, and later in his reign it was increased to one *akçe* for two sheep.[32] For the purpose of calculating the *resm-i ganem,* a lamb was equivalent to a mature sheep (thus, the tax for two lambs was still one *akçe*). General compilations, provincial compilations, and administrative treatises confirm that this tax rate remained the same throughout Anatolia during the later fifteenth and sixteenth centuries.[33]

A regulation from the end of Mehmet the Conqueror's reign tells us of the manner in which the sheep tax was collected: "In the province of Karaman, the judicial representatives perform the registration when it is necessary to count the sheep. They ask a shepherd about the sheep he tends, 'whose sheep are these? How many are yours? How many someone else's?' The judges' men register the count in that way, and the collector gathers the taxes according to their count."[34]

Let us now turn to the impact of the sheep tax on the pastoralists' security and well-being. In early Mongol practice, herds below a certain size were exempt from the sheep tax. This preserved the capital of poor nomads, who might otherwise have had too small a base for further pastoral activity. Exempting the marginal pastoralists from taxation enabled the Mongols to keep the maximum number of mobile nomads in the field. The Ottomans, concerned first and foremost with securing a financial and political return on their tolerance of nomads, adopted a different set of fiscal procedures.

A number of features of the sheep tax indicate that the welfare of the pastoralists' herds, a primary feature of nomadic taxation, meant little to the Ottomans. They did not care—or knew only too well—that there is a limit beyond which taxing the herd destroys it and the livelihood of the pastoralist, forcing him to settle—or to revolt. The size of the herd after taxation is the vital variable in this relationship; if the result of the taxation is to remove too many sheep (for conversion into money to pay the taxes), the herd will not be able to reproduce itself, to grow, and to support the family of the herder.

A few words about the natural determinants of herd size may help us understand why it is so crucial a factor in pastoral welfare. First come the quality and quantity of pasture, along with the availability of water.[35] Changes in weather, such as an early frost, can and do have crippling effects on the size and health of a herd.[36] Physical factors, such as reproduction rates, differential life spans, and disease, are also direct influences on herd size. In another vein, the rate of movement of the herd through terrain is inversely proportional to the herd size. Finally, if the herd is too small, the sheep will tend to stray from the path of the leaders, they will fail to reproduce as a result of the failure of the herd to cohere as a social unit, and the size of the herd will decline further.[37] From these remarks, the Mongols' concerns with the size and welfare of their herds are clear. From what follows, the opposite hopes of the Ottomans will emerge.

The first step toward controlling the nomads, or even settling them through beggary, was to require that *all* pastoralists pay a minimum tax independent of the meagerness of their herds. Thus, even if a nomad's herd had dwindled to fewer than twenty-four animals, the *yürük* was termed *kara,* lowly, and he owed a tax, the *resm-i kara,* no matter whether his herd consisted of the full twenty-four sheep, fewer, or none. This was fixed at twelve *akçes,* equal to the sheep tax on twenty-four sheep.[38] This minimum herd tax was based not on considerations of herd stability but on the desire to obtain a tax from each nomad at least equal to the ground tax due from the lesser categories of landed peasants.[39] Only in Aydın province, where a special statute existed for the Karaca Koyunlu nomads, were the actual requirements for herd maintenance a minor factor. Those nomads whose sheep tax totaled less than thirty *akçes* (implying a minimum herd size of sixty animals) paid the full thirty *akçes,* unless they had no sheep at all, in which case they paid twelve *akçes,* while the very poorest tribesmen paid six *akçes.*[40] Here the uncapitalized or ex-nomads owed the taxes charged to the poorer peasants, while marginal pastoralists paid a much higher minimum tax than their counterparts in other provinces. Thus a nomad with thirty sheep in some other province would pay only fifteen *akçes,* while his Karaca Koyunlu counterpart with thirty sheep would still owe thirty *akçes,* double the "normal" burden. The special statute for the Karaca Koyunlu provided a faster way of running down the pastoralist's herd, forcing him to convert more of his capital into cash. It dispersed the herd yet more quickly and led to the nomad's ultimate settlement and payment of the normal taxes of the stable, poor, dependent peasant.

The structure of the sheep tax, as it developed in the fifteenth century, included one more feature inimical to the prosperity of the nomad. While the rate of taxation remained fixed at one *akçe* for two animals, the collection date shifted. The time of year for assessment and collection of the sheep tax affected the revenues (and the taxpayers), just as would an alteration in the rates. Up until some time in the reign of Mehmet the Conqueror, the sheep tax was collected during the summer or, more frequently, towards the beginning of autumn. Regulations stated that formerly, the tax was assessed and collected when the lambs were shorn of their fleece (or, in one case, when the lamb joined the herd). Two late references to early collection practice state that the tax was collected when the lambs were sold or killed. All these texts imply that the collection took place in June at the earliest.[41] One reason for sending out the tax collectors at the time of fleecing is that the herdsmen gathered the herds together and sheared them systematically, much as cows were once branded in the American West. As the lambs and sheep came through the funnel to be clipped, enumeration and even on-the-spot payment would be facilitated. Mehmet the Conqueror changed this practice: his later code declares that the sheep tax is to be assessed in May, after lambing.[42] With the exception of the provinces of Boz Ok, Karaman, Iç Il, and Diyarbekir, where the tax continued to be due in May, in the rest of Asia Minor all collections of Bayezid II and his successors specify that the sheep tax was due in early April, after the lambing season.[43]

Why the change to April? The regulations merely state that these taxes were due after lambing and, in some cases, weaning.[44] In fact, in much of present-day Turkey the weaning time remains on or about the beginning of April.[45] The regulations do emphasize that in the count sheep and their lambs are equal. Thus, the count took place when the herd was at its greatest size for the year, before there were any losses to the lambs on the march up to summer pasture. This change, then, reflects a desire to gather the maximum revenues from the nomads. It might have been more convenient to make the count and collect the taxes later on during the fleecing season, but, from the late fifteenth century on, increasing the revenues came to prevail over ease of assessment as an Ottoman concern.

If the tax on sheep had originally been conceived as a nomadic tax in old Ottoman days, it had by the sixteenth century long ceased to be levied in the interests of the taxpayers. Nomadic taxation is occasional, since it is required only in time of need. The mobility, relative self-sufficiency, and lack of specialization of tent life restricts the need for a bureaucracy, and thus there is no need of regular taxation for salaries and the like. Imposition of the tax must be occasional, since nomads try to avoid the concentration of power in the hands of a "government" unless it becomes necessary. The tax rate must also take into account and protect the nomad's ability to pay. If the nomad cannot pay, then his ability to continue as a nomad will disappear, and along with it, his support for the chief.[46]

The Ottoman sheep tax was, then, not a customary tax for nomads. It was an annual, regular impost, which did not take into account the nomads' ability to pay. The rate for small flocks was at least indentical to the rate for large flocks. A nomad with a marginal flock might be forced to sell sheep to obtain money for his tax payment. Such a sale might lower the size of his remaining herd below the minimum necessary for natural reproduction, to make up for attrition or disease.[47] Since it touched all flocks regardless of size, the sheep tax was no longer an exaction appropriate to nomadism. Its tendency would be to reduce poor, under-capitalized nomads below the herd size level at which they could continue pastoral nomadism. Among other things, then, the sheep tax served as a device for transforming poor nomads into poor landless peasants.

A modern analogy of this process exists among the Saçıkara *yürük* of southeastern Turkey. Two generations ago, when pasture land was abundant, a herd of fifty sheep was sufficient for a family to remain economically independent.[48] Presently farmers own and cultivate these pastures, so the shepherds must have more income (and capital) to rent the pasture they formerly claimed as of right. Further, "The *yürük* migratory schedule is adapted to the agricultural cycles of the various villages, not because it is the optimum for grazing, or because it coincides with other productive requirements of the *yürük*. It is a political adjustment."[49] The implication of the necessity to rent pasture is that herding is no longer viable for families with fewer than one hundred sheep. The mean Saçıkara herd is now 268 sheep, the mode 290, and this figure agrees with a preferred herd size of 300 among nomads further to the west.[50] In the fifteenth century, taxation raised the minimum size of a viable herd; in the twentieth century, rental of pasture performs the same operation.

Previous discussion has, I hope, demonstrated that the Ottoman sheep tax became a threat to the pastoral base of nomadic life. It may be useful to attempt a less subjective examination of the impact of this tax on a "standard" herd of 300 and then on a marginal herd. Such calculations must be based on certain assumptions which I shall attempt to justify in the documentation.

To begin, we must have a model of the structure of a herd. Such a model is difficult to find, because modern manuals of animal husbandry describe herds destined for rather different purposes than the herds of a fifteenth century pastoralist; for example, to suit the modern palate the age distribution in such a herd is skewed to produce more lambs. Medieval European herding and husbandry manuals, emphasizing production for the wool trade in a damper climatic regime, are equally unhelpful.[51] It thus seems wise to follow the accounts of ethnographers who have given detailed accounts of the economics of herding practiced by their nomad hosts. Unfortunately, few modern anthropologists have studied herds as closely as they have studied the herders. The two best studies applicable to this study are by Barth and Bates, and Barth's work has provided the model for the following calculations.[52]

Let us assume, following Barth, that the distribution of sexes in a herd will be ten percent males and ninety percent ewes. Each ewe may be expected to bear one lamb per year. The rate of attrition in the herd is fifteen percent per year. Thus, fifteen percent of the lambs born in any year must be reserved for replacement of stock. In a herd of 300 sheep, there should be thirty males and 270 ewes. The herd produces 270 lambs in one year.[53] For stock replacement, a herd of 300 will require forty-five lambs. In one sense, the gross animal profit is 270 lambs, and the net animal profit 225 lambs.

Before considering taxes (which are, of course, levied after lambing), it will be useful to compute the value of the herd. In order to perform this computation we must first know the age distribution of the herd, since lambs, yearlings, and adult sheep fetched different prices.[54] The herd will consist of 270 lambs, 255 adult sheep, and forty-five yearlings (the fifteen percent replacement stock of the year past). Using figures from the regulations, we assume an adult sheep was worth fifteen *akçes,* a yearling ten, and a lamb perhaps six.[55] Multiplying the number of sheep in each age group by its appropriate price, and then adding the products so derived, we conclude that the total animal capital, before taxes and stock losses, was 5895 *akçes.* This is the gross animal capital of our herd. In a like manner the gross profit is the value of 270 lambs, or 1620 *akçes.* The net pre-tax profit is the value of 225 lambs, or 1350 *akçes.*

It is useful to look at these figures in terms of working capital. This working capital is the total value of adult and yearling sheep, or 4275 *akçes.* The net profit then represents a thirty-one percent return on working capital.

Now we may examine the impact of the sheep tax on our herd of 300 sheep and 270 lambs, 570 animals in all. Assuming a tax rate of one *akçe*/two sheep, the tax bill is 285 *akçes.* This represents twenty-one percent of the net profit, and six percent of the gross animal capital. The tax bill, paid in kind, would remove nineteen adult sheep from the herd, that is, six percent of the herd before lambing, three percent of the herd after lambing. Taken by itself, this represents a manageable burden for a herd this size, even though it is more than the burden of strictly nomadic taxation.[56]

As noted above, it is important to examine the impact of the tax not only on a "standard" herd, whose numbers soften that impact, but also on poorer nomads. Let us take Barth's poorest viable herd of sixty animals.[57] This herd will contain fifty-four ewes and six males. During the year fifty-four lambs will be born, nine of which must go for stock replacement. The net pre-tax profit will then be forty-five lambs, or 270 *akçes.* The tax will fall, after lambing, on a herd of 114 and will come to fifty-seven *akçes* or four adult sheep, four percent of the herd, seven percent of the herd before lambing. The tax burden on the old Saçıkara minimum viable herd of fifty is of the same order.

For our minimum viable herd of sixty adults to survive, forty-five lambs must be born. We have seen what the tax on sheep does to such a herd. How much should the herd of adult sheep be increased to preserve this new-born supply of forty-five lambs? Our herd of sixty must be increased to a size of seventy-seven adult sheep, in order both to remain viable and pay the sheep tax. Seventy-seven sheep implies sixty-nine ewes and sixty-nine lambs. This is a total herd of 146 sheep, from whom seventy-three *akçes* tax will be due. If we reckon this tax in lambs, and deduct as well a fifteen percent replacement of stock, from the total herd of seventy-seven, we achieve the goal of a net, post-tax remainder of forty-five lambs. Thus the sheep tax forces an increase in the viable minimum herd size of seventeen adult sheep, or twenty-five percent. For a poorer herd, then, the impact of a sheep tax levied regardless of herd size may have a noticeable impact. One authority complains that in modern Mongolia, taxes of five percent and ten percent, like the sheep tax here, were considered "unmanageably high."[58]

In sum, the sheep tax was a major Ottoman impost on the capital and income of nomadic pastoralists. Its rate and schedule of collection were suited to governmental, not nomadic, considerations, and its impact doomed the nomadic future of the less fortunate Anatolian pastoralists. Since a spell of bad weather or an epidemic might decimate even the largest herds, any nomad might feel the potentially "settling" influence of this tax.

In addition to the impact of the sheep tax on small herds, the uses made of the revenues were un-nomadic. The occasion for a nomad to pay taxes usually provided its own justification. Military or tribal necessity were clear and present dangers. Here, however, the nomads were taxed just as settled Ottoman subjects, so the reason for the tax and its justification to the nomad taxpayer is lost. Had the nomads still formed a major part of an Ottoman army, such levies for self-help might have seemed tolerable. But, as we saw in the preceding chapter, by the reign of Orkhan the Ottoman use of nomads was on the decline. Their role in the sixteenth century Ottoman military was minor, even déclassé: army labor gangs, ship construction, road work, transport services (carrying rice, biscuits, charcoal for the mines), digging saltpeter, and the like.[59] Such duties were not "occasions!"

In addition to the head-tax on sheep levied in the spring, a pen or fold tax, a "pen-due," also was assessed.[60] This *resm-i agıl* or sheep-fold tax was assessed in the fall, when the sheep were mating, confined within a small area and not spread out over pastures. The rate prescribed for this tax varied over time and by province. In the later code of Mehmet the Conqueror the rate was two *akçes* per sheep-fold, afterwards raised to three, as it appears in a code of Selim I.[61]

In the provincial codes, the rate varied from one *akçe* to five per herd of 300 sheep,[62] although it could be as high as one *akçe* for ten sheep.[63] The total burden of this tax, since it was levied only once in the year, was small, although for marginal herds in the east it was quite high and its ten percent rate aided in their depopulation and acted as a goad to settlement.

Still, it was not a nomad's own tax. True, in west Anatolia, its assessment took into account a minimum herd size below which there was a minimal tax or none at all, and this provision meets one elementary requirement of nomadic taxation, the preservation of the nomads' ability, in capital terms, to continue the pastoral routine. Nonetheless, its regularity, the annual fall imposition, mark it as a source of revenue for meeting the continuing exigencies of settled, and not the emergencies of tribal, life.[64]

The regulations describing the pen-due also imply that the *total* tax on nomads in Ottoman lands may have been a burden for any nomad, and especially for the under-capitalized nomad, as was the sheep tax. As our earlier discussion implied, this standard herd size, 300, is considerably larger than the minimum needed for subsistence and reproduction. Among the Basseri of South Persia, the subsistence level is sixty sheep, while very few herd owners possessed more than 200.[65] The earlier Saçıkara figures tell the same story. This minimum figure for the Basseri is by no means low for the Near East: it is greater than minimum herd figures for the Marri and Brahui of

Baluchistan or the Kababish, all of whom live in an environment of straitened circumstances in comparison with Anatolia.[66] The high herd figure in the Ottoman regulations probably reflects the added capitalization a nomad had to possess in order to shoulder the burden of Ottoman taxation, far above and beyond the basic requirement in sheep for subsistence of family and herd. Although its impact was small, perhaps one percent (in western Anatolia) of the annual profits computed above, the pen-due, like the sheep tax, had a confining purpose on nomadic activities and numbers.

The two annual taxes on sheep and their folds were not the only fiscal demands made upon the nomads. There were also recurrent fines. The Ottoman government did not tax nomads on their customary or prescribed winter and summer pasture areas, collectively called *haymana yurdu.*[67] The Ottomans fined them, however, if the flocks strayed from customary or assigned routes to and from those pastures, and fines were incurred if for any reason the nomads sought better favored summer and winter pastures. These fines were the *resm-i yaylak, resm-i kışlak, resm-i otlak,* and perhaps the *resm-i duhan.* The purpose of these fines was clear. Minor climatic variations often affect the line of march by nomads, who seek the best grazing for their flocks during the strenuous marches to and from their accustomed summer or winter pastures. These fines had the purpose of forcing nomads to use specific routes whose convenience lay in the government's improved ability to locate the nomads and not in the welfare of the sheep. The fiscal impact of one fine was not very noticeable; but repeated violations in the same year, caused by climatic necessity, would have a deep impact on herds already weakened by the scarcity of pasture and the longer marches to find it. Settling the nomads in unalterable and predictable routes where they could more easily be found was a major step in forcing their sedentarization.[68]

The *resm-i yaylak,* summer grazing fine, appears in the provincial codes for central and eastern Anatolia. Since it appears also in some texts which repeat regulations of the Ak Koyunlu ruler Uzun Hasan, the fine must have been imposed at least as early as the last quarter of the fifteenth century. A herd, usually defined as three hundred animals, was not subject to fine if it moved along its assigned routes and summered in its assigned summer pasture; these pastures were inscribed in the Ottoman cadastral registers. The nomad and his herd could pause at another pasture while *en route* to assigned summer pasture, but only for fewer than three nights. A longer stay subjected him to the summer grazing fine. Regulations from the reign of Selim I, some of which, however, quote Uzun Hasan's, state the fine as ca. 640 grams of oil, clarified butter, or fat from each tent.[69] Later, during Süleyman's reign, the tax rate was increased: each tent paid the same amount of fat, but in addition each herd of 300 sheep owed one sheep of the best quality.[70] After 1578, the code for Çankırı states that the summer grazing fine is due in coin, because the tax collectors were asking for more than the specified tax in kind, and it also forbade the collectors from requiring this tax from settled farmers on their customary pastures.[71]

In sum, this fine was an incentive for nomads to stick to particular lines of march, or, if forced to detour, to travel rapidly lest their herds graze in cultivated land and consume young seedlings. Intended to control and hinder the pastoralists' adaptation to a constantly changing environment, it was clearly not of nomadic origin. Nor did any of its revenues come to nomad chiefs or serve nomadic purposes.

As the summer grazing fine covered migration up to summer pastures, so did the *resm-i kışlak,* winter grazing fine, deal with the return. The general codes tell us about this fine. In the late fifteenth and early sixteenth centuries, the rule was that if a herd not assigned to a particular area entered and wintered there, the nomad offender owed in fine a one-year-old ewe if his herd were large, and six *akçes* (the presumed value of a lamb) if his herd were poor.[72] Later, a regulation of 952/1545 stated that the fine was owed if the herd settled in for a prolonged stay, that is, if the herd was not on the move. This clause parallels the three nights provision of the summer grazing fine. A herd in good condition would pay a one-year-old ewe, a middling herd paid ten *akçes,* while the poorest of herds would pay six. If the herdsmen, however, settled and cultivated the land, paying taxes on the land and its products, they were not liable to this fine.[73] A number of provincial codes mirror the provisions of the imperial collections.[74]

A few provincial codes had a different fine structure. In these provinces the fine was levied on nomads and not on herds. If a nomad wintered on land not assigned to him, he owed a tax of six *akçes* (in some cases, less, if he were a bachelor). If he became a cultivator and paid tithes and taxes, however, he would not be liable to the winter grazing fine.[75] This version of the fine is similar to a fine known as the *resm-i duhan* (or *resm-i tütün*), a smoke or hearth fine whose intent was to define the winter pasture of nomads and confine them to it.[76]

For nomads, the winter grazing fine was, again, designed for herds which did not follow their "normal" track nor wintered on their accustomed pastures. In the lowlands, of course, the grounds on which they might winter would be more likely to be under exploitation and tillage. The fine was, like the summer grazing fine, restrictive. It took no account of the exigencies of the seasonal migrations, and it brought no return to the nomads. Closely allied to it was a "smoke tax" to keep nomads from spending the entire winter on pastures other than their own.

A final impost, the pasture fine or *resm-i otlak,* combines features of the two grazing fines and served to confine the nomads to their customary summer pastures. The general codes again provide the best introduction to the pasture fine. When nomads kept their herds within the confines of the pastures registered under their names in the cadasters, government officials were forbidden to take more than the sheep tax from them. When, however, nomads let their herds wander onto other pastures where the fine was collected, or even as far as other provinces, they then had to pay the pasture fine. Up till late in the reign of Mehmet the Conqueror, the fine was one average sheep per herd. Then, and generally afterwards, it was graded: a fine herd owed a sheep valued at twenty *akçes,* an average herd owed a sheep worth fifteen *akçes,* while poor herds owed a sheep worth ten *akçes.*[77] The provincial regulations generally followed this rate.[78]

The general code of 952/1545 tried to consolidate some of these practices. The tax on sheep was to suffice for areas not subject to one of the fines, should nomads remain in those areas for any period. In each province, however, there were lands subject to the pasture fine. They would be entered in appropriate registers. The fine fell only on sheep from another province who entered these pastures and grazed them. Some of the lands so designated were on the confines of the customary summer pastures of the nomads, and the fines were usually collected while the sheep were there. The fine here was an incentive to confine the herds and nomads to particular, defined pastures in their own province. The collector of fines was either a designated timariote or the governor of the province. Old usage and custom had set the fine at one sheep per herd: in the sixteenth century, herd size, quality, and governmental need determined the rate. The shepherds could pay in money or in kind, either twenty *akçes* for a large sheep, fifteen for a normal sheep, or ten for a yearling. The maximum fine was twenty *akçes.*[79]

The winter and summer grazing fines were intended to control the nomads and their herds on the long marches to winter and summer pasture. The "smoke" and, in some provinces, the winter grazing fines, served to keep the wintering herds on their accustomed pastures. The pasture fine was the summer pasture version of the "smoke" fine. It helped to keep the herds where, in the government's eyes, they belonged. While one violation would not harm an average herd, there was no limit on the number of times the officials could levy this fine upon a herd whose customary pastures were too poor and which had to seek new routes or greener seasonal grazing.[80] Thus the pasture fine aided in preserving (and enforcing) the customary land utilization and summer *termini* of the nomad's routes, while the other fines helped to define the routes themselves.

These, then, are the Ottoman regulations touching nomads. The Ottoman dream of a sedentary paradise with its regular, predictable revenues from pacific farmers had no place for pastoral nomads. The nomads followed small-scale changes in climate to maximize their access to good pasture and sweet water; consequently they were always on the move. This mobility represented independence, and thus a potential for conflict with the central Ottoman regime. These two factors, mobility and independence, made the nomads a threat the Ottomans wanted to control. The Ottoman fiscal regulations played a major role in that control.

The Ottoman government's taxation of nomads went considerably beyond the forms of levy which nomads customarily employ among themselves. The Ottoman taxation was regular and permanent in order to meet the needs of government and not of pastoralism. The tax rates were fixed without regard for the pastoral taxpayer's ability to pay, and the rates therefore forced the minimum herd size for nomadic success to rise far above the normal animal capitalization of the unencumbered pastoralist.

The sheep tax forced marginally capitalized nomads out of the pastoral cycle and into settlement. The fines along the lines of march prevented nomads from escaping the effects of irregular rainfall upon their customary pastures while on the move. The pasture and "smoke" fines penalized them when they felt a need to find new pasture during summer or winter. These fines left many marginal nomads to the vagaries of uncertain rainfall along one line of march and within two uncomfortably well-defined sets of pastures. The Ottoman policies of taxation of nomads, then, were attempts to settle the nomads, or at least to settle them in one well-known routine, and to minimize their numbers.

The poor pastoral nomad was forced to take extreme measures if he wished to preserve his herd, as he has always had to do. He had to find the best pastures to keep his stock healthy, and he was thus often tempted away from a line of march, or a seasonal pasture, which had not been blessed with rain in a given year, to find nearby pastures that had fared better. He soon found himself paying repeated fines, whose cumulative impact could impoverish him unless he kept moving. Under the impact of the sheep tax and fines the poor nomad had the final choice of settlement or revolt. The Ottomans expected the nomad to settle and be "delivered" from nomadism. As we shall see, some nomads sought greener pastures and more attractive politics elsewhere.

Further, because the impact of these taxes on well-to-do nomads was not immediately threatening, the use as well as the amount of the taxes influenced their outlook. These taxes went to settled timariotes, to provincial governors, or to the grand fiefs of princes, and not for the benefit of the nomads. Nomads who served the military enterprise found themselves with demeaning duties. One of the appeals of Shah Ismail may thus have been his placing of nomad military units in the first rank of his armies and of nomad chiefs high in his councils. The Ottoman taxation may not have sedentarized the strong and wealthy nomads, but it surely antagonized them.

Notes to Chapter Two

1. For a theoretical treatment of the growth of a political body based upon the position of a mediator who "articulates" between "differentiated" populations, see P.C. Salzman, "The Proto-State in Iranian Baluchistan," in Ronald Cohen and Elman R. Service, eds., *Origins of the State* (Philadelphia, 1978), pp. 125-40; Meyer Fortes and E.E. Evans-Pritchard, eds., *African Political Systems* (London, 1940), pp. 9-10.

2. Joel Shinder, "Early Ottoman Administration in the Wilderness: Some Limits of Comparison," *International Journal of Middle East Studies* 9 (1978), pp. 497-517.

3. I. Beldiceanu-Steinherr, "La conquête d'Andrinople par les Turcs: la pénétration turque en Thrace et la valeur des chroniques ottomanes," *Travaux et mémoires* 1 (1965), pp. 439-61, a brilliant and stimulating study.

4. *EI*[2], art. "Kanun." It is important to distinguish collections of *kanuns* from legal codes or compendia such as the *Institutes* of Justinian. Collections of *kanuns* resemble much more that emperor's *Novels.* As for Islamic law, note that its immutability was established at the same time that a quite contrary view gained prominence in the medieval west, namely that "new forms" demand new laws.

5. See the remarks of V.L. Ménage in *Bulletin of the School of Oriental and African Studies* 43 (1980), p. 146.

6. Marshall G.S. Hodgson, *The Venture of Islam* (Chicago, 1974), vol. 2, p. 406. H. Inalcik, art. "Kanunname," in *EI*[2], justly remarks: "it is significant that codified *kannunnames* appeared only in Iran, Anatolia, Iraq and India—places with firmly established Turco-Mongol traditions and dynasties—and in regions of the Ottoman Empire where the typical Ottoman laws and administration were in force, *sc.* in Rumelia and Anatolia."

7. Barth, *Nomads,* p. 77.

8. I. Beldiceanu-Steinherr, "En marge d'un acte concernant le penğyek et les aqınğı," *Revue des études islamiques* 37 (1969), p. 23. The works of Mme. and M. Beldiceanu are essential for the study of Ottoman regulations.

9. See the excellent article by H. Inalcik, "Kanunname," in *EI*[2], and his earlier "Osmanlı hukukuna giriş," *Ankara üniversitesi siyasal bilgiler fakültesi dergisi* 13 (1958), pp. 102-26.

10. There is much current dispute about the chronology and contents of certain *kanunnames.* I try here to steer a middle ground which I hope is consistent with the evidence available to me. The reader may follow the arguments in this fascinating discussion in the bibliography cited *infra.*

11. The early *kanunname* was published by Friedrich Kraelitz-Greifenhorst, "Kanunname Sultan Mehmeds des Eroberers," *Mitteilungen zur Osmanischen Geschichte* 1 (1921-1922), pp. 13-48. See also Konrad Dilger, *Untersuchungen zur Geschichte des Osmanischen Hofzeremoniells im 15. und 16. Jahrhundert* (Munich, 1967). The later *kaṇunname* has been published twice: Mehmed Arif, "Kanunname-i al-i Osman," 72 pp., published as supplements to fascicules 15-19 of *Tarih-i Osmani encümeni mecmuası* (1912-1913); Nicoara Beldiceanu, *Code de lois coutumières de Mehmed II* (Wiesbaden, 1967). On the date, see V.L. Ménage, *Bulletin of the School of Oriental and African Studies* 32 (1969), pp. 165-67, and Beldiceanu's reply, "A propos du code coutumier de Mehmed II et de l'oeuvre juridique d'Ahmed Hersekzade," *Revue des études islamiques* 38 (1970), pp. 163-72.

12. N. Beldiceanu, in *Journal of the Economic and Social History of the Orient* 17 (1974), p. 213; H. Inalcik in *Der Islam* 43 (1967), pp. 138-40. Two manuscripts of *kanunnames* ascribed to Selim I were published in facsimile by Anna S. Tveritinova, *Kniga zakonov sultana Selim* I (Moscow, 1969). For a general discussion, H. Inalcik, "Suleiman the Lawgiver and Ottoman Law," *Archivum Ottomanicum* 1 (1969), pp. 105-38.

13. N. Beldiceanu, "A propos d'un livre sur les lois pénales ottomanes," *Journal of the Economic and Social History of the Orient* 17 (1974), pp. 208-209; N. Beldiceanu and I. Beldiceanu-Steinherr, *Recherches sur la province de Qaraman au XVIe siècle* (Leiden, 1968), pp. 9-11; Walter Hinz, "Steuerinschriften aus dem mittelalterlichen Vorderen Orient," *Belleten* 13 (1949), pp. 745-69; Hinz, "Das Steuerwesen Ostanatoliens im 15. und 16. Jahrhundert," *Zeitschrift der Deutschen Morgenländischen Gesellschaft* 100 (1950), pp. 177-201.

14. Difficulties of preservation and the hazards of rebinding have caused the loss of the first and last pages of many cadasters, so in some cases dating the cadaster and its partially preserved *kanunname* is a complex task. Barkan, pp. lviii-lxiii, 52.

15. Uriel Heyd, *Studies in Old Ottoman Criminal Law,* ed. by V.L. Ménage (Oxford, 1973). See also the reviews by Inalcik in *Bulletin of the School of Oriental and African Studies* 37 (1974), pp. 696-98, and by N. Beldiceanu, *Journal of the Economic and Social History of the Orient* 17 (1974), pp. 206-14. For a discussion of manuscripts containing diverse collections of *kanuns,* see N. Beldiceanu, *Les actes des premiers Sultans conservés dans les manuscrits turcs de la Bibliothèque Nationale à Paris,* 2 vols. (Paris, 1960-1964).

16. The basic problem facing the scholar is that there are no published chronological lists of the lesser members of the bureaucracy. To compile such a list, however desirable, would of course be a thankless and tedious task. For an excellent beginning see I. Beldiceanu-Steinherr and N. Beldiceanu, "Reglement ottoman concernant le recensement (première moitié du XVIe siècle)," *Südostforschungen* 37 (1978), pp. 1-40.

17. Early literature on the nomads of Asia Minor does not throw light on these matters, but does provide valuable lists of tribal names and locations: Dr. M. Tsakyroglou, *Peri Giouroukon, ethnologike melete* (Athens, 1891). Doctor Freiliz and Eng. Rawlig, *Türkmen aşiretleri,* translated from the German (Istanbul, 1334). The only scholar who seems to have shown much interest in this work is M. Tayyib Gökbilgin, *Rumeli'de yürükler, tatarlar ve evlad-i fatihan* (Istanbul, 1957), p. 8. In general, Gabriel Ardant, *Histoire de l'impôt* (Paris, 1971), vol. 1, p. 15.

18. Also, in sedentary slang, "to die."

19. Beldiceanu, *Qaraman,* p. 70. The *sipahi* was a mounted soldier holding a "fief" from the central government in return for military service. *Çift resmi* was the annual tax due from the amount of land which a pair, *çift,* of yoked oxen could plow, *cf.* the iugum. Its antecedents were almost certainly Byzantine. *Bennak resmi* was the tax payable by a landless or land-

poor peasant. *Caba resmi* was the tax paid by a landless bachelor. It was less than the *bennak resmi*. See also H. Inalcik, "Osmanlılarda raiyyet rüsumu," *Belleten* 23 (1959), pp. 575-610.

20. Beldiceanu, *Qaraman*, p. 63. Hadiye Tuncer, *Osmanlı imparatorluğunda toprak kanunları* (Ankara, 1965), p. 166.

21. H. Tuncer, *Toprak kanunları*, p. 104. Barkan, p. 190, a *kanun* from Çemişgezek, 948/1541-1542.

22. Tuncer, *Toprak kanunları*, p. 110.

23. *Ibid.*, pp. 87, 104, 110.

24. *Ibid.*, pp. 23, 110.

25. Barkan, p. 37, dated 986/1578-1579.

26. Tuncer, *Toprak kanunları*, pp. 173-87.

27. *Ibid.*, pp. 166, 16.

28. Kraelitz-Greifenhorst, "Kanunname," pp. 24, 28 (pp. 39, 43 of his translation).

29. Hamilton A.R. Gibb and Harold Bowen, *Islamic Society and the West* (Oxford, 1950), pp. 250-51. On the Ottoman silver *akçe* or asper, see N. Beldiceanu, *Les actes des premiers Sultans* (Paris, 1960), vol. 1, pp. 173-175.

30. Bertold Spuler, *Die Mongolen in Iran*, 3rd ed. (Berlin, 1968), pp. 306, 308-309.

31. Beldiceanu, *Qaraman*, p. 59.

32. Kraelitz-Greifenhorst, "Kanunname," pp. 22, 29 (pp. 36, 45 of his translation); N. Beldiceanu, *Les actes des premiers Sultans* (Paris, 1964), vol. 2, pp. 202, 300-301.

33. A. General *kanunnames:*
    Late Mehmed II: Beldiceanu, *Code*, ff. 25v - 26r = Arif, "Kanunname," p. 30.
    Selim I: Tveritinova, ff. 12b, 14a.
    Süleyman: Joseph, Freiherr von Hammer-Purgstall, *Des Osmanischen Reichs Staatsverfassung und Staatsverwaltung* (Vienna, 1815), vol. 1, p. 197.
    B. Ayni Ali's Treatise: H. Tuncer, *Osmanlı devleti arazi kanunları* (Ankara, 1962), pp. 58, 99, 101, 131, 139, 146.
    C. Provincial *kanunnames:*
    Ahisha *ca.* 1030/1620: H. Tuncer, *Osmanlı imparatorluğunda toprak hukuku, arazi kanunları ve kanun açıklamaları* (Ankara, 1962), p. 169.
    Aydın 935/1538-1539, 937/1530-1531, 1039/1629-1630: Barkan, p. 12; Tuncer, *Toprak hukuku*, p. 460, 288.
    Ayntab 982/1574: Tuncer, *Toprak hukuku*, pp. 346, 489.
    Bayburt 1516, 1530: Ismet Miroğlu, *XVI. yüzyılda Bayburt sancağı* (Istanbul, 1975), p. 154.
    Biga 922/1517-1518: Barkan, pp. 19-20; Tuncer, *Toprak hukuku*, p. 454.
    Bolu 935/1528-1529: Barkan, p. 31.
    Bozok n.d.: Barkan, p. 129.
    Diyarbekir 947/1540-1541, 973/1565-1566: Barkan, p. 133; Tuncer, *Toprak hukuku*, p. 183, possibly also p. 256.
    Erivan 997/1588: Tuncer, *Toprak hukuku*, p. 465.
    Erzincan 922/1516-1517: Barkan, pp. 181-84; Tuncer, *Toprak hukuku*, pp. 452-54, 486.
    Erzurum 1000/1591-1592: Tuncer, *Toprak hukuku*, p. 173.
    Hüdavendigar 892/1486-1487: Barkan, p. 3; Tuncer, *Toprak hukuku*, p. 499 (misdated).

Içil 922/1584-1585: Barkan, p. 50; Tuncer, *Toprak hukuku*, p. 260.
Şebinkarahisar 1022/1613-1614: *Ibid.*, p. 223 (as Karahisar-i Şarki).
Karaman 935/1528-1529: Barkan, p. 47; Beldiceanu, *Qaraman*, p. 50.
Karası 1576: Barkan, p. 22.
Kayseri 906/1500-1501: Barkan, p. 57.
Konya 966/1587-1588: Tuncer, *Toprak hukuku*, p. 401.
Kütahya 935/1528-1529: Barkan, pp. 24, 31.
Mardin 975/1567: Tuncer, *Toprak hukuku*, p. 275.
Pasin 988/1580: *Ibid.*, p. 352.
Siverek 924/1518-1519: Barkan, pp. 170-171.
Yeni Il 991/1583-1584: *Ibid.*, p. 77.

The *kanuns* which the Ottomans took over from the fiscal practice of Uzun Hasan of the Ak Koyunlu dynasty in southeast Anatolia deserve a separate study, for they preserve a notion of taxation which is closer to the nomads' own idea of taxing herds. Whenever possible I have referred to the texts in Barkan's collection, because the transcriptions of Tuncer are often abridged and occasionally inaccurate.

34. Beldiceanu, *Code*, ff. 25v - 26r = Arif, "Kanunname," p. 30.

35. For general remarks on the relationship between geology, geography, and carrying capacity, see Claudio Vita-Finzi, *Archaeological Sites in Their Setting* (London, 1978), pp. 71-88.

36. The fortuitous impact of weather is a leitmotif found in all field studies of pastoralism. Because of the unpredictable micro-climate, wealthy pastoralists transform the "excess" sheep in very large herds into land or other more secure forms of investment if they can. On the large, or perhaps more modest, rate of return on the capitalization of sheep among the Basseri, see Hillard G. Huntington, "The Rate of Return from the Basseri's Livestock Investment," *Man* 7 (1972), pp. 476-79. Huntington's point is that when labor cost, or "opportunity costs," are considered, the Basseri's rate of return falls considerably. The difficulty lies in considering herding to involve the cost of foregone opportunities elsewhere. Since such "opportunities" might involve poorer health, taxation, or conscription of the young adult, it is hard to see herding as a "cost" from the nomad's point of view.

37. Barth, *Nomads*, pp. 21-22; for a general discussion of herds, see Brian Spooner, *The Cultural Ecology of Pastoral Nomads* (Reading, 1973), pp. 9-15, especially his remarks on allelomimetic behavior.

38. In general, Inalcik, "Osmanlılarda raiyyet rüsumu," pp. 586-87; Hüdavendigar 892/1486-1487, Barkan, p. 3; Kütahya 935/1528-1529, *ibid.*, p. 24; later *kanunname* of Mehmet II, Beldiceanu, *Code*, f. 57r = Arif, "Kanunname," pp. 61-62; *kanunname* of Selim I, Tveritinova, ff. 12b, 14a; *kanunname* of Süleyman the Magnificent, Hammer-Purgstall, pp. 197-98. Beldiceanu, Tveritinova, and Hammer give a minimum figure of twenty animals rather than twenty-four.

39. *Bennak:* Kütahya 935/1528-1529, Barkan, p. 24; *caba:* Miroğlu, p. 154; Yeni Il 991/1583-1584, *ibid.*, p. 77, where the *resm-i caba* was thirteen *akçes*, so the minimum herd size was put at twenty-six.

40. Tveritinova, f. 13a; Barkan, p. 12, dated 935/1528-1529.

41. Shearing times of lambs are dependent to some extent on the local climate. Between coastal, plateau, and mountainous sections of Anatolia there are noticeable differentials in dates of the routine of husbandry. For one published calendar of the cycle, see Jean-Paul Roux, *Les traditions des nomades de la Turquie méridionale* (Paris, 1970), pp. 239-44. In general, the first

clip of the lambs took place in a period spanning late May and June, although some animals were shorn only around the time of the autumn clip, at the equinox. *Cf.* Kazim Riza, *Die türkische Landwirtschaft und ihre wichtigsten Betriebszweige* (diss. Leipzig, 1935), p. 153. *Kanuns* describing the earlier Ottoman collection practice: Hammer, pp. 198, 200; Tveritinova, ff. 12b, 14a; Beldiceanu, *Code,* f. 57v = Arif, "Kanunname," p. 62; Hüdavendigar 892/1486-1487, Barkan, p. 3; Kütahya 935/1528-1529, *ibid.,* p. 24; Tuncer, *Toprak hukuku,* p. 499; Tuncer, *Arazi kanunları,* p. 131, a general *kanunname* of 952/1545-1546.

42. Beldiceanu, *Code,* ff. 25v - 26r = Arif, "Kanunname," p. 30.

43. The provincial *kanunnames* requiring collection in May reflect a later lambing season on the plateau: Tuncer, *Toprak hukuku,* pp. 183, 260; Beldiceanu, *Qaraman,* p. 50; Barkan, pp. 47, 57, 129. Early April collections: Hammer, pp. 198, 200; Tveritinova, ff. 12b, 14a; Beldiceanu, *Code,* f. 57v = Arif, "Kanunname," p. 62, probably an addition; Aydın, 935/1528-1529, Barkan, p. 12; Bolu, n.d., *ibid.,* p. 31; Kütahya, n.d., *ibid.,* p. 24; Hüdavendigar, 892/1486-1487, *ibid.,* p. 3; Yeni Il, 991/1583-1584, *ibid.,* p. 77; Bayburt, 1516 and 1530, Miroğlu, p. 154; Ayntab, 982/1574, Tuncer, *Toprak hukuku,* p. 346; Erivan, 997/1588-1589, *ibid.,* p. 465; Erzurum, 1000/1591-1592, *ibid.,* p. 173.

44. Barkan, p. 12; Tuncer, *Toprak hukuku,* pp. 460, 489; Tuncer, *Arazi kanunları,* pp. 99, 146, 139.

45. Roux, p. 240.

46. John M. Smith, Jr., "Mongol and Nomadic Taxation," *Harvard Journal of Asiatic Studies* 30 (1970), pp. 60-67.

47. *Ibid.,* p. 63; Barth, *Nomads,* pp. 16-17; Herbert Harold Vreeland, *Mongol Community and Kinship Structure,* 2nd ed. (New Haven, 1957), p. 32.

48. Barth reports that the minimum herd size among the Basseri was sixty animals; Barth, *Nomads,* p. 16.

49. Daniel G. Bates, "The Role of the State in Peasant-Nomad Mutualism," *Anthropological Quarterly* 44 (1971), p. 126.

50. Daniel G. Bates, "Shepherd Becomes Farmer," in Peter Benedict, Erol Tümertekin, and Fatma Mansur, eds., *Turkey, Geographical and Social Perspectives* (Leiden, 1974), pp. 100, 127; Bates, "Role of the State," p. 126, with a discussion of the tendency to settle permanently; Bates, "Differential Access to Pasture in a Nomadic Society: The Yörük of Southeastern Turkey," in William Irons and Neville Dyson-Hudson, eds., *Perspectives on Nomadism* (Leiden, 1972), p. 55, statistics from a survey taken in the late summer, including the previous spring's lambs (born in early to mid-March); Bates, *Nomads and Farmers: A Study of the Yörük of Southeastern Turkey* (Ann Arbor, 1973), pp. 162, 174, 219; herd of 300, cf. Roux, p. 226; for a general statement of the impact of pasture rents, Wolf-Dieter Hütteroth, *Bergnomaden und Yaylabauern im mittleren kurdischen Taurus* (Marburg, 1959), pp. 104, 152-53.

51. Dorothea Oschinsky, *Walter of Henley and Other Treatises on Estate Management and Accounting* (Oxford, 1971); B.H. Slicher van Bath, *The Agrarian History of Western Europe A.D. 500-1850* (London, 1963), pp. 167-68, 286-88.

52. Ethnologists are beginning to gather more of these data: see the remarks of N. Dyson-Hudson, "The Study of Nomads," in Irons and Dyson-Hudson, eds., *Perspectives,* pp. 24-25. For Barth's data, see his *Nomads,* pp. 16-17, and, in greater detail, his "Capital,

Investment and the Social Structure of a Pastoral Nomad Group in South Persia," in Raymond W. Firth and B.S. Yamey, eds., *Capital, Savings and Credit in Peasant Societies* (Chicago, 1964), pp. 70-71; Bates' pastoralists are integrated into a market economy, so I have not used his data, although in many respects they are fuller than those of Barth. The age distribution in herds over a period of years is particularly clear in Bates' work. In general, I believe that calculations based on Bates' herds yield results quite similar to mine: Bates, *Nomads and Farmers,* pp. 143-53; for comparison with herds from Turkestan, see A. Golf, *Die Karakulzucht in ihrem Heimatlande Turkestan* (Berlin, 1933), and Irons, "Variations in Economic Organization: A Comparison of the Pastoral Yomut and the Basseri," in Irons and Dyson-Hudson, *Perspectives,* pp. 93-94.

53. Twinning was rare for the breeds of sheep under consideration here: Riza, *Landwirtschaft,* p. 151, based on pre-World War I husbandry practice in the Ottoman Empire.

54. The vocabulary of sheep rearing in Turkey emphasizes these distinctions between lambs, yearlings, and adults, especially since ewes do not breed until their second winter. Lambs are called *kuzu* after they are forty days old (these first forty days of life after the March birth were obviously the most precarious, and we have seen that the Ottoman tax collectors, beginning their work in early April or even in May, caught all or most of the runts in their tax net); male yearlings of six months and over are called *toklu,* females of one year are called *şişek,* and the adult rams are called *koç,* the ewes *koyun.* The difference in date among the yearlings comes from the modern practice of selling some of the males during their first winter. Riza, *Landwirtschaft,* p. 149; Bates, *Nomads and Farmers,* p. 147; Roux, p. 225 n. 1; Hamit Z. Koşay, "Türkiye halkının maddî kültürüne dair araştırmalar, III, hayvancılık," *Türk etnografya dergisi* 3 (1958), p. 39, with local dialectical variants on pp. 13, 25-27, 30, 32, 34, 36, 38.

55. These values are derived from the *kanuns* on herd fines, discussed *infra,* especially the *resm-i otlak.* The six *akçe* value for a lamb is not found in those *kanuns,* but it occasionally appears as a figure for the most destitute of herds, and since the value of a lamb was not as great as that of a strong adult sheep who had passed through one or more winters, this value seems reasonable. This "price" scale, fifteen-ten-six, agrees also with price statistics from ethnographic reports and studies of traditional animal husbandry. Riza, *Landwirtschaft,* pp. 156-57; Roux, p. 75; Bates, *Nomads and Farmers,* pp. 143-44, 147; Dieter Ehmann, *Bahtiyaren, Persische Bergnomaden im Wandel der Zeit* (Wiesbaden, 1975) p. 113. The American Department of Agriculture publishes full price statistics for animals, but the American palate's insistence upon lamb and its distaste for mutton reverses the Ottoman price structure.

56. Cf. Spuler *apud* n.30 above. Note also that if we accept Huntington's argument, in his "Rate of Return," pp. 477-78, the tax practically consumes all the net profits of herding, even for such a sizeable herd.

57. In fact, despite the many variables (besides taxes) which can affect herd size, minimum viable herds seem to hover between fifty and sixty sheep in most areas similar to Asia Minor pastures: see the general discussion of Hütteroth, *Bergnomaden und Yaylabauern,* pp. 88, 90-91; Irons, "Variations," p. 96; comparative remarks by the contributors to Cynthia Nelson, ed., *The Desert and the Sown* (Berkeley, 1973), pp. 40 n. 13, 132, 147. In all cases, smaller herd sizes are due to a mixed economy of pastoralism and cultivation, or alternative employment opportunities herding someone else's larger herd.

58. C.R. Bawden, *The Modern History of Mongolia* (New York, 1968), pp. 150, 169. The remarks of Huntington are even more appropriate here, if we accept his assumptions. On the impact of overtaxation, see Gyula Kaldy-Nagy, "Rural and Urban Life in the Age of Sultan Suleiman," *Acta Orientalia* 32 (1978), p. 297.

59. Gibb and Bowen, pp. 55, 101; Salahaddin Çetintürk, "Osmanlı imparatorluğunda yürük sınıfı ve hukuki statüleri," *Ankara üniversitesi dil ve tarih—coğrafya fakültesi dergisi* 2 (1943-1944), pp. 111-12; Cengiz Orhonlu, *Osmanlı imparatorluğunda aşiretleri iskân teşebbüsü (1691-1696)* (Istanbul, 1963), pp. 25-26.

60. For good illustrations of typical stone sheep-folds in Lycaonia, see Louis Robert, *Hellenica* 13 (Paris, 1965), plates 5 and 6.

61. Beldiceanu, *Code*, f. 57v = Arif, "Kanunname," p. 62; Tveritinova, f. 14a; Hammer, p. 200.

62. In the province of Hüdavendigar, each herd in 892/1486-1487 owed three *akçes*. In Aydın, in 935/1528 and 937/1530, the rate was three *akçes*, but one century later, in 1039/1623, it was two *akçes*. In 935/1528 the tax was three *akçes* in Kütahya. From Karaman, *kanuns* from Süleyman's reign and from 996/1587 give a rate of five *akçes* on a herd of 300 sheep. Three hundred sheep made an "official" herd. In Içil, in 992/1584, five *akçes* were due from each herd of 300. In Pasin, in 988/1580, the tax, collected when the flocks had arrived at their winter pastures or *kışlaks*, was one *akçe* per hundred.
Hüdavendigar: Tuncer, *Toprak hukuku*, p. 499.
Aydın: *ibid.*, p. 461. Barkan, p. 12. Tuncer, *Toprak hukuku*, p. 289.
Kütahya: Barkan, p. 24.
Karaman: Beldiceanu, *Qaraman*, p. 51. Tuncer, *Toprak hukuku*, p. 401.
Içil: *ibid.*, p. 260. Barkan, p. 50.
Pasin: Tuncer, *Toprak hukuku*, p. 353.
Of course, for a "standard" herd of 300, the Pasin *resm-i agıl* becomes three *akçes*.

63. In eastern Anatolia the collectors took the pen-due in kind. In these provinces (Ahisha, Bayburt, Diyarbekir, Erzurum, Şebinkarahisar, Urfa) the tax was called *resm-i yatak*, berth-tax. When the sheep arrived at winter pasture their numbers were to be estimated. Each herd owed one sheep of medium size in tax. From herds smaller than the standard 300 a money payment of one *akçe* on ten sheep was due. Tuncer, *Toprak hukuku*, pp. 183, 173, 223, 169; Miroğlu, p. 154. Not only the user, but also the owner of sheep-pens owed tax; a *kanun* of Süleyman (952/1545-1546) states that each pen "owed" two *akçes;* and in the early seventeenth century this tax was three *akçes*. Tuncer, *Arazi kanunları*, pp. 59, 131, 140.

64. That the nomads had to pay a tax on the pens in which their sheep mated is a further indicator of the extent to which their winter grazing possibilities were circumscribed by sedentary society. The sheep folds would be the common stock of the tribe in a nomad-based economy, and rights to them would vest in all members of the tribe. For one instance in which nomads in modern Turkey acquire pasture rights, alluded to above, see Bates, "Differential Access," pp. 48-59.

65. Barth, *Nomads*, p. 16.

66. Robert N. Pehrson, *The Social Organization of the Marri Baluch* (Chicago, 1966), p. 8; W.W. Swidler, "Adaptive Processes Regulating Nomad-Sedentary Interaction in the Middle East," in Nelson, ed., *The Desert and the Sown*, p. 40.

67. Beldiceanu, *Qaraman*, pp. 62-63.

68. Once these routes were settled, farmers could cultivate some of the better, now forbidden, pastures along the boundaries of the fixed route, and this process would hem in the nomads even more (while showing them a government-approved model for rural life.).

69. The quantity of fat was fixed at one *nevgi* (or *nügü*), a scoop measuring some two hundred *dirhems* in weight: Nejat Göyünç, *XVI. yüzyılda Mardin sancağı* (Istanbul, 1969), p. 139 n. 1. Kanuns: Bayburt, 1516, 1530, Miroğlu, p. 154; Mardin, 924/1518-1519, Barkan, p. 158; Erzincan, 922/1516, Tuncer, *Toprak hukuku*, pp. 452-54.

70. Mardin 975/1567, Tuncer, *Toprak hukuku,* pp. 275-76, 353; Diyarbekir 947/1540-1541, Barkan, p. 134; Çemişgezek 948/1541-1542, Barkan, p. 190 (pay either one sheep or thirty *akçes*); Arapgir 976/1568, Tuncer, *Toprak hukuku,* pp. 241-42.

71. Barkan, pp. 36-37.

72. Beldiceanu, *Code,* f. 38r-v = Arif, "Kanunname," p. 43; Tveritinova, ff. 13b-14a: if, however, the nomad cultivated the land and paid produce tithes and taxes, he did not owe *resm-i kışlak.* Similarly, a *kanun* of Süleyman the Magnificent, Hammer, p. 200 (where the poorest herd owed fifty *akçes*, which I take to be an error).

73. Tuncer, *Arazi kanunları,* pp. 100, 122, 147.

74. Karaman, 935/1528-1529, Barkan, p. 47, and Beldiceanu, *Qaraman,* pp. 53-54, similar but of uncertain date; Hüdavendigar 892/1487-1488, Barkan p. 4, merely states that the fine is proportional to the herd size; Yeni Il 991/1583-1584, *ibid.*, p. 77; Çemişgezek 948/1541-1542, *ibid.*, p. 190: for each herd of 300, an animal worth thirty *akçes*, and proportionately higher or lower depending on herd size; Diyarbekir 947/1540-1541, *ibid.*, p. 134; Urfa and Diyarbekir, 973/1565, Tuncer, *Toprak hukuku,* p. 185; Mardin 975/1567, *ibid.*, p. 276; Arapgir 976/1568, *ibid.*, p. 242; Pasin 988/1580, *ibid.*, p. 352.

75. Provincial practice was not uniform: Aydın 935/1528-1529, Barkan, p. 12 (three *akçes*), Tuncer, *Toprak hukuku,* p. 288 (from 1039/1629); Erzincan and Kemah 927/1521, *ibid.*, p. 485.

76. Its relation to the Byzantine "kapnikon" tax remains to be clarified. *Resm-i duhan* kanuns: Aydın 937/1528-1529, Barkan, p. 12; Aydın 937/1530-1531, Tuncer, *Toprak hukuku,* p. 460; Bayburt 1530, Miroğlu, p. 154; Diyarbekir 947/1540-1541, Barkan, p. 134; Süleyman's *kanun* of 925/1545, Tuncer, *Arazi kanunları,* p. 102.

77. Beldiceanu, *Code,* ff. 37v - 38r = Arif, "Kanunname," pp. 42-43, f. 57v = p. 62; Tvertinova, ff. 13b, 14a; Hammer, pp. 199-200.

78. Hüdavendigar 892/1487-1488, Barkan, p. 4 (without a rate); Karaman 935/1528-1529, *ibid.*, p. 47; Kütahya 935/1528-1529, *ibid.*, p. 26; Aydın 935/1528-1529, *ibid.*, p. 12, and 937/1530 in Tuncer, *Toprak hukuku,* p. 460 (a money fine of seventeen *akçes* if the *yürük* grazed his herd on a *timar*).

79. Tuncer, *Arazi kanunları,* pp. 100-101, 122, 131, 147.

80. See, for comparison, the sedentarizing (or settling) effect of the repeated payments which the Saçıkara must make to own village lands: Bates, *Nomads and Farmers,* pp. 132 n. 3, 135. For a contrary case, in which the large herds of powerful herdsmen wintered in the Develi plain and paid a fee of only two sheep per hundred in a herd for the entire period September-April, see Reşat Izbırak, *Develi ovası ve ekonomik gelişmesi* (Ankara, 1953), p. 20.

Chapter Three:

The Horse Drovers of the Axylon

The Ottomans praised their nomadic past in courtly chronicles and prescribed their nomads' future in mundane decrees. The impact of Ottoman tax policy and the alienation of nomad revenues were far from pleasing to the tribesmen. As far as the administrators cared, the nomads were, or were soon to be, subjects. Just as other subjects were registered in doomsday books, so were the nomads subject to occasional registration for tax and census purposes. These cadasters *(defters),* many of which have survived in whole or in part, sometimes allow a scrutiny of the organization, variety, and productivity of life in the Ottoman countryside. Entries describing nomads, listing adult male tribesmen, locating their pastures, and summarizing their financial obligations, help us to perform some primitive, incomplete, but nonetheless suggestive fieldwork among medieval pastoralists. Examining successive cadasters also affords one advantage which few ethnographers enjoy, the opportunity to follow a group's fortunes over the generations. This chapter attempts the study of some Anatolian nomads as they appear in the cadasters.

Many of the provincial cadasters for Asia Minor contain entries describing nomads. In one type of cadaster, the nomad groups appear singly between the descriptions of villages, towns or suburban areas. Such an organization can help the historian to fit the nomads into their geographical niche, for it implies that the registrars wrote up villages or groups as they came upon them: reading the cadaster with the aid of a good map lets us follow the registrars on their rounds. Where nomads appear between the entries for two villages, it is likely that either their routes of migration or their summer pastures lay between the villages.[1] The cadasters in which nomads appear as occasional intruders among villages and cultivated fields describe areas whose nomadic population was small and unrepresentative of the population as a whole. A second group of cadasters, whose provinces felt a larger nomadic presence, registered nomads in a separate section.[2] Here the clerks found it more convenient, in transcribing a fair copy from the field notes of the registrars, to differentiate the large number of nomadic from sedentary subjects for easier reference and uniformity of treatment. A variant of this type is the cadaster devoted solely to the tribes of a province, although this form appears but rarely among the surviving doomsday books. The province of Karaman, including Lycaonia, Cappadocia, and parts of Isauria, centered upon the Axylon—a great treeless plain surrounding the Salt Lake—was one province whose nomads were registered separately.[3] By far the largest tribe in Karaman was the Horse Drovers (*At Çeken,* occasionally appearing in the records in Persian as *Esb Keşan*), whom we shall study from the evidence of a cadaster of 1500-1501, the work of the registrar Haydar ibn Nasuh, known as Hatipoğlu, and his scribe Ali. For comparative purposes we have a cadaster of 1523, composed by Mustafa Çelebi and his scribe Ruşeni ibn Hacı Hüseyin.[4]

There are certain dangers in studying any record which, because of its convenience, stands out. No doubt the regulations whose impact on nomads formed the subject of the last chapter could be, and should be, studied from the scattered entries listing nomads in a large number of cadasters. The possibility that the Horse Drovers may give a false picture is increased by their numbers and a special statute that concerned them. Further, because all the Horse Drover entries follow each other, it is very difficult to determine the location of a group, a problem which most cadasters, sprinkling the nomads among fixed settlements, avoided. On the other hand, their homeland, Karaman, has been well studied and was always a haven for pastoralists. Also, Hatipoğlu's cadaster is the earliest extant (and presently dated) survey of nomads in the Ottoman orbit. An examination of the Horse Drovers may reveal the Ottoman impact on nomads at a crossroads: one generation after the Ottoman conquest of Karaman, Hatipoğlu went into the field with his scribe at the very moment when Safavid missionaries were coming to recruit nomad supporters.

Central Anatolia was already a pastoral center long before Hatipoğlu's visit. The Hittites herded sheep, goats, and horses on the plateau.[5] According to Strabo, "Cappadocia paid the Persians yearly, in addition to the silver tax, 1,500 horses, 2,000 mules, and 50,000 sheep. . . ." A late Roman author claimed that the empire's best horses were raised on the slopes of the Taurus. Finally, Strabo remarked of the sheep grazing south of the Salt Lake, "Although the country is unwatered it is remarkably productive of sheep; but the wool is coarse, and yet some persons have acquired great wealth from this alone."[6] The slightly rolling ground, gentlest in Anatolia, and the slopes of occasional mountains provided superb pasture. As a later traveler noted: ". . . many a place marked on our maps as a morass, was on the contrary fine pasturage and covered with flocks, with neither reeds nor rushes, nor even the coarse grass that indicates marshy ground."[7]

Hamilton, an English observer who passed through in the 1830s, paid more attention to the horses: "The Turcomans of this district, like their Cappadocian predecessors of old, are great breeders of horses, which, of course, they sell as soon as possible to other parts of the country, keeping the mares only at home; these they ride, but never use as beasts of burden.... Those I saw were neat, though small, and generally active, and were followed by their young foals."[8] A few years earlier Macdonald Kinneir, another observant traveler, noticed that "The plain was covered by Yoorooks (nomads), who are breeders of horses, and whose tents were pitched on small conical hills resembling tumuli, which seemed to preserve a perpetual verdure, whilst the remaining part of the country was parched with drought."[9]

Where in Karaman did the Horse Drovers live? As nomad pastoralists they had neither villages nor fixed residences with names to check on a map. They did, however, have routes and pastures. Depending on the pattern of rainfall and the number of animals to be grazed, the nomads each year chose well-watered lines of march and pastures for summer and winter from among their accustomed routes and pastures.[10] Plotted on a map, this collection of routes and pastures outlines an area shaped like a dumbbell. Among the Basseri of South Iran it is called the "il-rah" or tribal route. At a particular moment of the seasonal cycle, the nomads were at some point along the il-rah. Both routes and pastures might be altered with changing climatic or political fortunes; the tribe laid claim to a pasture or source of water only when the herds were encamped there. The seasonal migrations of the Horse Drovers were not as long as those found in some other areas of the Near East. Summer pastures might lie up the slopes of one of the extinct volcanic cones dotting the Axylon, while winter pastures would be spread around its base. On the other hand, the migration might lead from the northern slopes of the Taurus to the plains bordering the Salt Lake, or, finally, from the northern ridges of the Sultan Dağı to the outlying branches of the upper Sakarya south and west of Ankara.[11]

Settlement, slow or sudden, played an important role in circumscribing and defining the area where the Horse Drovers lived. In 1500 Hatipoğlu registered them in three indistinct and overlapping districts *(nahiyes):* Eski Il, Bayburd, and Turgud. The notion of an il-rah explains this fuzziness and overlay. Pastoralists of Bayburd might graze a pasture during, say, March, and once they had moved on nothing would prevent a herd of Turgud, or even a settled cultivator, from enjoying it in April. Unlike a settler, the nomad claims use of a specific point only at a particular time. Rights to a pasture in May do not imply claims to that pasture in July. The 1500 census shows that the At Çeken were far from permanent settlement.

In 1518 the great Ottoman historian and man of affairs Kemalpaşazade and his scribe Hüsam Dimaşki prepared a full cadaster of Karaman for Sultan Selim I.[12] In this cadaster Turgud and Bayburd appeared as *kazas* or judicial circuits of Konya, while Eski Il was a circuit of Larende.[13] The modern Eski Il is the area immediately south of the Salt Lake. It is closer to Konya than to Larende, some eighty km southeast of Konya. For Eski Il to have been a circuit of Larende it must have been rather large, or at least rather long. In fact, the circuit of Eski Il overlay much of the circuits of Aksaray, Sahra-i Konya, and Insuyu, while Turgud included at least parts of Said Ili, Ilgın, and Zengicek.[14] The Horse Drover circuits of 1518 must therefore reflect the pastoral il-rahs, whose extent, integrated over the full year, is large, while at any particular time it is restricted to the smaller areas grazed on that date. It does appear, however, that the Horse Drover circuits of 1518 were smaller than their districts of 1500-1501, and in fact the entire province was divided into smaller segments in 1518 than during Bayezid II's reign.[15]

Kemalpaşazade's circuits still reflect the pastoral cycle of the Horse Drovers, but the mixture of settled districts with fixed boundaries and nomadic il-rahs whose inhabitants preferred flexible borders, along with the difficulties inherent in overlapping jurisdictions, cannot have pleased the Ottoman administrators. As a result of the Ottoman policy of settling, or at least rendering the movements of their subject pastoralists routine or predictable, the cadasters show an evolution of the Horse Drover circuits into smaller, compact areas ultimately indistinguishable from, and no longer encroaching upon, settled districts.

Sultan Murad III had a cadaster of Karaman prepared in 1591 by Mehmed ibn Kara Ali and his scribe Ahmed ibn Bostan.[16] Although a cadaster of tribesmen, the 1591 census is also a cadaster of settled farmers who had not shed their past labels; as a "nomad" cadaster, it is an example of bureaucratic conservatism. The Horse Drovers, in 1591, were no longer grazing three circuits but were settled in seven smaller ones: Turgud, now a town north of Akşehir; formerly part of Turgud, Mahmudlar became a town, now called Müneccimöreni, some thirty km southeast of Konya;[17] Insuyu, a village west of the modern Cihanbeyli;[18] Korayş Özü, formerly a part of Turgud; Korayş, formerly a part of Bayburd; Eski Il, with the remainder of Korayş, and Bayburd.[19]

In 1500-1501, however, the districts of the Horse Drovers were sizeable and largely nomadic. The largest was Turgud, since it included Turgud, Mahmudlar, and Korayş Özü, an area southeast of Larende on the north slope of the Taurus, above Fisandon.[20] Somewhat lesser in extent was Eski Il, which included the south shore of the Salt Lake and the present hamlet of Eski Il as well as routes stretching as far south as Larende and parts of Korayş. The much smaller Bayburd, southeast of Larende, is the only nomadic il-rah which has left no trace on modern toponymy. Due to the overlap with settled circuits, and the nature of the route and schedule which define an il-rah, the three districts had boundaries not only in space but also in time. For administrative purposes, the districts consisted of the locations of the nomads at the moment they were sought. In 1500 the district was the il-rah. Once the nomads began to settle, the il-rah disintegrated, slowly, into circuits of towns and villages and became a vague memory. When Hamilton passed Kadınhanı, between Konya and Akşehir, he was told that the plains extending north in the direction of Ankara were called At Çeken.[21]

Our purpose in this chapter is to view the Horse Drovers through the lens of Ottoman cadasters. Therefore, our emphases will be upon the cadaster data and their interpretation as illustrating a method of research into the history of nomads. At the same time, the cadasters do not offer a full chronicle of the Horse Drovers. In order to place them in the proper perspective we need to look into their earlier career, and for this there are other sorts of texts for us to ponder.

There are only two sources, both popular in style, to lend us hints about the origins of the Horse Drovers. Two branches of the Horse Drovers appear in the life of a local dervish, the "Tales of Dediği Sultan." The "Tales" is a poem of 484 couplets "translated into Turkish," whose surviving manuscript was completed in 1814. As it awaits its editor, no other information about its composition and age are available.

According to the "Tales," Dediği Sultan was born in Khurasan.[22] He was purportedly a cousin of Hacı Bektaş, and a descendant of Ahmed Yesevi. Whatever his origins Dediği Sultan left Khurasan with the forty felt-covered tents of Turgud and Bayburd, who were his close friends. He dispatched them to Anatolia and went for pilgrimage and further study to Mecca. Later, Dediği Sultan arrived in Beyşehir and came into rivalry with another divine, Seyit Harun Veli, who died in 1320. When Dediği Sultan attended his funeral, some of the Seyit's followers struck him, causing forty drops of blood to flow from his nose. He rubbed some of the blood on his headgear, which the impressions of his fingers turned red in five stripes. Later, the Christians of Seydişehir rioted and Dediği Sultan expelled them, driving them off the plateau south to Antalya.

Celal al-Din Rumi invited Dediği Sultan to Konya, but "like Adam, Jesus, Moses and Muhammad," he preferred the seclusion of the mountains to the city. Dediği Sultan did not stand apart, however. He aided the Seljuk Sultan when Konya was besieged and he performed public miracles.

In their wanderings Turgud and Bayburd entered Anatolia. They did not find Dediği Sultan, and the people they did find attacked them. While seeking a stallion, one of Turgud's mares met Dediği Sultan by chance on Ala Dağı. Dediği Sultan massaged the mare from tail to mane and offered prayers. The "Tales" assures us that the "famous horses" of Turgud were foaled of this mare. The episode led to a reunion.

Dediği Sultan came to Ilgın and continued to perform miracles. The

Sultan gave him land there. Later, when Dediği Sultan went to inspect his future tomb, he doled out milk from a herd of stags to the onlookers. The close friendship with Turgud continued until his own death.

Dervish legend suffuses the story of Dediği Sultan. His connections with Hacı Bektaş, Ahmed Yesevi, and Rumi lend him stature.[23] His preference for the distant, visible hills, for animals before men, and his distinctive red striped cap, all are the stock in trade of the late medieval Anatolian holy man.

Some of these traditions concerning the Horse Drovers may be sound. Having left Khurasan, perhaps in flight before the Mongols, the nomads of Turgud and Bayburd came to Anatolia, to the lands around Akşehir, where they were known for their horses by the early fourteenth century. The house and supporters of Turgud were more visible than Bayburd.[24]

Another source is the popular chronicle attributed to Şikari, which will be a major concern in the next chapter. In 1275, according to Şikari, when Mehmed ibn Karaman installed the pretender Cimri on the Seljuk throne at Konya, he divided the open country between Konya and Ankara in two and assigned half to Turgud Bey and half to Bayburd Bey. In this way the two areas received the names by which they were known in the sixteenth century, Turgud Ili and, in the southeast, Bayburd Ili.[25]

There is a fifteenth century tradition linking the Mongols to one of the groups in Eski Il, the Kuştimur. When the grandfather of Osman, Süleyman Şah, died crossing the Caber, he had seven companions, all members of the Üç Ok federation. One of these was Kuştimur, who remained in the Çukurova section of Cilicia with the area around Tarsus as winter pasture and Bulgar Dağı in the Taurus as summer pasture.[26] Some of the Kuştimur groups bore the Mongol name Samagar, however, and this implies that some of the later Kuştimur served in those Mongol armies which invaded Anatolia in the thirteenth century. Kuştimur, by this line of thought, was the name of the group which some of the Samagar joined after the Mongols dispersed.[27]

The Horse Drovers were important in the history of the emirate of Karaman. In Şikari, some of the influential Karaman emirs share names with groups of Horse Drovers. The army of Karaman which fought against Murad I contained elements of the Turgud, Samagar, and Bayburd groups.[28] While Murad II was occupied with the revolt of Düzme Mustafa, the Karaman emirs raised an army of rebellion which included Turgud groups.[29] In 1466 Mehmet the Conqueror annexed the emirate to the Ottoman domains. As part of the campaign the grand vezir, Mahmud Paşa, tried to subdue Turgud, whose followers fled over Bulgar Dağı into the safety of the rocky Taurus.[30]

The Ottomans spent the rest of the century consolidating and pacifying their conquest. The Horse Drovers often rebelled during this period. In 1470 Kasım Bey of the Karaman dynasty tried to reestablish himself in Konya. He recruited soldiers from the tribes of Varsak, Kosun (associated with Turgud),

Turgud, Kökez, and Bayburd.[31] In 1475 Kasım Bey joined Uzun Hasan in opposition to Mehmet. His troops included the Varsak, Turgud, Çini (of Turgud), Kosun, and Kuştimur nomads.[32]

In 1481, upon the death of Mehmet, his sons Bayezid II and Cem fought over his succession. Cem had been governor of Karaman, and when he fought Bayezid at Yenişehir the Varsak (used as infantry!), Turgud, Bayburd and Kosun nomads supported him, as did Kasım Bey.[33] When Bayezid defeated Cem, Kasım Bey fled to Taş Ili, the Isauria of antiquity. The Varsak and Turgud emirs joined him there.[34] Cem fled to Egypt, and an Ottoman pursuit force under Hadım Ali Paşa arrived in Karaman. Kasım Bey defeated this army near Larende and besieged Konya. Gedik Ahmed Paşa then led an Ottoman army against Kasım, who lifted the siege and withdrew, first to Taş Ili, then to Tarsus, and ultimately to Damascus. This sworn enemy of the Ottomans died in 1483.[35]

The death of Kasım Bey did not end the tribal unrest. Mahmud Bey, of the Turgud emirs, raised an army from the Turgud and Varsak, but he too met defeat at the hands of the Ottoman general Karagöz Paşa, who also forced the submission of the Kuştimur, Kosun, and Kara Isalu.[36] Mahmud Bey's rising is interesting because it appears that he enlisted both foot and mounted soldiers from the tribes, which suggests that some of the nomads had begun to settle. It is also, perhaps, an indication of the breakdown of tribal unity that some of the Kosunlu tribesmen fought alongside Karagöz Paşa.

In 1487-1489 Turgud and Varsak tribes in Cilicia aided the Mamluks against the Ottoman grand vezir Davud Paşa. Although he obtained their submission in the summer, each succeeding spring brought new tribal support for the Mamluks in their struggle for the Cilician plain.[37]

I do not believe that these risings betray suppressed loyalties to Cem, the emirs of Karaman, or the Mamluks in Egypt. What they do reveal is a strong and continued desire to avoid the Ottoman centralizing administration. As the regulations studied in the last chapter informed us, so in some way must these nomads have learned that the Ottomans threatened the continuation of their ways. And in response to this storm, the nomads sought any port.

The next revolt, in the summer of 1500, began as Hatipoğlu's cadaster neared its completion. In fact, Hatipoğlu and his scribe Ali may have played a role in arousing the nomads. Bayezid II was in the Morea, engaged in the conquest of Coron and Modon. The Turgud and Varsak emirs, and also some soldiers unhappy with the rates of taxation, revolted in the name of Mustafa Bey, a Karaman cadet who had grown up in Persia. Mustafa and the tribesmen fell on Larende, looted the environs, and placed the citadel under siege. When news of the revolt reached Bayezid, he ordered his sons Ahmed, governor of Amasya, Şehinşah, governor of Konya, and his grandson, Mehmet Şah, governor of Beyşehir, to put down the rebellion. The three

Ottoman forces gathered and lifted the siege of Larende. The rebels fled across the Taurus and, as winter approached, Ahmed, Şehinşah, and Mehmet Şah returned to their duties. The following March Bayezid ordered Vezir Mesih Paşa to end the unrest. Mesih Paşa marched forth to Larende and constructed a strong fort at Avgadı, between Larende and Taş Ili. He left a garrison at Avgadı and scoured the mountains in search of Mustafa Bey, who fled in disguise to Tarsus and Aleppo. The Varsak and Turgud emirs sued for peace.[38] This was the last revolt in the name of Karaman.

Hatipoğlu and Ali went about their work during the troubles, and much of that work survives. In the field they prepared a full cadaster, a listing by area of persons and property. The full cadaster, called a "detailed" *(mufassal) defter,* survives only in part, as TT40 (covering Konya and environs), TT42 (Niğde and environs), and TT46 (Karahisar and Develi).[39] From the detailed cadaster of the province scribes extracted information and organized it in other books devoted to particular groups of people or forms of property. TT32, the register of tribes, is one such cadaster. Others remaining from the cadaster of 1500-1501 are TT33, a register of military holdings and private property in Kayseri,[40] and TK565, listing the pious foundations of Karaman, Kayseri, and Iç Il.[41]

In the provincial cadaster, as we have seen, a *kanunname* opened the volume.[42] Since the cadaster of 1500-1501 lacks both beginning and end any regulations which it may originally have possessed are now lost. However, sixteenth-century codes with sections on the Horse Drovers have survived, and these provide us the statutes under which the Horse Drovers were supposed to live.

Manuscripts in Paris and Leiden contain, besides other codes, regulations concerning the Horse Drovers copied from the cadaster of Ebu'l Fazıl. The date of this cadaster is not known, but it must have been between 1544 and 1570.[43] Unfortunately, like the other regulations concerning the Horse Drovers, Ebu'l Fazıl's statute is "extremely confused."[44] A second code stands at the head of the Horse Drover cadaster of 1591, TT636. In addition to new provisions concerning the settled farmers who retained their former, nomadic label, this code contains summaries of previous regulations affecting the Drovers.[45]

Any discussion of the Horse Drover regulations must be prefaced by the admission that the actual treatment of the Drovers was harsher than the statute ordered; in fact Ottoman officials, tax farmers, and of course the Horse Drovers themselves, all evaded the provisions of the imperial rules. The cadaster records demonstrate that the rules were often ignored. Some of the confusion in the Horse Drover statutes results from official cognizance of the problem, attempts to rectify the situation, and final exasperation at the imperial inability to control imperious officials. It is not surprising, then, that the Horse Drover statutes are concerned with taxes, to the virtual exclusion of other topics.

In drawing up the statute of 1591 an examination of the earlier cadasters and statutes was made. According to a cadaster prepared for Bayezid II, which would be either the 1500-1501 or the 1483 doomsday book, the Horse Drovers were excused from land taxes, produce taxes, and extraordinary levies, because they raised horses and, as nomads, did not cultivate the soil. They did pay the sheep tax, fines and fees, and a horse tax *(at resmi* or *resm-i esb).* This horse tax was peculiar to the Horse Drovers and was assessed annually among units of population called horse heads *(at başı),* that is, units each containing twelve households. In Bayezid's reign each horse head paid a horse tax of 300 or 360 *akçes.*[46]

At some time between Kemalpaşazade's cadaster of 1517 and Mustafa Çelebi's in 1523, the 1517 cadaster was corrected and reviewed by Bayezid Çelebi. The horse tax was increased to 500 *akçes* and the Drovers became subject to a pen due of five *akçes* per herd of 300 sheep. The manner of apportioning the horse tax among the households of a horse head was clarified: honest tribesmen would divide the sum according to the households' ability to pay, with the greater burden resting on the wealthy, even should they be widows or young children.[47]

After 1544, when Ebu'l Fazıl began his survey of the status of the Horse Drovers, he found a changed situation. By his time most of the Drovers had settled and were farming the land. The central fiscal authorities decided to abolish the peculiar statute of the Drovers and register them as settled subjects owing land and produce taxes which, the registrars felt, would amount to many thousands of additional *akçes.* For their part, the Drovers' wealthiest chiefs argued that they were not subjects and that they should continue under their former statute. They offered, as a compromise, to pay a higher horse tax of 700 *akçes* per twelve households. At some point in one or the other of his two tours of duty as Grand Vezir, Rüstem Paşa came to Karaman and agreed to the compromise.[48] This compromise was easily effected because he was in the thick of a succession dispute which threatened to rend asunder the fabric of the ruling dynasty, and his own position, as a participant in the intrigues, was precarious. The exact manner in which the Horse Drovers were taxed was far from his mind when he entertained their submissions,[49] unless, of course, he was concerned about the loyalty of the tribesmen of Turgud and Karaman.[50]

Although the basic terms of the new statute recounted by Ebu'l Fazıl seemed to acquit the Drovers from the taxes of other sedentary farmers, additional sections of his statute (omitted in the 1591 summary) provided grounds for tax collectors who wished to collect tithes and land taxes to do so. Since, for example, some lands produced more than others, an additional sum supplemental to the horse tax was allowed, and this additional tax was based on the produce of the soil. Further, it appeared that many of the Drovers did not pay a horse tax apportioned among members of a unit such as the horse head but paid the taxes of a settled subject.[51] In fact, the cadasters will demonstrate that for most Horse Drovers the horse tax was simply another term for the sum of the normal taxes which the Drovers paid. The repeated issuance of these regulations with new provisos and exemptions tells a tale of regulations ignored, not regulations enforced. The statute ceased to bear a resemblance to the actual practice once the right to collect the horse tax was sold to the highest bidder and the Drovers became subject to his concern for an adequate return on his investment.[52] This development led to the final settlement of the Drovers. The later folios of the statute of 1591 thus deal with poor farmers, not nomads, and for that reason we may leave its provisions and promises to students of Ottoman decline.

The cadasters will yield the story of the settlement of the Drovers in greater detail than the statutes, and they show it beginning already at the turn of the sixteenth century. Thus, although the statutes claim that the Drovers were free of land taxes until the 1520s, the cadaster of 1500-1501 contains listings of such payments. More interesting, and surprising, is the absence of horses from the cadasters. Although most summary revenue entries are labeled "totals from the horse tax," there is not a horse in sight. The horse tax, reckoned in the field, was not determined by counting horse head units and multiplying their sum by the relevant tax. The horse tax was always the sum of other taxes: sheep, fines and fees, produce, and occasional land taxes. If there was a brisk trade in Turgud's famous horses, neither cadaster was concerned with it.[53] The sixteenth-century settlement of the Horse Drovers and their poverty after a few generations of settled tax collections[54] demonstrate that the Horse Drovers could not hide, that they could not have been very mobile, and that, during the sixteenth century, therefore, the label Horse Drover contained more irony than description. The fact that they settled, and settled so soon, reflects not only Ottoman strength but also a lack of horses.[55]

What is the cadastral record? It is a list and description of "*cemaats,*" groups ordered by tribe. *Cemaats* of Eski Il are described together, then those of Turgud (in 1500-1501; in 1523, Bayburd follows Turgud). Tribal names are an integral part of the *cemaat* descriptions: the headings read "*cemaat* X, part of Eski Il (or Bayburd or Turgud), Horse Drover." In the headings the term *cemaat* always appears. In the body of an entry, however, the terms *cemaat* and *kabile* may be used, often with the implication that the registered *cemaat* is part of a *kabile,* a larger body. For example, a number of the Kuştimur entries take the form "*cemaat* of X from the *kabile* of Kuştimur."[56] Within the Emir Hacilu *cemaat* of Bayburd, there was another *cemaat,* the Duydilar.[57]

Beneath the heading comes a list of all adult males, usually five (in 1500-

1501) or seven (in 1523) per horizontal row. Occasionally the first name is that of the imam or headman of the group. Each entry follows the form "X son of Y" or "Z brother of X." In the case of brothers, each is listed in turn. Thus the adult males of a nuclear family would be listed as Ahmed son of Mahmud, Hamid his (Ahmed's) brother, Mehmet his (Hamid's) brother.[58]

A symbol beneath a man's name will denote the amount of cultivated land at his disposal. There are separate symbols for different amounts and tenures. The old are listed if they are infirm, and cripples are labeled as such. Notations of land tenure among members of a group usually imply that it consists of settled cultivators. Comparison of land and sheep taxes will confirm or invalidate this impression. Since the tax on sheep provides an index of herd size, the comparison of sheep and land taxes gives a clear indication of the reliance by each household on pastoralism or cultivation.

Immediately following the names of the male tribesmen come two totals. The first, *"nefer,"* is a count (usually accurate) of the names written above. The second total, *"hane,"* is a count of heads of households, and in a completely nomadic environment this is in fact a count of tents and families.[59] As a check on the scribes, a good approximation of the number of households in any group may be obtained by subtracting the number of bachelors from the total of males. The bachelor notation, however, usually appears only when the group contains farmers. Among the pastoral groups there is normally no listing of a man's marital status. Neither cadaster mentions women or minors.

Below the census appears a summary of taxes under the heading "tax product" or "product of the horse tax." The tax of non-cultivator groups turns out to be the sum of the sheep tax and the *"bad-ı hava,"* a catchall sum including fines and fees.

The sheep of the Horse Drover herds were mostly of the Karaman or fat-tailed breed. While the wool of this breed is not as fine as the product of the Ankara goat, it makes for cheap, coarse, but warm garments as well as carpets. And, as a nineteenth-century traveller observed, "the flesh of the animal is superior to any other breed on the face of the earth. . . . The natives fully appreciate the economical value of the broad-tailed sheep, and it has nearly supplanted every other breed in the peninsula. Fine rams fetch a high price, and you see them kept in all parts of the country solely for breeding purposes."[60] The tail is valuable for its fat, delicate enough to replace butter in cooking. Unfortunately the weight of the tail could become a problem: "In the older sheep they sometimes reach such a size that they have to be laid on a little platform on two wheels, so that the sheep may drag what they cannot carry."[61] In the nineteenth century "tail's fat" was marketed at a price between tallow and butter.[62]

As the cadasters show, other taxes fell on groups whose members tilled the soil. The cultivators paid land taxes; large cultivator groups and, in 1523, small ones as well, paid a tax on the wheat they raised based on the produce revenues. The harvest was assessed, roughly, in *kiles* (the Ottoman bushel), and each entry listed first the number of *kiles* and then the estimated produce revenue in *akçes*. In 1500-1501 this assessment must have depended on quality as well as quantity, since the revenue was never an even multiple of the number of *kiles*. In 1523, by contrast, the tax was five *akçes* per *kile*.

After the tax listings, to complete each entry, came a list of the *mezraas*, customary or assigned, of that group. This term has occasioned some discussion among Ottoman historians. In surveys of villages it probably meant "cultivated field" or perhaps "deserted village."[63] In the context of the Axylon its likely meaning is cultivable pasture; there were too many in Karaman for each to have been a village.[64] In compound names of pastures, the most common descriptive terms are "summer pasture," "winter pasture," and "well." The pasture listings often indicate that they were shared among two or (rarely) more groups, either at the same time or, as the notion of an il-rah would lead us to suspect, in turn.

Appendix One, consisting of three tables setting forth the cadastral information, provides the basis for the following discussion. In order to facilitate the historical comparisons, the statistics for the year 1523 appear, for each group, below the 1500-1501 figures. We may then use the tables to look at the changing status of Horse Drover groups, to examine the pattern of settlement pursued by the nomads, and also to derive a clearer meaning for the term *cemaat*. Finally, we should be able to realize why the cadaster was a useful instrument of Ottoman policy against the nomads.

Perhaps the most striking apparent change is that of population between 1500-1501 and 1523. If adult males are considered as an index, there were four times as many groups reporting increases as decreases; if households are considered, there were over three times as many with increases as decreases. These proportions are also valid for each separate district. It is very difficult, however, to judge the import of these raw figures. Any conjecture about the demography of the Horse Drovers must, to be fair, rest upon an understanding of population movements in the Axylon as a whole, in the towns and countryside both; and that task lies beyond this study. If rural population rose at a greater rate than did the number of Horse Drovers, our initial impression of expansion will soon fade. For example, there may have been non-biological causes for a rise in the number of Horse Drovers, through in-migration or accretion. The next step in this study would be, then, to examine the individual male lines from cadaster to cadaster in the attempt to reconstruct male linkages through fathers, sons, and brothers. Although errors due to the repetition of common names would tend to overemphasize biological ties within a group, this procedure might still yield some notion of the extent to which the tribes were recruiting outside their ranks.[65] In short, although there may have been more Horse Drovers in 1523 than in 1500-1501, it would be unwise to draw any conclusions from that fact at the moment.

When we turn to the animal population, we are on more solid footing. The crucial figure to examine is the number of sheep per household, that is, the herd which sustained that household. One drawback of the Karaman cadasters is that the sheep tax is registered as a total sum for each group, and so the tables present an average herd size per household; additionally, since we are doubling the sheep tax sum to obtain herd size, the total herd size will always be an even number.[66] Changes in the average herd size per household help us to evaluate the success or failure of a family's pastoral activities. The two cadasters present a clear picture of declining household herds: over three times as many herds declined in size as grew. In Eski Il, where the comparative figures are fewest, the ratio was over two to one; in Bayburd, nine to one; in Turgud, over three to one. In addition, many average household herds had fallen below sixty sheep, so more of the 1523 herds were inadequate to support a pastoral household. The notes to Appendix One also show a correlation between high fines and small herds. This implies that the poorer groups, unable to prosper under Ottoman rules, were turning to predation, or at least attempting to nourish their animals on forbidden farmlands. In general, then, pastoral nomadism was in decline as the major economic resource of the Horse Drovers.[67]

Other general features of the two surveys support this conclusion. On the one hand, Hatipoğlu's cadaster lists relatively few cultivators, that is, adults who farmed plots of land. Mustafa Çelebi, in 1523 on the other hand, listed quite a few cultivators, even though few of them possessed an entire family farm.[68] More of the Drovers were looking for plough, rather than raiding, animals.

Revenue statistics, however crude they may be, also can best be explained by a turn to peasant farming. The 1500-1501 cadaster listed the *mezraas* of each group after the tax summaries; almost all of them were used as pasture. By 1523 the situation had changed, and in the new context it would be more apt to translate *mezraa* as cultivated field than as pasture. In all parts of the Axylon the registrars noted the produce revenues of the farming activities of the Horse Drovers. Many, perhaps most, of the *mezraas* registered for the first time to the Horse Drovers in 1523 were cultivated, as their revenues demonstrate. In general, then, a glance at the two cadasters reveals the settlement of the nomadic Horse Drovers and the transformation of their means of livelihood.

What made them change? 1523 was a generation distant from the high hopes and raised daggers of Safavid irredentism. In 1501 Shah Ismail was about to taste power; by 1523 he had already swallowed bitter defeat and was soon to die. The controls Bayezid II had once contrived to put on nomad separatism were harshly applied by Selim I: the rising of Shah Kuli was broken, the Safavid horse pulled up short before the Ottoman cannon at Chaldiran, and Ismail's defeat in that 1514 battle severed the close ties between the Anatolian tribesmen and their failed messiah. Here and there in the tables we can glimpse groups which both gained agricultural prosperity and kept their herds intact. Cultivating fields and hiring shepherds, they may have seen the virtues of collaboration early, before taxation or punishment for treason ground them down and crippled their herds. These tribesmen would have served as a model, even a beacon, to their fellows. If capital in the form of sheep produced declining returns in an unfriendly environment, then it might be best to convert that capital into another investment rather than attempt its violent conservation, as Ismail had done. Let us now look at this process of settlement in greater detail.

The first of the Horse Drover districts was Eski Il. Eski Il meant old or former tribe, a tribe which had departed or dissipated.[69] This former tribe was probably a Mongol unit, Samagar or a part thereof, to which the Horse Drovers were attached as a support group responsible for providing remounts. Upon the departure of the Mongols, Turkish nomads moved into the region, perhaps under the leadership of Kuştimur in alliance with Karaman, recalling in their name for this district that it had been, and in the fourteenth century still was, Mongol territory.

Eski Il comprised pastures between Konya, Aksaray, Karapınar, and Akçeşehir.[70] In 1500-1501 the district contained more than fifty-six groups, but as the cadaster lacks its opening pages, we cannot say just how many more. The remaining pages list 2314 adult males, while the sum total of adult males for the district was 5095.[71] In 1523 the Eski Il circuit consisted of seventy-seven groups and thirty settled villages.

Leaving the villages aside, how should we define the status of the groups? The terminology of the cadaster itself is little help. The phrase "*sakin der . . .*," which could be rendered as "settled in or near . . . ," is no more than a guide to the location of the customary pastures of 1500-1501. If we use this definition, we should conclude that the Kara Çelik (Table 1: no. 69) were settled, but each of their household herds had an average of 342 sheep; without any indication of land tax or produce revenues it is plain that the Kara Çelik still were pastoralists. Since, then, the language of the cadaster provides no sure test, perhaps the best way of determining the status of a group is to compare the size of its herd with the amount paid in land or produce taxes. In Table 1, then, a column lists the sheep tax as a percentage of the total taxes paid by each group. Since it is possible for sedentary cultivators to engage in small-scale sheepherding, but very difficult for pastoralists to cultivate large areas, the presence of many land holdings indicates a settled population. At that time, sedentary cultivators would have found it difficult to pasture large herds and protect the crops both on fields near their village.

Already by 1500 some groups were in transition from nomadism to settled agriculture. The Ahmedler (1:63) represent one such transitional group. The group was split in two: the larger section traveled in Bayburd and grazed sheep, while the others lived in a village called Ahmedler. Although the villagers—three adult males—were few (even assuming dependents), they represented a break which became complete in 1523, when they were no longer considered members of the group and were not entered in Mustafa Çelebi's cadaster of tribesmen. Those who remained within Mustafa Çelebi's purview were faring poorly in 1523, with average household herds less than half the size of those in 1500-1501.

In calculating the sheep/household ratio, which yields a rough average herd size for the households of a group, it is important to bear in mind the sixty sheep minimum herd size required for continued nomadism, discussed in the previous chapter. In those groups for which we can calculate average household herd size in both 1500-1501 and 1523, a number fell below the minimum herd sizes of the Basseri or Saçıkara, with the expected result: the appearance of cultivators as a major element in the population of the groups.[72] The tables use the minimum figure of sixty as the boundary between adequate and inadequate household herds, but similar results appear even if a liberal estimate of fifty-five animals is used as the minimum. Of the eighteen villages listed in the 1523 cadaster, only four had a household herd size above the minimum. In short, even though the gap at the beginning of the 1500-1501 cadaster does not allow a full comparison, what is available to us proves that the "Former Tribe" was well on its way to becoming a population of former pastoralists.

Bayburd's district stretched north, east, and southeast of Larende; by the nineteenth century it was just a small judicial circuit southeast of that town.[73] It was the smallest in population of the Horse Drover districts, with twenty-three groups. One obvious contrast between Eski Il and Bayburd is the comparative absence of settled or cultivator groups. On the whole, Bayburd groups preserved their pastoral status, even though nineteen of their average household herd sizes declined. Of those who fell below the expected minimum herd sizes one, the Karaca Alilü (2:6), had ten cultivators in 1523, while another, the Çelik (2:22), paid high fines and fees, perhaps reflecting the cost of supplementing their incomes with predation.

Unfortunately, the 1500-1501 figures for the sheep tax of the Kayı (2:10) are mixed in with the proceeds of the land tax, but the land symbols in the census leave little doubt that less than one quarter of the Kayı taxes came from sheep. The settlement of the Kayı was a success, since their agricultural revenues increased while their herds dwindled in numbers and importance. By 1547 the settled farmers no longer existed as an officially recognized tribal group but had been replaced in the registers by a number of villages called

Kayı.[74] These Kayı give us an early taste of the final result of the trends in Bayburd sheepholdings between 1500 and 1523.

Of the Horse Drover districts, Turgud was clearly the most troubled, and the cadasters' story helps us to understand the continued turbulence of the groups of this area.[75] Once again, the herd figures illustrate the broad trend: some fifty-one declines in average household herd opposed to fifteen increases; twenty-nine declines to a herd size below the minimum; finally, nineteen of the fifty-one groups with herd size declining to a figure above the minimum had cultivators. Of the fifteen groups whose household herds increased in numbers, six had cultivator members in 1523 (but some of these groups, even with an increase in herd size, still had inadequate herds by pastoral standards). Overall, some fifteen of the Turgud groups paid high fines and fees, and these had poor herds. I have already suggested that for those groups with small herds still involved in pastoralism, predation was the acceptable (and agreeably nomadic) means of survival. Perhaps these groups, with little to lose, were the once and future troublemakers of Turgud. As for settling, the increase in produce revenue figures (listed in the notes to Table 3), which were not a common feature in the cadaster of 1500-1501, shows that the majority of Turgud groups chose either to farm their pastures, or to obtain lands to cultivate, or were simply too weak to sustain a life of raiding (and Ottoman reprisals).[76] There are also occasional cases of settled groups with large herds. Their settlement, while not following the pattern just discussed, is also easy to understand. Owners of large herds possess surplus wealth in those herds, but capital in herds is subject to disease or climatic fluctuation. The temptation to secure a more stable income through investment in land may have been as great among successful Turgud pastoralists as it is among the wealthy Basseri at the present time. Perhaps the Turgud family monuments in and around Akşehir represent such a transformation of mortal sheep into monumental stone.

Friedrich Giese observed this settlement process among the nomads of Sultan Dağı, near Akşehir, in the summer of 1904. Some nomads would cultivate a large field, others would tend gardens, and others became beekeepers. Tent life was restricted to the summer. In other seasons families occupied a clay hut. Some families lived in the hut during the entire year, and, according to Giese, they differed from long-settled Turks only in the custom that the women's faces continued to be unveiled. Giese found them still claiming to be *yürüks,* not to be confused with the settled Turks.[77] Hamilton's Turcomans and *yürüks* of central Anatolia displayed a similar range between nomad and settler. The Turcomans resided in villages during the winter. They lived on the produce of their herds and seldom cultivated the ground. In the summer they moved into tents but did not ascend the mountains. Rather, they pastured their flocks over large, extensive plains when they could. The *yürüks,* on the other hand, had no villages and, in the nineteenth century, lived in rolling, hilly areas in black tents formed of twigs, wicker work, and rugs.[78]

Because so many of the Turgud tribesmen posed problems for and even revolted against the Ottomans, we can follow the history of Turgud more clearly than we can that of Eski Il and Bayburd. Here, for once, the cadaster records may be interwoven with other sources to produce a tighter fabric. Turgud's fortunes rose with the house of Karaman and attained a peak in the fifteenth century. Such manifestations of chiefly wealth as pious foundations and stately tombs only fell off in number after the Ottoman conquest later in the century.[79] Some ten structures (mosques, baths, dervish convents, tombs) from this period betray the Turgud pretensions—what they had gained and, after the Ottoman conquest, what they stood to lose.[80]

The area from which the Turgud drew their support was kidney shaped, ranging north and west of Konya to Akşehir, then north all the way to Cihanbeyli. As we have seen, it shrank in size during the sixteenth century, and by the nineteenth century Turgud was limited to the land between the present towns of Turgud and Cihanbeyli on the plateau west of the Salt Lake.[81]

The largest sub-group of the Turgud were the Yapa, whose memory persists in the town of Yapalı, just southeast of Cihanbeyli. A knotted string in the margin of the 1500-1501 cadaster separated them from the rest of the Turgud. Their 1500-1501 tax figures do not separate sheep and land taxes, so that an average herd size cannot be deduced. An explanation precedes each tax figure: "sum of the sheep tax, fines and fees, *bennak* land tax from those without sheep, and field revenues. The horse tax is not collected. . . ."[82] In 1523 the tribesmen paid taxes on produce, sheep, fines and fees. Those without sheep paid land tax.[83] In 1523, individual tax figures do appear, and so we learn that twelve of the twenty-one groups had inadequate household herds; eleven of them had cultivators (or households without sheep). We can only speculate that Yapa underwent the same pastoral decline that the rest of the Horse Drovers had endured.

The reader will note that many Yapa groups bear the same names as groups found elsewhere in Turgud. These are probably the survivors of a hiving-off process which did not provide the secessionists with new local chiefs after whom to name themselves. Before the enthronement of Shah Ismail there was only one great political upheaval in Karaman sufficiently broad to have led to such a sundering of loyalties: the Ottoman conquest. We do know of Yapa leaders who served the Ottomans.[84] It is likely that the Yapa was that group of tribesmen who chose to join the Ottoman advance, perhaps saying "Yapa," that is "Let them do it."[85] Yapa, then, unlike the unruly followers of the Turgud family, may have been the local exemplars of a process that has always tended to shrink the number of steppe nomads, a process which "cooks" those who are tempted to throw in their lot with settled administrators and enjoy their luxuries, while it further embitters those "raw" nomads who return to the steppe resolved to spurn further contact with the settled life and its tax collectors.

We can now refine our reconstruction of the history of the Horse Drovers better to fit our scattered information. At some earlier time the Drovers actually did provide horses, in all likelihood for the Mongols. Turgud and Bayburd, in association with a third unit supplying horses to the Mongol Samagar division (or perhaps that division itself), constituted the Horse Drovers. This third group was withdrawn with the other Mongols, probably following Timur east in the early fifteenth century, and (considering the horseless Horse Drovers) taking most of the remounts along. The departed third group was remembered as the "former (Mongol) tribe," Eski Il. Enterprising Anatolian nomad chieftains, such as Kuştimur, then took over the Eski Il pastures, along with some of the Mongol remnants.[86] When the Ottomans conquered Karaman in 1467, some of those groups whose members collaborated with the new order received a special organization, while the remaining Turgud pastoralists dug in their heels for a combat which lasted well over two generations.

In all of this the Horse Drover order was a shifting and changing one. Some groups decided to join Yapa, others remained with Turgud; and if the Reyhanlu are an example, this process continued into the sixteenth century. Some of the groups were also the creations of gifted chiefs, such as the Şah Bey Nökerleri and other groups with the Mongol term *nöker,* political follower, in their titles. Where the tribesmen of these groups came from and what happened to most of them with the passage of time is unclear. Only the Turgud were successful enough to create a tribe from family and followers. The impact of the Ottomans, however, turned the development of the Drovers away from pasture in the direction of the stockade fence of the stables (and the root meaning of the word stable is important in this context): Murad III's Horse Drover cadaster is the last official record of the confederation, and it is a list of villages, not of nomads.

Earlier in this chapter I suggested that the Ottoman cadasters could be used to observe the changes wrought among the nomads by the Ottoman occupation of Karaman. So far we have examined the earlier history of the Horse Drovers and the decline of their pastoral economy over a generation spanning the first quarter of the sixteenth century. I also hinted that the cadasters themselves would prove to be a weapon in the hands of the Ottomans, a weapon which aided in the reduction of the Horse Drovers to submission. In order to understand how this was possible we need to look at the manner in which the registrars organized their work. In particular, we need to be clear about the meaning, in this nomadic context, of the term *cemaat.* So far I have avoided discussing this term, relying on the very general rendering "group." Within the cadasters, however, the number of members in each "group" varies considerably. The registrars used it as an umbrella term to label certain segments of the tribe. What in fact lies hidden behind this term?

The traditional social organization of nomads is our key to answering this question, and Barth's study of the Basseri is a convenient source for this data. The actual nomad communities which first strike us are camps, with their people and animals. The camp is what the ethnographer, and the Ottoman registrar, first saw. Camps, however, do not retain permanent identities: their size and composition vary from summer to winter, and their membership fluctuates in response to personal animosities or outside opportunities. Moreover, camp formation is based as well on expediency in herding, joining together adequate manpower for tending the animals and grouping individual herds together into an optimally manageable herding unit. These factors can and do change quite rapidly, and so camps are very temporary social groupings. If, therefore, Horse Drover camps had names, and even if the registrars had extracted them and written them down, such a list would not have helped to keep track of the nomads over the long term. So the Ottoman administrators were not looking for camps to list; they sought, if possible, more permanent groups that would persevere over the decades.[87]

While the camp was therefore administratively awkward, the clan was not. Within a tribe clans served two special functions. A clan provided a permanent identity for individual tribesmen (justified in a genealogical idiom), and it was the prime administrative sub-unit of the tribe, with which the chief dealt in assigning pastures, organizing migrations, and raising cavalry. For the political puposes of chieftaincy the clan formed the most important structural segment of the tribe.[88] The Ottomans, as we shall see, found both these functions suitable for their own purposes. All they needed was a regular name to apply to the camp or group of camps they visited, and any official clan or patrilineal descent group name would do.

We may now determine what *cemaat* meant by comparing this description with the Horse Drover tables. We note, first, that our task is limited to the cadaster of 1500-1501. By 1523, when Ottoman policies were well under way, the large number of cultivators and villages obscures a strictly tribal, pastoral view of the Drovers. In 1500, however, the Ottomans were still feeling their way, so the framework for their future cadasters of the Horse Drovers is reflected most clearly in this cadaster (barring future discovery of the 1483 cadaster). What made a *cemaat* in 1500 is the question we must try to answer; this may lead us to understand why this form of registration was chosen.

To begin, let us see what the secretaries found. Significant variables here were herd size and number of households. There are maximum herd sizes in pastoralism, and, unfortunately, we do not know the herding capacity of the

Horse Drovers. As a rough guide, comparative material is available from field studies. The Mongols consider 1000 sheep the largest number that can be herded together, if all sheep are to obtain sufficient grazing. Camp size depends on this figure.[89] Barth's discussion does not include herd size in camps, but his figures allow an approximate computation. During the winter, camp herds total between 500 and 1000 animals, and the summer camps have perhaps 3000 sheep. Now the herd size of an At Çeken *cemaat* in the cadaster is simply double the total sheep tax. In examining the herds for the various *cemaats* we may reasonably argue that those *cemaats* with fewer than 1000 sheep could have operated as single camps. Those *cemaats* with fewer than 3000 might have. By this reckoning, in 1500 Eski Il had fourteen of thirty-two probable and nine of thirty-two possible single-camp *cemaats;* Bayburd had six of twenty-three possible; Turgud thirty-five of eighty-three probable, thirty-one of eighty-three possible. Turgud stands out with more single-camp *cemaats* than the more submissive Eski Il and Bayburd.[90]

It is also clear that the 1500 *cemaats* were small. Of Eski Il *cemaats* ranging in composition from three to eighty-eight households, the median consisted of seventeen households. Of twenty-three Bayburd *cemaats* ranging from ten to 260 households each, the median is fifty. Of seventy-five Turgud *cemaats* ranging from four to 152 households each, the median was eighteen households. Since the median Horse Drover *cemaats* turn out to have been smaller than the median Basseri tribal grouping, it must follow that these *cemaats* were sub-tribal units. For our purposes, it will be sufficient to conclude that the smallest groups, such as the Perakende, Dag Dere, Ali Fakihli, etc., of Eski Il, and their analogues in Bayburd and Turgud, were camps. Repeated names, such as Izz al-Din and Dag Dere, look to be two camps of a single clan. Given the evanescent nature of camps, it is not surprising that the smallest units in either one of the two cadasters under our view here are the ones most likely to be missing from the other. Clan, however, was probably the appropriate meaning for the larger *cemaats.* On the basis of *cemaat* size it seems reasonable to propose that the secretaries wished, whenever possible, to register clans, patrilineal descent groups without chieftains, throughout.

Let us move from what the registrars got to what they wanted. Because clans, unlike camps, are lasting entities, they wanted to count clans. Many, indeed most in Eski Il and Bayburd, of the *cemaats* they found must have been clans, considering the large numbers of sheep, far beyond the capacity of a single camp. The secretaries also would have wanted to deal with clans which had headmen, since these are the normal administrative sub-units of tribes.

That summer of 1500 Hatipoğlu counted some *cemaats* which were clans of only single-camp size, just as in summer the smallest Basseri clan could form a single camp. These clans had been diminished by some factor.

Especially among the Turgud, many of the clansmen were going off in revolt, so the secretaries might expect to find more of the single-camp clans. Perhaps the camps would not inform on fellow-clansmen out of sight over the hill. This interpretation fits the circumstances of submissive Eski Il and Bayburd as well as rebellious Turgud. Any alternative requires a certain simple-mindedness on the part of the registrars, working among tiny camps one day and much larger groupings another.

It is of crucial importance to bear in mind that these clans were sub-tribal units. Never do we see a chieftain. Each of these units had a non-tribal service to perform, as a unit of taxation in Ottoman governance. In the cadaster, following the heading identifying the *cemaat,* on the same line, is an entry listing the holder of rights to the taxes of the *cemaat.* Especially in Eski Il, some of the *cemaat* revenues formed part of a grant.[91] The timariotes' names are usually lacking, perhaps because they were placed in another cadaster. Most of the revenues of the Horse Drovers, however, were collected for the Ottoman prince who governed the province of Karaman. None of these revenues were devoted to the pastoral or political welfare of the nomad tribes.

In order to collect these revenues and use them for Ottoman purposes it was essential to circumvent the chief and neutralize his potential opposition. In some cases the Ottomans bought the chiefs off with revenue grants and offices elsewhere. In order, however, to sever his tribesmen's ties to him, it was necessary to reach below him, to reach into and divert sub-tribal units, our clans. Among the Basseri, "Perhaps the chief's most important function is to represent the tribe in its relations with the Iranian administration, and in conflicts with sedentary communities of persons."[92] The cadasters show the Ottoman government bypassing the chiefs, reaching down inside the structure of the tribe, dealing directly with the clans and their headmen, and thus requiring the headmen to act as agents of the Ottoman government instead of the tribal chiefs. This policy weakened the political structure, the most important structure indeed, of the tribes.[93]

This, then, has been the story of the Horse Drovers. The Ottoman cadasters list their men, their animals, their pastures, their settlements, and their financial obligations. The cadasters allowed us to watch their decay as pastoralists and their settlement into cultivator communities. We were much closer to their pastures, in a sense, than chronicle entries or imperial regulations could bring us, and we have followed the tribe over a longer period than an actual ethnographer could. Although we could, of course, not answer all the questions a field anthropologist would, we have had the advantage of compiling more limited data over many more years. Thus, the implications of the early Ottoman settlement and of the later Ottoman regulations worked themselves out for us in this case history from the Anatolian steppe. Finally, we saw that the very choices involved in drawing up a cadaster furthered the policies of the Ottoman government against the nomads. The fruition of these policies is Murad III's cadaster of ex-nomads, the full measure of the Ottoman secretaries' success. In truth, the pen is mightier than the horse.

Notes to Chapter Three

1. Since most of the cadasters appear to be the work of a summer, when the weather cleared the roads, the nomads would not be at their winter pastures. The cadasters do list the customary or assigned pastures of the nomads, but modern maps of Turkey do not have the scale necessary to identify individual pastures, and the official gazetteers not only exclude most pastures but also the occasional village. For Karaman see also Sırrı Üçer and Mesud Koman, *Konya ili köy ve yer adları üzerinde bir deneme* (Konya, 1945). There are other cadasters devoted solely to nomads: M.A. Cook, *Population Pressure in Rural Anatolia, 1450-1600* (Oxford, 1972), p. 59.

2. See N. Beldiceanu in *Turcica* 8 (1976), p. 264. The work of the Beldiceanus is as essential for the study of cadasters as it is for the comprehension of regulations.

3. For the older Turkish literature see Muzaffer Erdoğan, *Izahlı Konya bibliografyası* (Istanbul, 1952). The best geographical studies are Wolf-Dieter Hütteroth, *Ländliche Siedlungen im südlichen Inneranatolien in den letzten vierhundert Jahren* (Göttingen, 1968); Hermann Wenzel, *Sultan-Dagh und Akschehir-Ova, eine landeskundliche Untersuchung in Inneranatolien* (Kiel, 1932); H. Wenzel, *Forschungen in Inneranatolien,* two vols. (Kiel, 1935-37).

4. Neither of the cadasters bears a date. The Hatipoğlu cadaster, TT32, is described by I. Beldiceanu-Steinherr and N. Beldiceanu, "Deux villes de l'Anatolie préottomane: Develi et Qarahisar d'après des documents inédits," *Revue des études islamiques* 39 (1971), p. 380 and plates 1-8; Ibrahim Hakki Konyalı, *Konya Ereğlisi tarihi* (Istanbul, 1970), p. 247; Konyalı, *Şerefli Koçhisar tarihi* (Istanbul, 1971), p. 369; Konyalı, *Aksaray tarihi,* vol. 1 (Istanbul, 1974), pp. 831-45. The date follows from internal evidence. The cadaster's dimensions accord with those of cadasters composed for Bayezid II (1481-1512). Mehmet II's cadasters are shorter, Selim I's broader. References to two sons of Bayezid, Abdullah and Şehinşah, indicate that compilation took place after the death of Abdullah in 1483 and before the death of Şehinşah in 1511: TT32, pp. 2, 3, 56. Pious exhortations following their names establish that Abdullah was dead, Şehinşah alive: cf. A.D. Alderson, *The Structure of the Ottoman Dynasty* (Oxford, 1956), p. 22. A marginal note on p. 44 of the cadaster, entered after its completion, bears the date 16-25 August 1502 (*evasıt Safer* 908), and this must therefore be the *terminus ante quem.* A note in the text at p. 103 states that "deeds from Sultan Ahmed Bey are in the hands of the aforementioned persons." This contemporary entry establishes the *terminus post quem,* since Bayezid's son Ahmed, governor of Amasya province, came to Karaman only once, in 1500. Bayezid II ordered a cadaster of Karaman in 1500, and his only other cadaster of that province occurred in 1483: I. Beldiceanu-Steinherr, "Un transfuge qaramanide auprès de la porte ottomane," *Journal of the Economic and Social History of the Orient* 16 (1973), p. 155. Further, cadasters of the nomads were an integral part of every general cadaster of the province: TT636, dated 1591, lines 38-39 of the *Kanunname.*

Thus TT32 is part of the 1500-1501 cadaster which Bayezid II ordered Hatipoğlu and Ali to prepare.

The second cadaster, TT1061, is easier to date. It shares identical tax and summary figures with TT387, compiled in 929/1522-1523; since 929 Hicri began on 20 November 1522, I assume that these cadasters are products of the following year. Thus TT1061 is part of that year's general cadaster, the work of Mustafa Çelebi: Konyalı, *Aksaray,* p. 828; *Konya Ereğlisi,* pp. 248-50. Professor Nejat Göyünç kindly informs me that there was a general cadaster of the Ottoman domains in that year.

It is appropriate here to pay tribute to the works of Konyalı, Turkey's indefatigable local historian. His works contain a mass of source material for the history and geography of central Anatolia.

5. William L. Langer and Robert P. Blake, "The Rise of the Ottoman Turks and Its Historical Background," *American Historical Review* 37 (1932), p. 480.

6. T.R.S. Broughton, "Roman Asia," in Tenney Frank, ed., *An Economic Survey of Ancient Rome,* vol. 4 (Baltimore, 1938), pp. 617-19.

7. These observations were made in early May, on the way from Konya to Niğde: Mrs. Scott-Stevenson [Mary Esme Gwendoline Grogan Stevenson], *Our Ride Through Asia Minor* (London, 1881), pp. 283, 274, 311. See also the charts in Ferruh Sanır, *Sultan Dağlarından Sakarya'ya* (Ankara, 1948), pp. 81-87, and Zeki Afşin, *Konyanın iktisadi bünyesine bir bakış* (Istanbul, 1940), pp. 100-20.

8. William J. Hamilton, *Researches in Asia Minor, Pontus, and Armenia,* vol. 2 (London, 1842), pp. 243-44.

9. John Macdonald Kinneir, *Journey Through Asia Minor, Armenia, and Koordistan, in the Years 1813 and 1814* (London, 1818), pp. 215-16; Mrs. Scott-Stevenson, *Our Ride,* pp. 274-96, gives a description of such an encampment; see also Josef Strzygowski, *Kleinasien, ein Neuland der Kunstgeschichte* (Leipzig, 1903), pp. 1-2.

10. For the dynamics of herd management, see Gudrun Dahl and Anders Hjort, *Having Herds* (Stockholm, 1976), chapter 4.

11. Wenzel, *Sultan-Dagh,* pp. 40-44; Wenzel, *Forschungen,* vol. 2, pp. 77-111; Hütteroth, *Siedlungen,* map 2. Hütteroth's study, based in part on late sixteenth-century cadasters, is a marvelous study of settled life in the Axylon.

12. This cadaster is TT63: Konyalı, *Koçhisar,* p. 257; Konyalı, *Konya Ereğlisi,* pp. 360-61; Konyalı, *Aksaray,* vol. 1, pp. 763-75; for a description, see Beldiceanu, "Deux villes," p. 382. Kemalpaşazade's cadaster of the Horse Drovers has yet to be found. Such a cadaster must have existed, since later in Selim's reign or at the very beginning of Süleyman's reign, a certain Bayezid Çelebi corrected TT63 and the Horse Drover cadaster: see lines 11-12 of the 1591 *kanunname.* This text was published by Konyalı in photographic reproduction and in transcription, but a number of missing lines and printing errors mar the transcription: *Konya Ereğlisi,* pp. 263-78; *Aksaray,* vol. 1, pp. 741-54; *Koçhisar,* pp. 309-26.

13. TT63, p. 4; Konyalı, *Aksaray,* vol. 1, p. 765.

14. Konyalı, *Aksaray,* vol. 1, pp. 763-66, lists the administrative divisions found at the beginning of TT63; Hütteroth, *Siedlungen,* maps 1-3, 11, show the settled circuits.

15. Compare a 1471 list of circuits published by Konyalı, *Koçhisar,* pp. 363-64, with the list from TT63.

16. This cadaster is TT636 and contains the *kanunname* referred to in note 12 above. For a description see Konyalı, *Aksaray,* vol. 1, pp. 741-42.

17. See Hütteroth, *Siedlungen,* map 11.

18. West of the Salt Lake on the road linking Konya to Ankara, Cihanbeyli's former name was Esb Keşan, the Persian form of At Çeken.

19. Konyalı, *Koçhisar,* pp. 309-10, 339. An earlier cadaster, Maliyeden Müdevver 242 in the Başvekalet Arşivi, lists villages inhabited by former Horse Drovers.

20. See the 1869 map in Konyalı, *Koçhisar,* p. 379; all the surrounding areas are described as summer pastures.

21. Hamilton, *Researches,* vol. 2, p. 189. For *nahiyes* of possible nomadic origin (but without overlap onto settled jurisdictions), see Wolf-Dieter Hütteroth and Kamal Abdulfattah, *Historical Geography of Palestine, Transjordan and Southern Syria in the Late Sixteenth Century* (Erlangen, 1977), pp. 19-20.

22. The *yürüks* of Sultan Dağı, above Akşehir, told Friedrich Giese that they had come from Khurasan: Giese, *Materialien,* p. 7. M. Zeki Oral recounted the "Tales": "Turgut oğulları," *IV. Türk tarih kongresi 1948* (Ankara, 1952), pp. 148-50; Oral, "Turgut oğulları, eserleri-vakfiyeleri," *Vakıflar dergisi* 3 (1956), pp. 45-55. For a study of the architecture and administration of Dediği Sultan's tekke, see Ömür Bakirer and Soraiya Faroqhi, "Dediği Dede ve tekkeleri," *Belleten* 39:155 (1975), pp. 447-71.

23. It is improbable that Dediği Sultan was a contemporary of both Rumi (d. 1273) and Seyit Harun Veli (d. 1320). A pious transmitter may have introduced Rumi and Hacı Bektaş into the text. Dediği Sultan appears to have been a lesser, heterodox rival to Seyit Harun Veli.

24. This distinction persists: Faruk Sümer, articles "Turgut-Eli," "Turgutlular," in *Islam ansiklopedisi.* I know of no surviving monuments of the chief of Bayburd from any period.

25. SHK, pp. 44-45; in the 1330s a chronicler writing in Niğde wrote of various heretic tribes, among whom he numbered the Turgud and Kökperlü (a Turgud group in the cadasters): H. Sohrweide, "Der Sieg der Safaviden in Persien und seine Rückwirkungen auf die Schiiten Anatoliens im 16. Jahrhundert," *Der Islam* 41 (1965), p. 103.

26. Faruk Sümer, "Çukur-Ova tarihine dair araştırmalar," *Tarih araştırmaları dergisi* 1 (1963), pp. 32, 34; APZ, pp. 188-90.

27. Faruk Sümer, "Osmanlı devrinde Anadolu'da Kayılar," *Belleten* 12 (1948), p. 586.

28. Ismail Hakkı Uzunçarşılı, *Osmanlı devleti teşkilatına medhal* (Istanbul, 1941), p. 154 n.2.

29. Aşıkpaşazade, ed. Ali, p. 101.

30. Hammer, *Geschichte des Osmanischen Reiches,* vol. 2 (Pest, 1828), p. 88. M.C. Şehabeddin Tekindag, "Son Osmanlı-Karaman münasebetleri hakkında araştırmalar," *Tarih dergisi* 17-18 (1962-1963), p. 55.

31. Tekindag, "Son münasebetleri," pp. 57-59. One monument to the power of the Kosun was the *"Kosunlu bac,"* a passage duty levied on goods crossing the Cilician Gates, probably originally a fee for protection from nomad depredations. H. Inalcik, "Bursa and the Commerce of the Levant," *Journal of the Economic and Social History of the Orient* 3 (1960), pp. 142-43.

32. Tekindag, "Son münasebetleri," p. 66.

33. *Ibid.*; Hammer, *Geschichte,* vol. 2, p. 256; Brigitte Moser, *Die Chronik des Ahmed Sinan Celebi, genannt Bihisti* (Munich, 1980), p. 63.

34. Selahattin Tansel, *Sultan II. Bayezit'in siyasi hayatı* (Istanbul, 1966), p. 117.

35. Tansel, *II. Bayezit,* pp. 117-19.

36. *Ibid.,* pp. 120-21; Hammer, *Geschichte,* vol. 2, p. 256; M.C. Şehabeddin Tekindag, "II. Bayezid devrinde Çukur-Ova'da nüfuz mücadelesi," *Belleten* 31:123 (1967), pp. 350-51; *The History of Mehmed the Conqueror by Tursun Bey,* published by H. Inalcik and Rhoads Murphey (Minneapolis, 1978), f. 175b. The Kara Isalu had also given their name to a passage duty at the Cilician Gates: Inalcik, "Bursa," pp. 142-43.

37. Tansel, *II. Bayezit,* pp. 121-22; Hammer, *Geschichte,* vol. 2, pp. 294, 298-99; Tekindag, "Nüfuz mücadelesi," pp. 351, 358-61.

38. Tansel, *II. Bayezit,* pp. 123-25; I.H. Uzunçarşılı, *Osmanlı tarihi,* vol. 2 (Ankara, 1964), pp. 109-10; Hammer, *Geschichte,* vol. 2, p. 239; Aşıkpaşazade, ed. Ali, pp. 260-61; Müneccimbaşı, *Sahaif ül-Ahbar,* vol. 3 (Istanbul, 1285 H.), p. 428; Petra Kappert, *Die osmanischen Prinzen und ihre Residenz Amasya im 15. und 16. Jahrhundert* (Istanbul, 1976), p. 73. I would like to thank Professor V.L. Ménage for the correct reading of Avgadı.

39. Beldiceanu, "Deux villes," pp. 380-82; Konyalı, *Koçhisar,* p. 369.

40. Beldiceanu, "Deux villes," pp. 379-80. TT33 is identical, in its data, to Maliyeden Müdevver 20.

41. Konyalı, *Akşehir* (Istanbul, 1945), pp. 122-23; Konyalı, *Koçhisar,* pp. 235, 363-64; *Konya Ereğlisi,* p. 237; Konyalı, *Konya tarihi* (Konya, 1964), pp. 113-14, 248.

42. Uriel Heyd, *Studies in Old Ottoman Criminal Law,* ed. by V.L. Ménage (Oxford, 1973), p. 171.

43. This *kanunname* was first published by N. Beldiceanu and I. Beldiceanu-Steinherr, *Recherches sur la province du Qaraman au XVIe siècle* (Leiden, 1968), pp. 74-83. Since it refers to Rüstem Paşa as Grand Vezir, the text can be no earlier than 1544. The Beldiceanus later discovered and described two Karaman codes contained in Leiden, Cod. or. 305 (described in their "Deux villes," p. 378), the second of which was Ebu'l Fazıl's. His regulations concerning the Horse Drovers, ff. 35r-39r, are identical to those in Beldiceanu, *Qaraman,* pp. 74-83. I believe that the appropriate *terminus ante quem* for this code is 1570, when Ebu'l Fazıl left the finance office. Ebu'l Fazıl was, incidentally, the son of the Ottoman historian Idris Bitlisi.

44. Beldiceanu, *Qaraman,* p. 30; the 1591 code summarizes Ebu'l Fazıl's statute briefly and omits all the difficult passages, a loss of some five folios!

45. There are two other Horse Drover regulations extant. The first, published by Ferid Ugur in Konya, is unavailable to me: cf. Beldiceanu, *Qaraman,* pp. 3-4. The second, published by Hammer, seems to be a summary of the Ebu'l Fazıl statute: *Des Osmanischen Reiches Staatsverfassung und Staatsverwaltung,* vol. 1 (Vienna, 1815), pp. 260-64.

46. 1591 code, lines 4-11; for the annual sum of 360 *akçes* see Beldiceanu, *Qaraman,* p. 74 n. 7.

47. The statute of Bayezid Çelebi appears in Beldiceanu, *Qaraman,* pp. 74-75, and in the 1591 code, lines 11-25.

48. Beldiceanu, *Qaraman,* pp. 75-76; 1591 code, lines 26-37 (a summary of Ebu'l Fazıl's statute omitting most of the details in Beldiceanu, *Qaraman,* pp. 76-83).

49. For Rüstem Paşa's delicate position see Uzunçarşılı, *Osmanlı tarihi*, vol. 2, pp. 401-408, 549-550; Ş. Altundag and Ş. Turan, art, "Rüstem Paşa," *Islam ansiklopedisi.*

50. Şerafettin Turan, *Kanuni'nin oğlu şehzade Bayezid vak'ası* (Ankara, 1961), pp. 122, 129, 142.

51. Beldiceanu, *Qaraman*, pp. 77-78.

52. Hammer, *Staatsverfassung*, pp. 261-62.

53. In TT32, the sections listing Turgud and Bayburd treat most of the summary figures under the rubric *"hasıl"* with the phrase *"der resm-i esb"* added by a later hand.

54. 1591, code, lines 38-40.

55. This is, however, only a partial argument, since I have not been able to search for records of horse sales in the markets of Karaman. It is difficult, in any case, to imagine that the Horse Drovers would have submitted to the demands of tax farmers if they had had many horses, and therefore could have easily escaped. I would suggest, however, that in the seventeenth and eighteenth centuries the phenomenon of abandoned settlements was connected with and immediately prior to a resurgence of pastoralism, and also of horses, in the Axylon. As far as I know there is little evidence to support the assertion that the pastoralists of Karaman described by later travelers were lineal descendants of our Horse Drovers.

56. TT32, p. 1 (three entries); p. 4, *"cemaat-i. . . . an cemaat-i yuva-i Kuştimur"*; and *passim* in both cadasters.

57. TT32, p. 56.

58. What defined an adult male? For discussion of the demographic problems that this question raises, see Leila Erder, "The Measurement of Preindustrial Population Changes: the Ottoman Empire from the 15th to the 17th Century," *Middle Eastern Studies* 11 (1975), pp. 284-301; Geza David, "The Age of Unmarried Male Children in the Tahrir-Defters (Notes on the Coefficient)," *Acta Orientalia* 31 (1977), pp. 347-57.

59. I shall always translate *"hane"* as "head of household" or "household." "Hearth," a frequent rendering, has sedentary implications, while "tent" asserts too much of my case without proof. There is controversy about the exact denotation of this term: Amnon Cohen and Bernard Lewis, *Population and Revenue in the Towns of Palestine in the Sixteenth Century* (Princeton, 1978), pp. 14-15; Erder, "Measurement," pp. 295-96; Cook, *Population Pressure*, pp. 63-66; Justin McCarthy, "Age, Family, and Migration in Nineteenth-Century Black Sea Provinces of the Ottoman Empire," *International Journal of Middle East Studies* 10 (1979), p. 313.

60. Henry J. Van Lennep. *Travels in Little-Known Parts of Asia Minor*, vol. 2 (London, 1870), pp. 240-41.

61. *The Turkish Letters of Ogier Ghiselin de Busbecq*, trans. by Edward S. Forster (Oxford, 1927), pp. 46-47.

62. Van Lennep, *Travels*, vol. 2, p. 241; Mrs. Scott-Stevenson, *Our Ride*, p. 186; and, in general, Kazım Rıza, *Die türkische Landwirtschaft und ihre wichtigsten Betriebszweige* (Leipzig, 1935), pp. 146-47.

63. Cook, *Population Pressure*, p. 78; Cohen and Lewis, *Population and Revenue*, p. 168 n.57.

64. The major study of the meaning of the term *mezraa* is in Hütteroth, *Siedlungen*, pp. 169-70. The only deserted villages in the Horse Drover cadasters are those *mezraas* whose name ends in the term *viran.*

65. Let us say that Ahmed ibn Ali, a farmer, chose to leave the land in 1503 and join a pastoral *cemaat.* If an adult Ali were already registered in the 1500-1501 cadaster entry for that *cemaat,* it would be likely, though erroneous, that the new recruit would be considered, from the data in the 1523 cadaster, as a son of the 1500 Horse Drover Ali. Thus a reconstitution of agnatic links would result in a distribution skewed in favor of tribal genealogies. Of course, these problems also hold true for transfers from other *cemaats.*

66. In some other cadasters, such as those for Aleppo which Peggy Venzke will publish, herd sizes are registered for individual heads of households.

67. Cook, *Population Pressure,* p. 13 n. 3, considers the gross figures for sheep without attempting to derive trends for individual herds (but this was in any case not his purpose). We may wonder whether 1500 was an especially good year or 1523 a bad year. On the problems arising from this consideration see Cohen and Lewis, *Population and Revenue,* pp. 7-8. I believe that the cadastral data, although often approximate (there are a disturbing number of rounded sums), give a reliable picture of the resources available to the government. If anything, they paint too rosy a picture: Hütteroth and Abdulfattah, *Historical Geography,* pp. 10-11.

68. Cf. Cook, *Population Pressure,* p. 11.

69. For this rendering see J.G.C. Anderson, "Exploration in Asia Minor During 1898: First Report," *Annual of the British School at Athens* 4 (1897-1898), p. 77.

70. Sümer, "Çukur-Ova," p. 73.

71. TT32, p. 379.

72. See *cemaats* 74, 80, 84, for striking examples.

73. Konyalı, *Akşehir,* p. 148, citing the imperial almanac of 1848.

74. Sümer, "Kayılar," p. 577; Beldiceanu, "Deux villes," p. 354.

75. For the moment, I exclude Yapa from consideration, since its treatment is so different in the two cadasters.

76. This comparative discussion of the cadasters presupposes that the registrars caught most, if not all, of the groups. Leaving aside Eski Il, whose 1500-1501 record is incomplete, it seems that the record is a fair representation of the population. There are *cemaats* missing from either one of the cadasters, but there are few large *cemaats* found in one cadaster and missing from the other. If this view is reasonable, it may help demonstrate that the registration of the Drovers took place in 1500 rather than in 1501, when Mesih Paşa was hunting down the revolt's leaders in the Taurus.

77. Giese, *Materialien,* pp. 4, 6.

78. Hamilton, *Researches,* vol. 2, p. 220. David G. Hogarth pointed out that the existence of a summer camp may demonstrate that the families of a settlement may be descended from nomads, and he cites summer camps on the plateau that are no more "salubrious" than the winter village: *A Wandering Scholar in the Levant* (London, 1896), pp. 81-82. See also Kemal Güngör, *Cenubi Anadolu yürüklerinin etno-antropolojik tetkiki* (Ankara, 1941); for the terrain and agricultural possibilities, L. Jung, "Böden der Trockengebiete," and V. Horn, "Weideverhältnisse in den Gebieten Vorderasiens," pp. 51-59 and 99-113 of R. Knapp, ed., *Weidewirtschaft in Trockengebieten* (Stuttgart, 1965).

79. This conclusion follows from an examination of the data appended to the family trees published by Oral in *Vakıflar dergisi* 3 (1956), pp. 62-63.

80. *Ibid.*, pp. 31-64.

81. Konyalı, *Akşehir*, pp. 140-42.

82. TT32, p. 159.

83. TT1061, p. 133.

84. N. Beldiceanu, *Le timar dans l'état ottoman* (Wiesbaden, 1980), pp. 32, 62, 73.

85. Could *cemaat* 27b refer to followers of the Ottoman prince Şehinşah, sometime governor of Karaman?

86. The various Oğuz names among Bayburd suggest that it was formed out of a mix of conscripts gathered near Bayburd city.

87. Barth, *Nomads*, pp. 21-23, 25-47.

88. *Ibid.*, pp. 50-54.

89. Herbert H. Vreeland, *Mongol Community and Kinship Structure*, second ed. (New Haven, 1957), p. 35. Dahl and Hjort, *Having Herds*, gathers similar material. The works of Bates, Irons, Spooner, and Swidler, cited in the last chapter, yield comparable figures.

90. I have not made similar computations for 1523 thanks to the complicating factor of the cultivators.

91. This practice became common in Mustafa Çelebi's 1523 cadaster.

92. Barth, *Nomads*, p. 77.

93. For a later Persian parallel to this procedure, see Lois Beck, "Herd Owners and Hired Shepherds: the Qashqa'i of Iran," *Ethnology* 19 (1980), pp. 341, 347.

Chapter Four:

Conclusion

The nomadic and tribal aspects of the early Ottoman enterprise are barely visible through the dense and colorful veils that later court chroniclers wove, but they are there, and I hope the reader has at least caught a glimpse of them. The necessity of a complex administrative structure, borne in upon Osman and Orkhan as the towns of Bithynia capitulated one by one, led the Ottomans away from tribalism toward governing practices common to settled Muslim societies. They hoped that their fellow tribesmen would become their malleable subjects. The nomad, once a valued military specialist, became a potential enemy. The two preceding chapters have illustrated Ottoman attempts to control the nomads. The Ottoman administrative regulations and cadasters provide substantial documentation defining and describing the impact of Ottoman rule on the nomads. The experience alienated the nomads, who found that subjection to the sedentary Ottomans was not as enriching as allegiance to the tribal Osman.

Timur's victory over the Ottomans in 1402 gave the nomads breathing space, but Timur soon took his troops from Anatolia and the Ottomans relentlessly recouped their losses. The fifteenth-century Anatolian nomad had to look elsewhere for a worthy champion of his values and his ways. For the nomads of the Axylon, of Lycaonia and Cappadocia, whom we examined in the last chapter, one possible alternative was the emirate of Karaman, a constant foe of the Ottomans since Orkhan's time. How did the lords of Karaman view the nomads? We are fortunate in having a chronicle—or romance—of this ruling dynasty composed from the Karamanid point of view. This work, the Şikari chronicle, is our only pro-Karaman source for fifteenth-century Anatolian history and thus provides an invaluable view of the cultural assumptions and expectations which ruled in Karaman.[1]

Şikari's format is a string of stories associated with the fortunes of the emirs of Karaman. The coverage of these fortunes is uneven and, for the purposes of our search, sparse. Although Şikari knew something about the seventh-century Byzantine ruler Heraclius, he tells us nothing of the invasion of Baybars in the 1270s, nothing of the lengthy Mongol domination of

Anatolia, and nothing of the famous Mongol governor Timurtash, who is a central figure of early fourteenth-century Karaman. There is even no mention of the death of the great Seljuk ruler Ala ed-Din I, the putative patron of Şikari's main source. Where, also, are the nomads? The occasional mention of Turgud, Bayburd, and Varsak might incline us to suspect that nomads play a large role in the text, but they do not. Bayburd and Turgud join the Karamanid armies, but the actual names of their tribal chiefs are not mentioned. Turgud's nomads never appear, only "Turgud Oğlu/the son of Turgud" with x or y thousand men (and the term, "*er,*" means simply men, not horsemen).[2] This outlook colors and distorts the chronicle. Timur's victory over Bayezid I, which gave the Karaman and nomad emirs a generation free from Ottoman interference, appears as a single combat without nomad allies. The appearance of such tribal names as are found in the cadaster of Chapter Three indicates a tribal presence, but neither Şikari nor his heroes treat these forces as anything other than the troops, from whatever source and of whatever kind, of one general. The point of view is overwhelmingly sedentary and even legitimist. Şikari does not hesitate to call the Seljuk imposter Cimri, a Karamanid puppet on the throne of Konya in 1276, a thief.[3]

There can be little doubt that the heroes of whom Şikari wrote were aware of nomads. Şikari, however, did not see the history of Karaman in such a light. For Şikari, honoring a successful leader meant presenting the symbols of sedentary Muslim autocracies: drum, standard, and ceremonial robes.[4] Sedentary prerogatives also made Ala ed-Din a great sultan: twenty-four vezirs, 400 wrestlers, 2000 bodyguards, 60,000 palace servants, 400 muftis, sheykhs, ulema, and the like.[5] Karaman himself captivated the Seljuk with his adaptability: "Karaman mastered the court and council style, the military ceremonial, and the imperial manner. The Sultan so enjoyed their conversations that he did not even eat without Karaman."[6]

Şikari's (and his patrons') sedentary persuasion went further than this, for the rise of the Karamanids to power was allied to the desire to settle in sedentary splendor: "One spring both Türkmen and Oguz went up to summer pasture. Sad ed-Din passed away and they made Nur ed-Din (founder of the dynasty) bey. Hayr ed-Din, the Türkmen bey, said to Nur ed-Din, 'O Nur ed-Din bey, we are tired of nomadism. If only we could wrest Herakl's fortress from the kafirs' hands and settle down.' The Oguz beys approved these words."[7]

The search for legitimacy in the eyes of sedentary society pervades Şikari's Karamanid rulers throughout the work. The final chapters of Şikari provide striking proof of these aspirations. Consider Şikari's treatment of the Safavids: we learn that after Prince Cem fled Anatolia and Bayezid II became sole ruler, Karaman was at peace for twenty years. The Ottomans ruled all of

Taş Ili (rough Cilicia), and nobody could contend with them for it. When, however, the Safavid Shah Ismail was seeking troops, he somehow learned that the Karaman emirs were unhappy with Ottoman administration and were leaderless after the death of Kasım Bey. He then invited the emirs to join him, since he too was opposed to the Ottomans.[8] The religious propaganda, the appeal to nomads, the heterodox approach to politics and power, none of these elements caught Şikari's eye or moved his pen: to him, and to his heroes, Ismail and Selim were two contending sedentary rulers, and administration, not pastoral sympathy or god-like charisma, affected the house of Karaman. Here we see the distance between Şikari and his subject, his insistence upon viewing the history of Karaman through the prism of dynastic diplomacy rather than focusing on the supporters of nomadic independence. In this sense Şikari is perhaps the most sedentary-minded of historians.

In short, Şikari tells us that Karaman was not the appropriate political rallying-point for the nomads. The desire to settle, the court ceremonial, the lack of distinction between military formations recruited from a nomadic or a sedentary base, perhaps even the desire of one Karamanid to have his own Persian Shahname, all these show that the nomadic tradition was not for Karaman. Not the legacy of the Mongol-Turkic nomads, but the legacy of the Rum Seljuks and their Persianized sedentary administration and civilization defined the aspirations of the sons of Karaman.[9]

Thus, there was no tribal alternative to the Ottomans available from Karaman. The Ottoman vision of society promised paradise to the cultivator, and the Karamanid wish was for a recreated Persian *divan,* not life in the saddle. The pastoral subjects of the Ottoman dynasty had, however, another vision that laid a claim on their loyalty. The Safavids of Iran had Anatolian supporters and sought to raise even more. Their propaganda suffused the pages of the early Safavid chronicles, one of which (known as the Anonymous Ross) reproduces the Safavid vision as it was revealed to the nomads of Anatolia. Let us now view this revelation through the eyes of Dede Muhammad Rumlu.[10]

Dede Muhammad was a member of the Rumlu tribe, nomad supporters of the Safavids from central Anatolia, the land of the Seljuks of Rum. A sufi and dervish, he was a disciple of the holy man Hasan Halife Tekkeli. The Tekkeli comprised another tribe of Safavid supporters hailing from the former emirate of Tekke in southwest Anatolia. Hasan Halife, a member of the Safavid order, dwelt among the Rumlu and Tekkeli tribes. He had attended both Juneyd and Haydar, the earlier Safavi sheykhs who gave the order its shiite flavor and millenarian political ambitions. After testing Hasan Halife's zeal for fasting, Haydar stationed him in Tekke with the commission to prepare the way for Shah Ismail. After Hasan's death, his son Shah Kuli, "slave of the Shah," inherited this commission. Shah Kuli was later to embitter the final years of sultan Bayezid II by raising a heterodox tribal revolt in Anatolia.

In 905/1499-1500 Shah Kuli granted Dede Muhammad leave to go on pilgrimage to Mecca. He ordered him to return to Anatolia via Tabriz, where he would see the shii Shah Ismail assume power.

> When he had performed the circuit of Mecca and visited Medina, he turned towards Baghdad. Between Medina the Sanctified and Baghdad he got separated from the caravan and was overcome by sleep. On awakening he could find no trace of the caravan, and for three days he wandered through the desert, supported only by his spiritual power, until at length he fell exhausted to the ground, and his tongue hung out of his mouth. From sheer thirst he longed for death. When the mid-day sun shone straight down upon him he perceived an Arab youth riding towards him, who coming up to him said: "Oh! dervish, arise, for thou art not far from cultivated land." The dervish indicated by signs that he was too feeble to walk. The youth then took his hand, and no sooner was his hand in that of the youth than he felt all his strength return. So he arose and was led by the youth towards a hill: when they reached the summit of the hill he looked around and saw that as far as the eye could reach the plains were covered with verdure and roses and tulips, and that gold-embroidered tents and silk canopies had been spread out. Turning to his companion he said: "Oh! Arab youth, no one ever saw a place such as this in the deserts of Mecca and the Najaf-i Eshraf [the area about Kerbela, the burial site of the shii martyr Hussein]. What place is this? And who is the lord of these tents and palaces?" The young Arab replied, "You will know afterward." He then walked by the young man's side, until they came to a palace, whose cupola outrivalled the sun and moon. They then entered, and a delightful apartment met his view, the like of which he had never seen. Golden thrones were arranged side by side, and on one of the thrones a person was seated whose face was covered with a veil. Dede Muhammad, placing his hand on his breast, made a salutation, whereupon an answer to his salutation came from the veiled one, who, having bidden him to be seated, ordered food to be brought for him. The like of this food he had never seen in his life before. They also brought some cold water, which Dede Muhammad drank, nor had he ever tasted such refreshing water. As soon as he had finished his repast, he saw that a party of men had entered, bringing a boy of about fourteen years of age, with red hair, a white face, and dark-grey eyes: on his head was a scarlet cap. Being entered he made a salutation and stood still: the veiled youth then said to him: "Oh! Ismail, the hour of your 'coming' has now arrived." The other replied: "It is for Your Holiness to command." The prince then said: "Come forward." He came forward, and His Holiness taking his belt three times lifted it up and placed it on the ground again. He then, with his own blessed hands, fastened on the girdle, and taking [Ismail's] cap from his head, raised it and then replaced it. He wore a Kurdish belt-dagger: this His Holiness took from him and threw to the dervish, saying: "Keep this, for it will stand you in stead." His Holiness then told his servants to bring his own sword, which, when brought, he fastened with his own hands to the girdle of the child. Then he said, "You may now depart." Having recited the Fatiha [the first verses of the Quran] he entrusted the child to the two or three persons who had brought him in. When they had taken the child away, he made a sign to the young Arab to lead the dervish back to his caravan: and having brought him to it, said: "This is the caravan from which you were separated." When Dede Muhammad saw the caravan he said: "Oh! youth, tell me, for God's sake, who that prince was and who the child?" He replied: "Did you not know that the prince whom you saw was no other than the Lord of the Age [the hidden imam, object of shiite millenarian longings]?" When Dede Muhammad heard this name he stood up and

> said: "Oh! youth, for the love of God, take me back again that I may once more kiss the feet of His Holiness, and ask a blessing of him, perchance I might be allowed to wait on him." But the youth replied: "It is impossible. You should have made your request at the first. You cannot return. But you can make your request where you will, for His Holiness is everywhere present and will hear your prayers." The dervish then sought to return, but he could no longer see the rider, and ascending to the summit of the hill looked around in vain for any signs of those flowers and palaces. He uttered a deep sigh, and saw that his caravan had gone on far ahead. He was therefore obliged to rejoin the caravan.[11]

To the tribal following of the Safavi chief, Dede Muhammad's dream revealed the intimate connection between their sheykh and the messianic fulfilment of their expectations. The hidden imam, the scarlet surroundings, the expected "coming" of a purging savior, the sanctification of swords and daggers, all these justify and urge on a militant audience. The head-dress distinguished them from an uninitiated enemy. These were men set apart by choice and a mission, not settling together under the shade of a tree. Ismail's kızılbaş or "red-headed league," among whom were the Rumlu and Tekkeli tribes, were his earliest supporters, his army, forming a fifth column deep inside Ottoman Anatolia. In this dream the Lord of the Age approves the head-dress, the ends, and the Anatolian means: he hands Ismail's dagger to Dede Muhammad. This act does not simply imply approval for the dervish's propaganda. It is a call to arms.

The Lord of the Age in a desert paradise is a far cry from the humble sheykh who entertained Osman and presented him with a daughter, not a dagger. Details of the dreams confirm and extend this impression. Men diverting streams, the shade of a tree, such restful symbols are incompatible with the raising and lowering of weapons. The Ottoman dream was to create and preserve a secure and stable administration over the world. To Dede Muhammad the appropriate vision was one of cleansing and cutting off, purification rather than conservation. The shiite dream is of struggle, not success, martyrs, not bureaucrats.

We have noted that the Ottoman tree protected a sedentary world in which nomads, whose ways and allegiances were doubtful, were not welcome. Not so for the Safavids: their vision, with its oasis miraculously revealed in the desert, beckoned to the nomads with the promise of greener pastures. The Safavid millenarian vision was a pleasing option, since it was suffused with nomadic and tribal elements. After all, it was revealed to Dede Muhammad Rumlu, a tribal representative of a tribal leader, Hasan Halife Tekkeli (and note the tribal suffixes of Rumlu and Tekkeli). Surrounding the mysterious oasis, where conquest and predation were planned, was pasture aplenty: ". . . as far as the eye could reach the plains were covered with verdure and roses and tulips. . . ." The Safavid promise was for the nomads.

The Safavid connection with Anatolian nomads was already a generation old when Dede Muhammad went on pilgrimage. Indeed, the millenarian aspect of Safavid politics arose from the peregrinations of Juneyd, a Safavid sheykh, among Turkish nomads in the middle of the fifteenth century. Already by 1487 Bayezid II was concerned about Safavid partisans in Anatolia and Anatolians in the Safavid army. Among tribes (some of them newly named formations) supporting the Safavids were the Rumlu, Tekkeli, Karamanlu, and—perhaps echoing the last chapter—the Bayburdlu. The Safavids' political organization was openly tribal, and Safavid chronicles delineate the elements of the Safavid military by tribe. Of the eight tribes which joined Shah Ismail at Erzincan in eastern Anatolia in 1499, seven were Anatolian: Ustajlu, Karamanlu, Rumlu, Tekkeli, Zu'l-Kader, Avshar, and Varsak.[12]

This tribal organization clearly rivaled the sedentary structure of the Ottoman and Karamanid enterprises; it was modeled not on the Persianized bureaucracies of classical Islam, but on the Mongol political tradition, passed on in Anatolia by the Kara Koyunlu and Ak Koyunlu confederations. Shah Ismail was the grandson of Uzun Hasan, greatest chief of the Ak Koyunlu and defeated enemy of Mehmet the Conqueror. This tribal alternative was enforced by the presence among Ismail's constant companions of leaders who shared tribal concerns and bore tribal names. For us the most interesting of these were Rustem Bey Karamanlu and his uncle Bayram Bey Karamanlu, whose aid and comfort brought Ismail through to safety when, as a hunted youth, he was gathering supporters under enemy eyes.[13] The Safavis provided the nomads their acceptable alternative, and they seized it.

We have now come to the end of our long march. The sedentarization of Karamanid history reminds us of early Ottoman history. The Ottoman ceremonial herd of sheep at Bursa, now in the Istanbul zoo, is the outcome of our story. Osman and Orkhan found that the tribal institutions which they had at their disposal enabled them to unite the ex-nomads and ex-Byzantines of Bithynia in the troubled times of the later thirteenth century. Their success forced them to face the problem of a growing, more complex political and economic enterprise, for which the limited ends and means of tribalism have never sufficed. The classical Muslim political institutions, reinforced by the fourteenth century flow of schoolmen into west Anatolia, aided them in this political transformation and clothed their earlier activities in a religious zealot's habit. The Ottoman leaders moved away from their nomads and became less and more than chiefs in adopting the sultan's robes. They no longer served or represented nomadic tribesmen; instead they ruled their nomadic subjects.

This process ended those needs for which nomads occasionally bound themselves for the welfare of the tribe. Occasional nomad taxation exists for the sole purpose of defending a shared tribal interest. The regular Ottoman taxation of nomads took money and sheep away without a beneficial return to the tribe. Nomads who served the Ottomans found that their special skills were no longer needed and that such non-nomadic occupations as rowing demeaned their status and demonstrated the lack of return for loyalty. The taxes themselves showed no regard for pastoralists' ability to pay, and their impact upon poorly capitalized nomads could encumber them with the humiliation of sedentary unemployment. The nomads did not relish these fruits of subject status.

Ottoman taxation showed a disregard, and what was worse, disrespect, for the realities of nomadic and tribal well-being. Ottoman taxation threw nomadism into some peril. Ottoman administrative practice demonstrated dangers to the structure of the tribe. The census registration of units below the tribal level, in which the authority of the chief was undermined by the studied undercutting performed by the Ottoman secretaries, drove the chiefs into revolt. For when the tribesmen dealt with the Ottoman government directly, the chiefs would serve no further useful function. The tax registers of the Ottomans were not only witness to the process of settlement and subjection. They were weapons in that struggle. The Ottoman success is perhaps best reflected in the sedentary outlook of the Karamanids' own historian.[14]

All this was still very much in the balance in 1501. For as Dede Muhammad found upon his return to Rum (Anatolia), the greener pastures of the Safavids aroused the nomads' support for Shah Ismail. The success of this propaganda can be appreciated by recalling Bayezid II's response: in 1502 he deported Safavi supporters from Tekke and Hamid in southwest Anatolia, as well as from elsewhere on the plateau, to Coron and Modon in the Peloponnesus. In 1507-1508 Bayezid attempted to close his eastern frontiers in order to deny access to the Safavi strongholds. In 1511, finally, Bayezid had to put down a pro-Safavi revolt by Shah Kuli, "the Shah's slave," in which Bayezid's grand vezir was killed.[15]

The result of Ottoman sedentary success, the struggle of the sultans against the shahs in the sixteenth century, was seen by Ottoman intellectuals solely in its religious guise, a struggle against shiite heresy. Rulings of the great scholars and teachers soon labeled this a war for the faith. Thus, the nomads had traveled full circle in the estimation of Ottoman society, from ghazis at the roots of Ottoman history to objects of the ghaza when the Ottomans were in full flower. To the Ottomans, the nomads were now the ones who had lapsed somewhere along the path to Istanbul, the heretics in society as much as in religion.

The nomads, however, found their niche as Safavi warriors in Anatolia irredenta. Shah Ismail's propaganda beckoned to them with its promise of a pastoral emphasis (open fields rather than shaded, well-watered gardens), a political organization responsive to and based on tribal principles, and a military organization which offered nomadic predation in place of regimentation and oars. This promise was sealed by the sacred character of the Safavid propaganda mission. The millenarian shiite propaganda of the Safavis saw all opponents as justifiable objects of war. As Shah Ismail's brother commanded him, "For the die of heaven's choice has been cast in your name, and before long you will come out of Gilan like a burning sun, and with your sword sweep infidelity from the face of the earth."[16] Shah Kuli's mentor brought a like message to Anatolia: "Hasan Halife has come. Nay, he has brought to Teke Ili a living fire."[17] The nomads now had their religious sanction, and the battle lines of politics and theological justification were drawn. Shah Kuli's revolt brought the nomad dreamers and their Safavi dream into the Ottoman consciousness, as a nightmare.

This book has been a case history, as the reader will note, of a process common in the history of civilization: the formation and demarcation of frontiers beween acceptable society and "the barbarians." Our setting was the conflict between settler and nomad, cultivator and pastoralist, a contest whose first literary monument in our tradition is the story of Abel and Cain. The outcome of our version was identical to that of Genesis. Cain the settled cultivator murdered his brother the herder; the Ottomans and their modern epigones devoted extensive resources to the "pacification" of nomads. The perspective of this book has been based on the nomads' point of view, and this perspective may now be pleasing, coming at a time when extensive pastoralism's contribution to world protein supplies is receiving a sympathetic evaluation.

It is nonetheless true that this work and its explanatory framework is but a part of a much larger story. We might have seen parallel developments had we turned to American history, to cattlemen fighting sheepmen, to cowboys and dirt farmers, to immigrants and Indians. In all these, and other, cases, the label "barbarian" is merely another word for the less offensive "outsider" and both, of course, exist only in the mind of the self-anointed civilized. Thus, the Ottoman nightmare was merely a latter-day impression of the mark of Cain. Returning to our smaller stage of Anatolian history, we can see that the history of nomads in Ottoman society was almost a self-limiting phenomenon: success at conquest and at tribal recruitment created problems which only sedentarization ameliorated. But that settlement of the leaders soon estranged them from their tribesmen. And those powerful leaders were able to call the tune for the future. The Ottomans defeated Shah Ismail in 1514, and the Lord of the Age has yet to feed his sheep.

Notes to Chapter Four

1. For more on the chronicle and its text, see Appendix Two.
2. SHK, pp. 185 ff.
3. SHK, p. 44.
4. SHK, pp. 3, 14, 15, and *passim* for the robes, which seem to have attracted Şikari.
5. SHK, p. 9; these numbers, even adjusted for inflation, are not necessary to erect a tent or even to service the yurt of a Mongol chief.
6. SHK, p. 21.
7. SHK, p. 10.
8. SHK, pp. 206-8, preceded on pp. 204-6 by a vague account of the disturbances in Anatolia during the years 1500 and 1501. SHK also conflates Bayezid II and Selim I into one ruler. Can an author working just after 1517, as SHK claimed to be doing, have made such an error?
9. We could also have derived these concerns from Karamanid architectural patronage, a more concrete basis than the romance of Şikari: see, in the first instance, Ernst Diez, Oktay Aslanapa, and Mesud Koman, *Karaman devri Sanatı* (Istanbul, 1950), who give a clear notion of the massive and sedentary uses of the Karaman emirs' revenues.
10. The actual title of the manuscript is *Jihan-gusha-yi khagan-i sahib-giran;* the work, which is related to the *Habib us-Siyar* of Khwandamir, may be the earliest Safavid chronicle. Erika Glassen, *Die frühen Safawiden nach Qazi Ahmad Qumi* (Freiburg, 1970), pp. 13-14.
11. E. Denison Ross, ed. and tr., "The Early Years of Shah Isma'il, Founder of the Safavi Dynasty," *Journal of the Royal Asiatic Society* (1896), pp. 328-31. E. Glassen, "Schah Isma'il, ein Mahdi der anatolischen Turkmenen?" *Zeitschrift der Deutschen Morgenländischen Gesellschaft* 121 (1971), pp. 61-69. A shorter version of the story appears in the *Alam Ara-yi Shah Esmail* (Teheran, 1349), pp. 41-43.
12. V. Minorsky, *Persia in A.D. 1478-1490* (London, 1957), pp. 61, 69, 80; H. Sohrweide, "Der Sieg der Safaviden in Persien und seine Rückwirkungen auf die Schiiten Anatoliens im 16. Jahrhundert," *Der Islam* 41 (1965), pp. 132-33, 137; O. Efendiev, "Le role des tribus de langue turque dans la création de l'état Safavide," *Turcica* 6 (1975), p. 31; *A Chronicle of the Early Safawis, Being the Ahsanüt-Tawarikh of Hasan-i Rumlu,* trans. by C.N. Seddon (Baroda, 1934), p. 18; *Tadhkirat al-Muluk,* trans. by V. Minorsky (London, 1943), pp. 190-95.

13. Hasan Rumlu, pp. 2, 3, 18; Ross, pp. 258, 285, 332, 336; Sohrweide, "Der Sieg," p. 137.

14. F. Sümer, art. "Karaman-oghulları," *EI*², claims, without citing his source, that the Bayburd and Turgud tribes fought for Shah Ismail.

15. Sohrweide, "Der Sieg," pp. 138-64.

16. Ross, p. 262.

17. Hasan Rumlu, p. 59.

Appendix One:

Horse Drover Statistics

Table 1: Eski Il[1]

Cemaat	adult males	cultivators[2]	households	sheep	sheep/ hsehld	sheep tax as pct. of total tax	settled?
A. Kuştimur[3]							
1a. Kumral	7		5	200	40	34	S
b.							
2a. Hüseyin Şeyh[4]	7						
b. Hüseyin Şeyhlü	13	13					S
3a. Güzeller	42		29	1380	47	35	S
b.							
4a. Arablu	29	25	14	600	43		S
b.							
5a. Eyüpler[5]	77	70	42				S
b.							
6a. Perakende-i Kuştimur[6]	47		39				
b. Perakende-i Kuştimur	44	7	40	800	20	32	S
7a.							
b. Perakende-i Kuştimur in the village of ...Hacı	7	7	6	200	33	28	S

Cemaat	adult males	cultivators[2]	households	sheep	sheep/ hsehld	sheep tax as pct. of total tax	settled?
8a. Yuva-i Kuştimur	152	114	88	9204	105	56	S
b.							
9a. Koçu	9	9	9	300	33	27	S
b.							
10a. Taşgunlar	66	44	33	600	18	21	S
b.							
11a.							
b. Hasanlar	9	6	5	400	80	38	S
12a.							
b. Bulduklar		60		3200		29	S
13a.							
b. Avcılar	9	9	8	200	25	30	S
14a.							
b. Davud Hacılar[7]	237	219	129	10000	78	34	S
15a.							
b. Perakende-i Kuştimur in the circuit of Aksaray	30	26	25	2000	80	57	S
16a.							
b. Bölük-i....	32	27	25	2600	104	27	S

N.B. Groups 17-34 appear only in TT1061, registered as villages.

Cemaat	adult males	cultivators[2]	households	sheep	sheep/ hsehld	sheep tax as pct. of total tax	settled?
17a.							
b. Küçük[8]	47	19	38	400	11	18	S
18a.							
b. Gözen	14	10	12	80	7	12	S
19a.							
b. Yenice (near Ereğli)	27	9	26	180	7	14	S

20a.							
b. ....(near Ereğli)	40	10	32	400	13	20	S
21a.							
b.	16	2	15	800	53	54	S
22a.							
b. ....[9]	31	26	23	300	13	19	S
23a.							
b.	21	19	15	200	13	11	S
24a.							
b. Andi Kara	72	52	36	860	24	16	S
25a.							
b. Ahi Viran	48	41	30	1800	60	29	S
26a.							
b. Gelamazlar	34	28	25	800	32	28	S
27a.							
b. Ince In	17	17	14	800	57	42	S
28a.							
b. In Burnu	43	40	28	2200	79	37	S
29a.							
b. Dökenek[10]	26	26	21	1600	76	55	S
30a.							
b. ...Öyük	9	9	9	100	11	14	S
31a.							
b. Germiek[11]	88	86	51	4000	78	40	S
32a.							
b. Kızıl Çöllü	15	9	9	1000	111	46	S
33a.							
b. Dedelü	124	119	84	4000	48	32	S
34a.							
b. Hasanlar	116	109	90	2100	23	17	S
B. Çepni[12]							
35a. Perakende-i Çepni Bey							
b. Perakende an taife-i Çepni (village)	27	27	27	580	21	30	S

Cemaat	adult males	cultivators[2]	households	sheep	sheep/ hsehld	sheep tax as pct. of total tax	settled?
36a. Çepni	16	8	5				
b.							
37a. Çepni of Karaman Şah	18		12	1400	117		
b.							
38a.							
b. Village of Sar and Dovanış, also called Daslar	29	25	18	640	36	10	S
39a.							
b. Village of. . . .	4	4	3	20	7	4	S
40a.							
b. Village of. . . .	13	13	7	200	29	6	S
41a.							
b. Village of. . . .	4	4	2	40	20	6	S
42a.							
b. Village of Alemhan. . . .	10	10	6	100	17	8	S
43a.							
b. Village of Adamlar	45	45	24	600	25	12	S
44a.							
b. Village of Kavak, also known as. . . .[13]	10	9	5	40	8	3	S
C. Boynu Yumru							
45a. Boynu Yumru[14]	77		46		c.76		
b.							
46a. Boynu Yumru	75		47		c.76		
b.							
47a. Ali Fakihli	16		9		c.76		
b. Ali Fakihler	27		16	1300	81		
48a. Bey Vermişler	64		39		c.76		
b. Bey Vermişler	87	10	52	3800	73		

49a. Pınar	33		23		c.76		
b.							
50a. Kızıl Koyunlu[15]	38		28		c.76		
b. Kızıl Koyunlar	56	5	37	2400	55		?
51a. Alaca[16]	35		19		c.76		
b. Alaca	39		27	1950	72		
52a. Yok Çayır	17		14		c.76		
b.							
53a.							
b. Iki Ok[17]	93	16	69	3200	46		indequate average household herd
54a.							
b. Some Boynu Yumru[18]	111	13	68	4800	71		
55a.							
b. Şamlular[19]	14		9	600	67		
56a.							
b. Bulcalu	60	5	42	2500	60		
D. Kum[20]							
57a. Kumlu	29		16		c.70		
b. Kumlar	24		15	2000	133		
58a. Kumlu	91		46		c.70		
b. Kumlar[21]	152		122	10000	82		
59a. Kumlu	117						
b.							
60a. Baratlı	29		14	3512	251		
b. Barat	24		12	4000	333		
61a. Kumlu[22]	13		11	700	64		
b. Kumlar	27		26	4000	154		
D. Eski Il cemaats without intermediate affiliations							
62a. Veludlü [23]	4			100			S
b. Veledlü	11			400	36?	33	S

Cemaat	adult males	cultivators[2]	households	sheep	sheep/ hsehld	sheep tax as pct. of total tax	settled?
63a. Ahmedler[24]	20	3	11	1200	109		
b. Ahmedler	34		23	1000	43		inad. herd
64a. Köseler	29		10	1290	129		
b. Köseler	25		18	1200	67		
65a. Zekeriyalar	36		16	660	41		inad. herd
b. Zekeriyalu	38	4	23	1000	43		inad. herd
66a. Bereketlü	40		16	3600	225		
b. Bereketlü [25]	37	2	30	1000	33		inad. herd
67a. Keş	10		8				
b. Keş	17	4	11	400	36		inad. herd
68a. Koyuncular, also called Veled-i At Koyuncular	3		3	300	100		
b. Koyuncular	3	3	3	200	67	60	S
69a. Kara Çelik	39		24	8200	342		
b.							
70a. Bulduklar	72		49	7800	159		
b.							
71a. Korayş Melik Şah	169	71	63	10000	159	57	mixed?
b. Korayş Melik Şah	190	168	148	17400	118	55	settling?
72a.							
b. Korayş. . . .	262	217	176	13400	76	42	settling?
73a. Izz al-Din[26]	115		66	4200	c.64		
b. Izz al-Dinlü	115	27	78	4020	52		inad. herd
74a. Kara Gözlü [27]	98		73	2700	37		inad. herd
b. Kara Gözlü	125	118	88	2680	30	26	S
75a. Kelamazlar	9		7	1200	171		
b.							
76a. Yılmaz[28]	92		61	10500	172		
b. Yılmaz	118		74	10500	142		

77a. Yılmaz	17		13	8200	631		
b.							
78a. Perakende-i Farsak-i Hoşkadem	15		10	3000	300		
b. Perakende-i Varsak-i Hoşkadem[29]	31	11	19	3000	158		
79a. Dag Dere[30]	32		14				
b. Dag Dere, also known as Çoban Oğlanları	85	31	59	10000	169		
80a. Yum Hüseyin	38		20	2440	122		
b. Yum Hüseyin	40	12	35	1200	34		inad. herd
81a.							
b. Other Yum Hüseyin	20		15	800	53		inad. herd
82a. Kara Pinar	33		21	1780	85		
b.							
83a. Sultan....[31]	30	18	19		c.135		
b. Sultan....[32]							
Bölük-i Uşaklar ve Bulduklar	20	19	12	800	67	22	S
Bölük-i....	29	27	25	3000	120	69	S
84a.	29	22	18		c.135		
b. Bölük-i....	15	15	15	400	27	37	S
85a. Evlad-i Aziz	9		9				
b.							
86a. Kürekçiler							
b.							
87a. Araban near Kayacık	18	10					
b.							
88a. Salı Arab	41	18					
b.							
89a.	20	14					
b.							
90a. Okçular	72	55		500		20	S
b.							

Cemaat	adult males	cultivators[2]	households	sheep	sheep/ hsehld	sheep tax as pct. of total tax	settled?
91a. Hacı Osman	26	22	21	268	13	34	S
b.							
92a. Akçe Kethüda	50	43	44	426	10	22	S
b.							
93a. Halife	12	10	10	110	11	23	S
b.							
94a. Hacı Osman Kethüda	22	14	16	1180	74	67	mixed?
b.							
95a. .... Araban near Larende	10	10	10	100	10	22	S
b.							
96a.							
b. Kuncalar	57		41	1100	27		inad. herd
97a.							
b. Kendlü [33]	208	37	141	11000	78		
98a.							
b. Saru Muradlu[34]	45	2	26	2000	77		
99a.							
b. Hüccetli[35]	142	20	105	14000	67		
100a.							
b. Develü [36]	20	2	14	600	43		inad. herd
101a.							
b. ....[37]	689	36	467	42000	90		
102a.							
b. Davudlar, also known as Timurlar[38]	126	19	78	3400	44		inad. herd
103a.							
b. Sevilmişlü near village of Çekilsin[39]	111	20	69	4000	58		

104a.						
b. Other Sevilmişlü [40]	228	34	151	13000	86	
105a.						
b. Further Sevilmişlü [41]	51	4	34	3000	88	
106a.						
b. Karaman Şah[42]	35		16	1000	63	
107a.						
b. Melçik[43]	84	13	54	1000	19	inad. herd
108a.						
b. Yusuf Hacılar	22	7	12	400	33	inad. herd
109a.						
b. Naci, also known as	38	4	24	1000	42	inad. herd
110a.						
b. Delüler[44]	36	4	25	1380	55	inad. herd
111a.						
b. Kürtül[45]	49	3	35	100	3	inad. herd
112a.						
b. Ali Koca[46]	54	6	29	6000	207	
113a.						
b. .... Hacılu	23	6	15	1000	67	
114a.						
b. Yakublar[47]	87	8	54	3000	56	inad. herd
115a.						
b. Esen Beylü	39	12	29	2000	69	
116a.						
b. ....[48]	56	11	39	1760	45	inad. herd
117a.						
b. Serlaklar[49]	165	132	92	6500	71	mixed?
118a.						
b. Otluklu[50]	9		7	1000	143	
119a.						
b. ....[51]	174	121	85	13000	153	

Cemaat	adult males	cultivators[2]	households	sheep	sheep/ hsehld	sheep tax as pct. of total tax	settled?
120a.							
b. Danişmendlü [52]	11	11	7	2000	285		S
121a.							
b. Kul Hamza[53]	34	32	30	600	20		S
122a.							
b. ....[54]	53	48	30	3000	100		S
123a.							
b. Sakallar[55]	124	85	58	7300	126	54	mixed
124a.							
b. Village of Siranlu	41	40	27	700	26	17	S
125a.							
b. Village of Emir Ali	34	28	25	800	32	14	S
126a.							
b. Village of Kara Viran	61	53	43	1800	42	16	S
127a.							
b. Çobanlar	7	7	7	800	114	68	S
128a.							
b. .... Kavak Viran[56]	55	51	43	2000	46	38	S
129a.							
b. Araban	30	2		1200			
130a.							
b.	15	14	9	1200	133	41	S
131a.							
b. Ozanlar	25	25	25	200	8	15	S
132a.							
b. Another cemaat in the kışlak of Ozanlar	10	10	10	100	10	19	S
133a.							
b. Dervishes	9						S

134a.							
b. Türkmen near Obruk[57]			7	400	57	43	inad. herd
135a.							
b. Andi Kara settlers from Kuştimur	18						S
136a.							
b. .... not in earlier cadasters	21	20	17	1200	71	54	S
137a.							
b. Ömer Fakihler	8	8	8	200	25	36	S

Table 2: Bayburd[58]

Cemaat	adult males	cultivators	households	sheep	sheep/ hsehld.	sheep tax as pct. of total tax	settled?
1a. Emir Hacılu[59]	181		105	12000	114		
b. Emir Hacılu	163		128	10000	78		
2a. Tac al-Dinlü	98		76	9000	118		
b. Tac al-Dinlü[60]	195		111	8000	72		
3a. Sadık-i Siyah (also known as Dundarlu)	312		226	16000	71		
b. Dundarlu (also known as Kara Sadıklu)[61]	395		209	16600	79		
4a. Kuluslu	151		80	17046	213		
b. Kuluslu[62]	185		132	16000	121		
5a. Ogul Beylü[63]	206		139	18400	132		
b. Ogul Beylü	343		222	16000	72		
6a. Karaca Alilü	94		59	18166	308		
b. Karaca Alilü	120	10	85	5000	59		inad. herd?
7a. Murad Fakihlü (also called Akşehir Kara Keçilü)	114		77	8930	116		
b. Kara Kecilü (also known as Murad Fakih)	123		104	6000	58		inad. herd
8a. Türkmenlü (also known as Saruhanlu)	52		32	2728	85		
b. Türkmenlü	58		46	3000	65		
9a. Ak Ali	54		30	6080	203		
b. Ak Alilü	67		49	4000	82		
10a. Kayı	343	249	260				S
b. Kayı	680	n.a.	475	10000	21	34	S
11a. Aksaklu	77		50	6230	125		
b. Aksaklu	108		75	6000	80		

12a. Şekerlü	40		33	3200	97	
b. Şekerlü (associated with Tac al-Dinlü)	29		18	3200	177	
13a. Varsaklu	69		44	9000	205	
b.						
14a. Necib al-Dinlü	39		30	8690	290	
b. Necm al-Dinlü [64]	44	8	32	8000	250	
15a. Köse Receb	21		13	1200	92	
b. Köse Receblü	29		20	1000	50	inad. herd
16a. Kürd	122		74	7300	99	
b. Kürd	109		79	5000	63	
17a. Duydular	22		13	2400	185	
b. Duydular	33		21	2000	95	
18a. Peçenek[65]	25		10	11680	1168	
b. Peçenek	34		27	2000	74	
19a. Abd al-Müminինlü	178		138	13008	94	
b. Abd al-Müminin[66]	237		144	12000	83	
20a. Eylemişlü	163		113	11028	98	
b. Eylemişlü [67]	220		153	9600	63	
21a. Katrancı	24		14	2670	191	
b. Katrancı[68]	37		26	3000	115	
22a. Çelük (of Sadık-i Siyah)	22		12	1200	100	
b. Çelik[69]	29		22	1000	45	inad. herd
23a. Ibrahimlü [70]	42		17	2400	141	
b. Ibrahimlü	37		26	2000	77	

Table 3: Turgud[71]

Cemaat	adult males	cultivators	households	sheep	sheep/ hsehld.	settled?
1a. Oylı	15		10	1350	135	
b. Oylı[72]	22		16	1200	75	
2a. Ömer Yar	27		23	1550	67	
b. Ömer Yar[73]	59	6	43	2400	56	inad. herd
3a. Perakende-i Kökperlü	9			790		
b. Kökperlü Perakende	15		11	500	45	inad. herd
4a. Kökperlü [74]	10		7	540	77	
b. Kökperlü	22	3	16	600	38	inad. herd
5a. Kekçiler	14		8	472	59	
b. Gökçeler	12	1	10	400	40	inad. herd
6a. Göynler	60		40	2750	69	
b. Göynler[75]	66	7	44	3200	73	
7a. Duydılar, also known as Çöp Isalu	96		60	5100	85	
b. Dundılar, also known as Çöp Isa[76]	125	7	81	5000	62	
8a. Şahinler	40		22	2600	118	
b. Şahinler[77]	53	6	28	2000	71	
9a. Köşkler	28		14	1748	125	
b. Köşkler[78]	41	12	25	1200	48	inad. herd
10a. Lala Oğlu	10		7	630	90	
b. Lalu	21		17	1200	71	
11a. Sarı Hamza Akşehir Beyli	10		7	444	63	
b. Küllü, also known as Sarı Hamza[79]	10		8	200	25	inad. herd
12a. Melik Gazi	33		22	1400	64	
b. Melik Gazilü [80]	35	6	27	600	22	inad. herd
13a. Evlad-i Mübarek	42		30	3230	108	
b.						

14a.	Nökeran-i Turgud Bey	41		24	1144	48	inad. herd
b.	Nökeran-i Turgud Bey[81]	53	4	33	1200	36	inad. herd
15a.	Doganlı[82]	22		14	816	58	inad. herd
b.	Doganlu	28	4	19	600	32	inad. herd
16a.	Kayırcıklu	9		7	600	86	
b.	Kayırcaklu	12		7	500	71	
17a.	Küçük Danişmendlü	13		8	1800	225	
b.	Küçük Danişmendlü	34	6	24	1400	58	inad. herd
18a.	Ağzı Açıklar, also known as Pir-i Gani	19		13	1500	115	
b.	Ağzı Açıklu, also known as Pir-i Gani[83]	29	5	16	400	25	inad. herd
19a.	Develüler	26		20	1742	87	
b.	Develüler[84]	42		31	3000	97	
20a.	Yanko	4			150		
b.	Yankoz	4			100		
21a.	Emir Hacılu[85]	16		9	424	47	inad. herd
b.	Emir Hacılu	26		16	500	31	inad. herd
22a.	Bulcalar	18		17	100	6	inad. herd
b.							
23a.	Yemenlü	209		152	12000	79	
b.	Yamanlu[86]	325	22	180	12000	67	
24a.	Kalaycı, also known as Osmanlı Oğlu	38		30	1220	41	inad. herd
b.	Kalaycı[87]	39		37	700	19	inad. herd
25a.	Erdoğdulu	26		22	2000	91	
b.	Erdoğdulu[88]	25	3	15	2000	133	
26a.	Dükçür	39		34	4136	122	
b.	Dükçür	50	17	42	3000	71	
27a.	Ayaslar	17		10	500	50	inad. herd
b.	Ayaslar[89]	18		13	280	22	inad. herd
28a.	Koçlu[90]	9		7	80	11	inad. herd
b.	Koçalar	7		4	60	15	inad. herd

Cemaat	adult males	cultivators	households	sheep	sheep/ hsehld.	settled?
29a. Evlad-i Yadgan	11		8	340	43	inad. herd
b. Evlad-i Yadgan[91]	13		9	200	22	inad. herd
30a. Kosunlu	78		65	830	15	inad. herd
b.						
31a. Ibrahim Hacılu	31		24	1400	58	inad. herd
b. Ibrahim Hacılu[92]	31		22	1400	64	
32a. Alayundlu	105		72	13100	182	
b. Alayundlu[93]	227	17	125	12000	96	
33a. Hasan Beylü	9		7	788	113	
b. Hasan Beylü [94]	13		6	600	100	
34a. Yahşı Han	9		7	400	57	inad. herd
b. Yahşı Han, also known as Buslarlu[95]	21	8	19	400	21	inad. herd
35a. Durdu Dundarlu	46		30	4000	133	
b. Duy Dundarlu	86	3	48	3000	63	
36a. Zengan[96]	30		28	1800	64	
b. Zengan	41	11	29	1400	48	inad. herd
37a. Körpeler	4			100		
b. Körpelü [97]	4		3	200	67	
38a. Oğlan-i Bayezid	13		10	600	60	
b. Oğlan-i Bayezid	9		9	400	44	inad. herd
39a. Mahmudlar	169		111	16014	144	
b. Mahmudlar[98]	278	43	199	17200	86	
40a. Şüllü	53		36	4050	140	
b. Süllerlü [99]	78	28	47	3000	64	
41a. Saruca Ahmed	38		24	3000	125	
b. Saruca Ahmedlü	75	8	53	3000	57	inad. herd
42a. Bilcelü	54		40	2400	60	
b. Yenicelü [100]	77	10	60	2000	33	inad. herd
43a. Yoltimur	32		29	2440	84	
b. Yoltimur[101]	44	13	40	2400	60	

44a.	Gereklü	28		16	1200	75	
b.	Gereklü	45	7	30	1600	53	inad. herd
45a.	Hüseyin Beylü [102]	11		10	660	66	
b.							
46a.	Müşki	31		20	500	25	inad. herd
b.	Müşki	64	10	42	3000	71	
47a.	Insanlar[103]	4		4	60	15	inad. herd
b.							
48a.	Delüler	29		23	1640	71	
b.							
49a.	Toklıcaklu	25		18	1950	108	
b.	Toklıcaklu	34	5	23	3000	130	
50a.	Mürekkebler	14		10	300	30	inad. herd
b.	Mürekkeb. . . .	12		8	400	50	inad. herd
51a.	Nökeran-i Piri Bey	32		28	840	30	inad. herd
b.	Nökeran-i Piri Bey[104]	52	9	29	1000	34	inad. herd
52a.	Erkenkocan	13		12	1100	92	
b.	Erkenkocan	16		9	1100	122	
53a.	Dedelü [105]	14		8	1200	150	
b.	Dedeler	32	4	23	1200	52	inad. herd
54a.	Sarı Sakallu	25		16	1600	100	
b.	Sarı Ishaklu	26		17	1000	59	inad. herd
55a.	Kaya Hasanlar	8			190		
b.	Kaya Hasanlu	9		6	3000	500	
56a.	Reyhanlu	10	66	74	7774	101	mixed?
b.							
57a.	Kara Budaklar	11		7	276	39	inad. herd
b.	Kara Budak	18		10	400	40	inad. herd
58a.	Reyhanlu	22		16	400	25	inad. herd
b.	Tetimme-i Reyhanlu[106]	17	5	11	400	36	S
59a.	Katrancı	24		18	998	55	inad. herd
b.	Katrancı	25		19	600	32	inad. herd
60a.	Tur Ali Hacı	10		6	400	67	
b.	Tur Ali Hacı	13	3	6	400	67	settling?

Cemaat	adult males	cultivators	households	sheep	sheep/ hsehld.	settled?
61a. Altı....	26	21	21	1780	85	S
b. Altı....[107]	36	36	27	2000	74	S
62a. Künce	23		6	1260	79	
b. Küncelü	30		22	1200	55	inad. herd
63a. Aymalar[108]	120		100	7000	70	
b. Aymalar	188	13	148	8000	54	inad. herd
64a. Ulaş	6			30		inad. herd
b. Ulaş[109]	11		11	200	18	inad. herd
65a. Aysöz	18		7	526	75	
b. Aysöz[110]	26		16	700	44	inad. herd
66a. Çepni	43		31	2094	68	
b. Çepni[111]	55	8	44	1600	36	inad. herd
67a. Yugra Avratlu	135		95	11950	126	
b. Yugra Avratlu[112]	251	31	168	10400	62	
68a.						
b. Niğde	25		15	1000	67	
69a. .... Perakende	9		8	200	25	inad. herd
b.						
70a. Arıklar	22		15	384	26	inad. herd
b. Arıklar[113]	5		5	100	20	inad. herd
71a. Kırıklar	4	4				S
b. Kırıklar	23		17	1000	59	inad. herd
72a. Aga Beylü	37		30	1000	33	inad. herd
b. Aga Beylü [114]	42		28	1000	36	inad. herd
73a.						
b. Mancılu from Aga Beylü [115]	20		10	200	20	inad. herd
74a. Tirük	3					
b.						
75a. Kaziti	29	5	16	2100	131	mixed?
b. Kaziti	53		10	1400	140	

76a. Şalmanlu	35		28	4420	158	
b. Selmanlu[116]	29		20	2000	100	
77a. Durhacılar	13		8	360	45	inad. herd
b. Durhacılu[117]	19		13	200	15	inad. herd
78a. Nihallar	97		60	7000	117	
b. Nihallar[118]	182	6	122	8000	66	
79a. .... of Yavaşlu, also known as Hasan Beylü Yavaşlusu[119]	26		19	3126	165	
b. Yavaşlar, also known as Hasan Beylü Yavaşlusu	51	8	37	3000	81	
80a. Şahingitlü	114		70	10050	144	
b. Şahingit[120]	192	31	133	10000	75	
81a. Nökeran-i veled-i Tursun Bey ibn Turgud	31		28	3200	114	
b. Nökeran-i veledler-i Turgud[121]	43	6	36	3200	89	
82a. Çoban Karaca	56		41	4000	98	
b. Çoban Karaca[122]	73	16	66	6000	91	
83a. Yavaşlu	47		34	1620	48	inad. herd
b. Other Yavaşlu	79	11	55	3000	55	inad. herd
84a.	10		7	1020	146	
b. ....[123]	22	7	12	1000	83	
85a. Kaysar	67		31	1970	64	
b. Kaysar[124]	80	5	46	1200	26	inad. herd
86a. Tahirlü [125]	92	3	57	8934	157	
b. Tahirlü	127	11	94	8000	85	
87a.						
b. Evlad-i Aglarca, part of Saruca Ahmedlü [126]	13		9	400	44	inad. herd
88a.						
b. ....[127]	19		10	100	10	inad. herd

Cemaat	adult males	cultivators	households	sheep	sheep/ hsehld.	settled?
89a.						
b. ....[128]	20	7	13	200	15	inad. herd
90a.						
b.	14	5	8	100	13	inad. herd
91a.						
b.	68	10	41	2000	49	inad. herd
92a.						
b. Hisünler[129]	95	17	65	2000	31	inad. herd
93a.						
b. Acarlar	4		4	200	50	inad. herd
94a.						
b. Varsakan[130]	69		48	9000	188	
95a.						
b. Acarlar	16		11	600	55	inad. herd

Table 3a: Yapa of Turgud[131]

Cemaat	adult males	cultivators	households	sheep	sheep/ hsehld.	total taxes
1a. Gereklü	193		171			10274
b. Gereklü	197	187	147	8000	54 inad. herd	7960
2a. Yavaşlu	49		30			2175
b. Yavaşlu	45	43	35	2000	57 inad. herd	2570
3a. Duy Dundarlu	45		34			1936
b. Duy Dundarlu	52	51	30	1120	37 inad. herd	1764
4a. Yıkacık	90		70			4072
b. Yıkacıklu	91	72	65	8000	123	5640
5a. Bilcelü, also known as Davudlar	23		16			1280
b. Bilcelü, also known as Davudlar	25	25	20	400	20 inad. herd	740
6a. Toklucaklu	35		23			1718
b. Toklucaklu	45	43	32	2000	63	1570
7a. Alayundlu	41		28			1772
b. Alayundlu	49	48	40	5580	140	3530
8a. Delüler	11		4			790
b. Delüler	9	9	7	2000	286	1160
9a. Agalar	61		35			2150
b. Agalar	56	55	44	7000	159	4540
10a. Köseler	33		18			1350
b. Köseler[132]	19		17	200	12 inad. herd	980
11a. Mahmudlar	10		7			322
b. Mahmudlar	14	14	11	600	55 inad. herd	500
12a. Sakallu	9		7			500
b. Sakallar[133]	8		7	200	29 inad. herd	248
13a. Tazılar	12		10			582
b. Tazılar[134]	12		10	200	20 inad. herd	340

Cemaat	adult males	cultivators	households	sheep	sheep/ hsehld.	total taxes
14a. Yurd Bey and Yakublar	12		9			694
b. Yurd Beyler, also known as Yakublar	15	15	12	2400	200	1534
15a. Ali Bey veled-i Yapa	44		37			7565
b. Ali Bey veled-i Yapa[135]	48					
16a. Nökeran	249		210			9191
b. Nökeran-i Şah Bey[136]	286		156	6000	38 inad. herd	13952
17a. Germiyan Yahşılu	19		12			950
b. Germiyan Yahşılu[137]	20		12	400	33 inad. herd	614
18a. Haymanegan-i Celal Bey	38		30			2500
b. Haymanegan-i Celal Bey[138]	33		27	600	22 inad. herd	972
19a. Haymanegan-i Şah Bey veled-i Yapa	23		22			3000
b. Haymanegan-i Şah Bey[139]	23		20	3000	150	1968
20a. Haymanegan-i Kemal Bey veled-i Yapa	35		30			7000
b. Haymanegan-i Kemal Bey veled-i Yapa[140]	59		30	4000	133	2846
21a. Haymanegan-i Aydogmuş Çavuş						
b.						
22a. Dervish lodge Kol Fazıl near Yaylacuk	5					
b.						
23a.						
b. Reyhanlu[141]	109		76	5000	66	9528
24a.						
b. . . . .[142]	36		26	2000	77	2804
25a.						
b. Du'l Kadırlu[143]	6		5	100	20 inad. herd	170

26a.					
b. Evlad-i Seyit Harun	25		1000		770
27a					
b. Reaya-i veledler-i Şehinşah Bey[144]	11	11			252
28a.					
b. Yahyalar from Aga Beylü [145]	20	7	200	29 inad. herd	690

Notes to Appendix One

1. TT32:1-52; TT1061:2-79. Since the beginning of Eski Il is missing from TT32, some direct comparisons between 1500-1501 and 1523 are not possible. The order of presentation of the *cemaats* varies among the two cadasters, due to changes in the route followed by the registrars as well as changes in the pastures and schedules of the Horse Drovers; it was in the nature of things impossible for Mustafa Çelebi and Ruşeni to seek out a *cemaat* at the same point in its schedule as Haydar and Ali found it. Because of the large number of sub-groups to which *cemaats* in Eski Il belonged, I have clustered together *cemaats* under their sub-groupings, even though they were separate from each other in the cadaster. This allows a clearer view of their organization. In TT32 the sub-group member *cemaats* tended to be registered together. The Turgud, Bayburd and Yapa tables follow the order of registration in TT32. Entry a is always the 1500-1501 entry; entry b is the 1523 entry. Thus, the reader should be aware that the total number of *cemaats* is always greater than the number in either cadaster. This is especially true in TT32's Eski Il section, thanks to the missing pages.

2. In this column appears the total number of symbols indicating size or type of land cultivated, e.g. *çift, nim çift, bennak,* per *cemaat.*

3. TT32 begins with a Kuştimur *cemaat,* and it is likely that Kuştimur *cemaats* have been lost with the earlier pages of the cadaster. Lacunae in the tables are due to lacunae in the cadasters.

4. In 1500-1501, the Hüseyin Şeyh were part of the Yok Kuştimur. In 1523 they appeared to be settled and associated with a dervish lodge. The only figure given is for total revenues, *hasıl el-galle,* of a field, 100 *akçes* in 1523.

5. The Eyüpler were part of the Yok Kuştimur. Their taxes were listed as part of the totals of the Perakende-i Kuştimur.

6. Literally, Kuştimur dispersed or scattered, part of a village or a field, but no longer of a *cemaat.* In 1501 they were on the plain east of Konya, and their taxes included the taxes of the Eyüpler. The total herd of both *cemaats* was 1306 sheep, the average herd per household totaled sixteen, and fifty percent of their taxes came from the sheep tax.

7. With added produce revenues from *mezraas* of 1080 *akçes;* also listing the revenues from *mezraas* of a dervish lodge, 580 *akçes*. Most of these revenues were *haric ez defter,* that is, these *mezraa* listings were newly added after the previous cadaster, presumably the revision by Bayezid Çelebi.

8. A further fourteen adult males, (eleven households, with three cultivators) lived in Eregli, had eighty sheep (seven per household, on average), and paid twelve percent of their total taxes in the form of the sheep tax.

9. In addition to the regular taxes, produce revenues (*hasıl el-galle* and *zemin*) amounted to 1210 *akçes.* These produce revenues are not counted in the normal totals but are listed beneath the names of *mezraas.* Unless expressly stated, figures in the "percent" column do not include these *mezraa* products unless the main summary entry for taxes in the cadaster includes them.

10. Additional produce revenues: 150 *akçes.*

11. Also called . . . of the Boz Apa.

12. The Çepni registered in TT32 consist of three *cemaats;* in TT1061, the *cemaat* is registered as eight villages. First I list the three 1500-1501 *cemaats* (with their one obvious 1523 village), then follow the remaining villages of 1523.

13. Kavak enjoyed the use of some fields skirting Karaca Dağ and near Kökez (Kadınhanı).

14. The Boynu Yumru *cemaats* of TT32 have no separate tax listings. There were 17000 sheep scattered over the eight *cemaats,* and the average herd size per household figure listed is thus purely tentative.

15. In 1500-1501, this *cemaat*'s produce revenues were 1550 *akçes;* in 1523, 1750 *akçes.*

16. Produce revenues from fields in 1500-1501: 980 *akçes.*

17. Produce revenues in 1523: 300 *akçes.*

18. This *cemaat* may have consisted of the same families as 45a or 46a, and a comparison of the personal names would surely decide the question. I regret that in 1978 I had neither time enough to transcribe the personal names in TT1061 nor permission to photograph documents.

19. Produce revenues in 1523: 500 *akçes.*

20. The Kum (-lu and -lar) pastures were located near Zengicek in 1500-1501: the taxes for three of their *cemaats* were lumped together, so once again the average herd sizes are far from certain.

21. Produce revenues in 1523: 1000 *akçes.*

22. These Kumlu lived in the Konya plain. In 1523, their produce revenues were 850 *akçes.*

23. The Veledlü were settled in the village of Salurcık, north of Mahmudlar, and they cultivated a winter pasture called Veledlü. Mahmudlar, however, lay in the *nahiye* of Turgud.

24. Three of the 1500-1501 Ahmedler lived in a village of the same name (the village appears to have been removed from the 1523 cadaster). The rest of the Ahmedler traveled an il-rah which included Bayburd in the summer and Eski Il in the winter.

25. The Bereketlü paid a pasture tax, *resm-i otlak,* of 100 *akçes* in 1523. Their low herd size, which may already have compelled the two men to undertake agricultural activities, may also have caused them to seek better pastures on forbidden lands.

26. The Izz al-Din, in 1500-1501, were registered as two *cemaats,* although their taxes were entered as one total. They were probably traveling as two adjacent camp groups. Their produce revenues totalled 90 *akçes,* in 1523, 75 *akçes.*

27. The Kara Gözlü's fields lay at the base of Kara Dağ.

28. This entry consists of two *cemaats* with one total tax figure. Again, in 1500-1501 they may have been two camping groups. In 1523, the Yılmaz were one *cemaat,* paying produce

revenues of 2000 *akçes.* It is quite possible that the 1523 entry for Yılmaz also includes 77a below.

29. In 1523, produce revenues totalled 500 *akçes.*

30. The Dag Dere, in 1500-1501, consisted of sixteen adult males, fourteen households near Çoban Viranı, also called Çoban Oğlu, and sixteen further adult males near Çokçı (perhaps younger shepherds with herds that could not travel with the main camps).

31. The sheep taxes for 83a and 84a appear as one total. Between them they shared 5000 sheep in 1500-1501. 83a also paid a *resm-i bennak* of 216 *akçes.*

32. In 1523, Mustafa Çelebi came across this *cemaat* divided into two cultivating camps.

33. Produce revenues from fields in 1523: 700 *akçes.*

34. Produce revenues in 1523: 100 *akçes.*

35. 1523 produce revenues: 700 *akçes.*

36. 1523 produce revenues: 1100 *akçes.*

37. 1523 produce revenues: 8050 *akçes.*

38. 1523 produce revenues: 2900 *akçes.*

39. 1523 produce revenues: 3550 *akçes.*

40. 1523 produce revenues: 1100 *akçes.*

41. 1523 produce revenues: 350 *akçes.*

42. In 1523, the registered *mezraas,* whose produce revenues were 1100 *akçes,* were all recent, *haric ez defter,* acquisitions.

43. 1523 produce revenues: 70 *akçes.*

44. 1523 produce revenues: 2500 *akçes.*

45. The Kürtül's fines and fees were over eight times the amount of their sheep tax. They had, surely, become rather desperate as their herds dwindled; since so few of them had lands to cultivate in 1523, is it not possible that their herds had sustained a severe and sudden loss, so that deprivation had caught them unawares, and left them with little alternative other than to hunt, or steal, a living?

46. 1523 produce revenues: 1550 *akçes.*

47. 1523 produce revenues: 700 *akçes.*

48. 1523 produce revenues: 1650 *akçes.* The sheep tax was only half of this sum.

49. The Serlaklar, as well as the next five *cemaats,* were registered as timars. 1523 produce revenues: 3850 *akçes,* a bit more than the sheep tax.

50. 1523 produce revenues: 1300 *akçes.*

51. 1523 produce revenues: 9738 *akçes,* one-third greater than the sheep tax.

52. 1523 produce revenues: 4000 *akçes,* four times the sheep tax. I imagine that this *cemaat* hired shepherds to tend their herds.

53. 1523 produce revenues: 250 *akçes,* land taxes: 2480 *akçes.*

54. 1523 land and produce revenues: 3546 *akçes,* over twice the sheep tax.

55. The Sakallar were connected with a dervish lodge, and they were also cultivating a large number of fields which had not appeared in earlier cadasters. The 1523 produce revenues from these new fields came to 11270 *akçes.*

56. 1523 produce revenues: 1000 *akçes.*

57. 1523 produce revenues: 1500 *akçes.*

58. TT32: 54-95; TT1061: 149-180.

59. The Emir Hacılu had a *mezraa* near Tavşanlı, west of the road linking Mut to Larende and just south of the latter.

60. 1523 produce revenues: 290 *akçes.*

61. 1523 produce revenues: 2500 *akçes,* also a pasture fine of 600 *akçes.*

62. 1523 produce revenues: 500 *akçes.*

63. In the sixteenth century the Ogul Beylü became part of the Boz Ulus confederation. In the seventeenth they migrated to west Anatolia along with some of the Boz Ulus. Faruk Sümer, *Oguzlar* (Ankara, 1967), pp. 177, 191. 1523 produce reveneus: 1000 *akçes.*

64. Cf. TT32, p. 83; Beldiceanu, *Qaraman,* pp. 79-80 (TT32 gives the incorrect pasture assignments which allowed this *cemaat* to prosper).

65. The Peçenek had a *mezraa* near Akçaşehir, in Eski Il. 1523 produce revenues: 1200 *akçes,* slightly greater than the sheep tax.

66. 1523 produce revenues: 500 *akçes.*

67. 1523 produce revenues: 1750 *akçes.*

68. 1523 produce revenues: 1000 *akçes.*

69. 1523 produce revenues: 100 *akçes,* but Çelik's fines and fees came to 390 *akçes.* Were they supplementing their diminished herds by raiding?

70. Cf. the list of Bayburd *cemaats* in Tekindag, "Son münasebetleri," p. 58 n. 69.

71. TT32: 96-178; TT1061: 81-131.

72. 1523 produce revenues: 1000 *akçes,* 1.67 times the sheep tax.

73. 1523 produce revenues: 6250 *akçes,* five times the sheep tax.

74. Kökperlü pastures were located near Ilgın.

75. 1523 produce revenues: 1800 *akçes* from fields near Akçaşehir; all the fields were recent acquisitions.

76. 1500-1501 produce revenues: 196 *akçes;* in 1523, 500 *akçes.*

77. 1523 produce revenues: 275 *akçes.*

78. 1523 produce revenues: 1000 *akçes,* 1.67 times the sheep tax.

79. The fines and fees equal the sheep tax, implying that income from theft supplemented the inadequate herds of the *cemaat.*

80. Criminal fines and fees were two-thirds of the sheep tax. The 1523 produce revenues amounted to 750 *akçes,* 2.5 times the sheep tax, and one of the cultivated fields was a 1500-1501 winter pasture for sheep.

81. Criminal fines and fees were greater than the sheep tax. This *cemaat* shared a pasture with the Ayaslu.

82. Some of their pastures were near Ilgın.

83. 1523 produce revenues: 200 *akçes,* equal to the sheep tax.

84. 1523 produce revenues: 1000 *akçes,* equal to the sheep tax.

85. They shared pastures with the Yugra Avratlu. In 1523, their fines (for theft?) and fees were greater than the sheep tax.

86. The Yamanlu also had an associated group of ten dervishes.

87. Their fines and fees equalled their sheep tax.

88. 1523 produce revenues (from recently acquired fields): 500 *akçes,* also pasture fines of 60 *akçes.*

89. Their 1523 fines and fees were greater than their sheep tax.

90. In 1500-1501, fines and fees were greater than their sheep tax; in 1523, 2.3 times greater.

91. Their 1523 fines and fees were greater than their sheep tax.

92. Their 1523 produce revenues (from newly acquired fields): 750 *akçes.*

93. Their 1523 produce revenues were 1000 *akçes,* and a group of dervishes was associated with the *cemaat.*

94. In 1500-1501, their produce revenues were 413 *akçes* on fields near Said Ili (Kadınhanı); in 1523, 50 *akçes.* The 1523 cadaster specifically states that it was the tribesmen who cultivated the field.

95. Their cultivated field was called Buslar, near Said Ili (Kadınhanı). In 1523 their produce revenues were 75 *akçes.*

96. Zengan is a village north of Cihanbeyli: Hütteroth, *Ländliche Siedlungen,* map 11.

97. Their fines and fees were greater than their sheep tax.

98. 1523 produce revenues: 900 *akçes.*

99. Produce revenues in 1500-1501: 100 *akçes;* in 1523: 350 *akçes.*

100. 1523 produce revenues: 600 *akçes.*

101. 1523 produce revenues: 250 *akçes.*

102. A new group in the 1500-1501 cadaster.

103. This *cemaat* consisted of Musa ibn Insan and his three brothers (plus, of course, unregistered women and children): thus it was simply a small family camp in 1500-1501. I would guess that this tent was part of another *cemaat* in 1523.

104. 1523 produce revenues: 5900 *akçes,* almost twelve times the sheep tax.

105. 1500-1501 produce revenues: 560 *akçes.*

106. Fines and fees were greater than sheep taxes.

107. The 1523 cadaster lists this *cemaat* as former At Çeken.

108. Aymalar's pasture lay near Konya and Zengicek, and their 1500-1501 il-rah presumably ran between the two; their 1523 produce revenues were 2850 *akçes.*

109. Fines and fees were greater than total sheep taxes.

110. 1523 produce revenues: 750 *akçes*, more than twice the sheep tax.

111. 1523 produce revenues: 500 *akçes*, from recently acquired fields.

112. The 1500-1501 listing includes ten members of the Niğde *cemaat*. Some fields were also used by the Emir Hacılu of Turgud. 1523 produce revenues: 3670 *akçes*, mostly from recently acquired fields.

113. Fines and fees equalled the sheep tax.

114. 1523 produce revenues: 200 *akçes;* fines and fees: 450 *akçes*.

115. This *cemaat* did not appear in previous cadasters. Their 1523 produce revenues were 150 *akçes*, fines and fees 200 *akçes*.

116. 1523 produce revenues: 1000 *akçes*, equal to the sheep tax.

117. 1523 produce revenues: 250 *akçes*, 2.5 times the sheep taxes, which were also much less than the total fines and fees.

118. 1523 produce revenues: 120 *akçes;* winter pasture fine, 20 *akçes;* pasture fine, 40 *akçes; resm-i duhan*, 60 *akçes*.

119. Yavaşlı is north of Turgud in the modern district of Akşehir. The 1523 produce revenues were 300 *akçes*.

120. In 1500-1501 this *cemaat* paid a water-mill fee and shared pasture with the Emir Hacılu. In 1523, their produce revenues were 2000 *akçes*, and many of their cultivated fields were newly acquired.

121. In 1500-1501, Piri Çelebi, the son of Tursun Bey ibn Turgud, cultivated one of the fields, even though other members of the *cemaat* remained pastoralists. By 1523, there were more cultivators, and the produce revenues from recently acquired fields were 100 *akçes*.

122. 1523 produce revenues: 150 *akçes*, from recently acquired fields.

123. 1523 produce revenues: 500 *akçes*, equal to the sheep tax.

124. Produce revenues in 1500-1501 and 1523: 1500 *akçes*.

125. In 1500-1501 they also paid winter pasture and pasture fines of 50 *akçes*. 1523 produce revenues from recently acquired fields: 3500 *akçes*. See also Tekindag, "Son münasebet-leri," p. 55 n. 55.

126. 1523 produce revenues: 125 *akçes*, from a field confirmed to them by Selim I.

127. Fines and fees were four times the sheep tax.

128. Fines and fees were twice the sheep tax.

129. 1523 produce revenues: 100 *akçes*.

130. 1523 produce revenues: 11000 *akçes*, 2.75 times the sheep tax.

131. TT32: 157-178, TT1061: 133-148 (called Yapalu).

132. The Köseler paid land *(bennak)* taxes in 1523; their fines and fees were considerably larger than their sheep taxes.

133. In 1523, The Sakallar paid land *(bennak)* taxes; their fines and fees equalled their sheep tax.

134. In 1523 the Tazılar paid land *(bennak)* taxes and fines and fees which were much greater than their sheep tax.

135. In 1500-1501, the total revenues included produce tithes *(öşr)* and pasture fines; in addition, a field yielded 30 *akçes* in produce revenues. This *cemaat*'s position was verified by a deed from Murad II (TT32, p. 170). In 1523 the *cemaat* paid pasture fines of 900 *akçes,* winter grazing fines of 600 *akçes,* and produce revenues of 6700 *akçes.*

136. In 1523, the Nökeran paid *bennak resmi.*

137. In 1523, produce revenues were 3250 *akçes;* the *cemaat* also paid land taxes *(çift, caba, bennak),* as well as fines and fees greater than the sheep tax total.

138. The Haymanegan paid *bennak resmi;* their fines and fees were greater than their sheep tax.

139. They paid, in 1523, *bennak* and *caba* taxes.

140. In 1500-1501 their produce revenues were 400 *akçes;* in 1523, 250 *akçes;* they also paid *bennak* and *caba* land taxes in 1523.

141. The Reyhanlu, who may be the same *cemaat* as the Turgud Reyhanlu of 1500-1501, paid *çift, bennak,* and *caba* taxes.

142. This *cemaat* paid *çift, bennak,* and *caba* taxes.

143. In 1523 they paid *bennak* taxes.

144. They paid *bennak* taxes.

145. They paid *çift* and *caba* taxes. Their fines and fees were twice their sheep taxes. In general, compare the list in Tekindag, "Son münasebetleri," pp. 59 n. 70, 76 n. 153.

Appendix Two:

Şikari

In the early years of this century Halil Edhem, the eminent Ottoman numismatist, epigrapher, and historian, was preparing a series of articles describing sources for the history of the emirate of Karaman. Tahir Bey, a former mayor of Larende (now Karaman), had come across a resumé of information about Larende and sent it along. Later, Tahir Bey obtained a complete copy of this work, a history of Karaman composed by a certain Şikari. Halil Edhem eagerly began to copy the work but was soon unhappy with its contents. It contained no dates and he thought it replete with unnecessary stories. In short, its value for an exact chronology appeared doubtful, and Edhem chose not to use it. Both manuscripts are now lost.[1]

Sceptics, however, including Halil Edhem himself, came to have second thoughts about Şikari when they discovered that this work was not simply nineteenth century folklore. The seventeenth century Ottoman historian Ahmed b. Lutfullah, called Müneccimbaşı, a scholar known for his interest in and use of noteworthy older chronicles, had used Şikari from a text copied c. 1025/1615. This discovery brought Şikari much closer to the deeds which his work elaborated.[2] The debate over Şikari has continued until the present. Paul Wittek felt compelled to treat Şikari as a source for the early history of the Menteşe emirate, even though he voiced doubts about the work and relegated discussion of it to an appendix.[3] Claude Cahen despaired of making a successful separation of truth and legend among Şikari's (oral?) traditions.[4] In more recent times the dervish scholar Abdülbaki Gölpinarlı has attacked the work's worth, which has been defended (promising later proof) by the folklorist Cahit Öztelli.[5] The latest scholarly appreciation of this work is from Faruk Sümer, who states that it "should not be used without confirmation through other sources."[6]

The tales Şikari recounts have long puzzled scholars tantalized by, and perhaps eager to trust, a source some two hundred printed pages in length. Perhaps from fear that the work may be a magnificent humbug, they have shied away from the basic tasks of establishing the development of the text and identifying its author. These tasks do, however, deserve some effort, for even (at worst) a forgery has an interesting history to reveal.[7]

The final publication of a text of Şikari is bound closely to the origins of modern historical scholarship in Turkey. Among the influential members of the Ottoman Historical Society, the Tarih-i Osmani Encümeni, was Arifi Pasha, governor of Konya province from 1909 to 1911. Arifi Pasha became interested in the history of the emirate of Karaman and learned of a manuscript history of Karaman, composed by our Şikari, which belonged to a wealthy citizen of Larende, Hadimizade Enver Efendi. Arifi Pasha had the manuscript copied by Ibrahim Aczi Efendi, the census registrar of Larende. Seeking to please his patron, Ibrahim Aczi later produced a more detailed anonymous history of Karaman. This longer work, written in a more modern Turkish, omitted the prefatory couplet identifying Şikari as author, lacked all the enmity against the Ottomans which Şikari displayed, and contained not only footnotes but even some transcribed French. This new discovery met with Arifi Pasha's perhaps naive enthusiasm. On Arifi Pasha's death his daughter gave both manuscripts to the library of the arts faculty of Istanbul University.[8] Not content with one *"edition critique"* of Şikari, Ibrahim Aczi later sold Mesud Koman an anonymous Persian prose history of Karaman, which he claimed to have copied from a manuscript belonging to a telegraph guard in Ermenak.

Ibrahim Aczi's longer version of the Karaman history was used in a series of articles in the *Ikdam* gazette during 1921 by Necib Asım, an instructor at Istanbul University. These articles produced a reply from the bibliophile and collector Ali Emiri, who possessed a Şikari manuscript dated 1119/1707. Ali Emiri had purchased this manuscript from a former Ottoman finance minister, Ragip Bey, who had obtained it from a governor of Konya, Izzet Pasha. The Arifi Pasha manuscript (the short, Şikari text, now Istanbul University MS TY 646) lacked an ending and various phrases found in Ali Emiri's manuscript, which became the "standard" Şikari text for the next generation of scholars, led by Wittek.[9]

Hadimizade Enver Efendi's Şikari, the basis of Arifi Pasha's copy, was twice sold and ended its journey in the Konya Public Library, where Ferid Ugur was able to unite to it the missing end folios. Although the manuscript bears no colophon a dated marginal note on p. 5 established 1023/1613 as the *terminus ante quem* for its production. The printed text published by Ugur and Koman at Konya in 1946 is based on this manuscript and lists important variants from Ali Emiri's eighteenth century manuscript.[10]

In forming an opinion of the value of the Karaman history, it would be helpful to know just who Şikari was and how he went about his business. Şikari, however, tells us nothing about himself; his name, if it is his name and not a nom de plume, appears only once, in a short Turkish verse: "If you wish to know this speck of dust, he is the dirt beneath your feet, that is, Şikari."[11] Scholars have thus had to search for Ottomans who were called Şikari, and have come up with a few candidates: an Ahmet or Haydar Şikari, who died in 1506 or 1584, the son and grandson of high Ottoman officials, and the author of an incomplete Mesnevi treatment of the story of Yusuf and Zuleyha;[12] a judge of Malkara whose name appears in an official register dated 1567;[13] or Şikari Çelebi, a judge and minor poet of the reign of Ahmet I.[14] Although Ahmet or Haydar Şikari, who was described as an "unconventional" personality, might seem the most likely candidate, there is absolutely no evidence to link him, or any of the other known Şikaris, with the modest author of our Karaman history.[15]

The text of the Karaman history does not allow us to identify its compiler with any confidence. It does provide a description of the method of composition, in an aside. According to Şikari, the Seljuk Sultan Ala ed-Din Keykubad I, impressed by Firdawsi's Persian *Shahname,* commissioned the poet Dehhani to prepare a Seljuk Shahname in Persian verse.[16] The Karamanid emir Ala ed-Din (1356-1391) desired a Karaman Shahname and ordered a certain Yarıcani to prepare a Persian imitation. According to Şikari, Yarıcani's work was unpopular, probably because Persian verse fell upon deaf ears in an increasingly Turcophone society interested in a literature of the spoken language. Şikari thus took it upon himself to prepare a prose translation into Turkish.[17] He was not content with a mere translation, however, for his book continues to describe events into the fifteenth and sixteenth centuries, until the middle of the reign of Selim I.

It is difficult to accept the assertion that the bulk of Şikari's work represents a translation from the Persian. There is no distinction in style and especially in diction between the "translated Yarıcani" and the Şikari "continuation." Nor does the manner of presentation differ: individual tales preceded by the introductory phrases *"ezincanib," "ravi eyder," "raviler rivayet ederler kim,"* indicating "The story goes that. . . . " There are, it is true, verses scattered through, some of which are in Turkish.[18] In most cases Şikari attributes the poetry to his Persian model, but it is still very difficult to believe that the colloquial conversations which enliven the work are the raw simplifications of a polished verse which the translator elsewhere saw fit to quote. In addition, there is no discernible break in style or coverage anywhere in Şikari's treatment of the Karamanid Ala ed-Din. Must we then conclude that Şikari, master of a crude oral style, was such a gifted joiner of pieces as to reduce the vocabulary of Persian poetry to his own prose? It seems hard to believe. Easier to understand is Şikari's fitting poetic snatches into a prose history of Karaman and authenticating his work by a bogus commission to Yarıcani. Dehhani's Seljuk *Shahname*, after all, has never turned up, nor have any works of Yarıcani.[19]

Notes to Appendix Two

1. Halil Edhem, "Karaman oğulları hakkında vesaik-i mahkuke," *Tarih-i Osmani encümeni mecmuası* 2:11-14 (1327), pp. 697-698, esp. n. 2. On the lack of dates, see Claude Cahen, "Quelques mots sur Şikari," *Wiener Zeitschrift für die Kunde des Morgenlandes* 70 (1978), p. 56. Bursalı Tahir Bey's copy was presumably complete, while Halil Edhem's, copied from Tahir Bey's manuscript, presumably was not.

2. Max Van Berchem and Halil Edhem, *Matériaux pour un corpus inscriptionum arabicarum, 3me partie, Asie Mineure,* fasc. 1-2 (Cairo, 1917), pp. 44, 101.

3. Paul Wittek, *Das Fürstentum Mentesche: Studie zur Geschichte Westkleinasiens im 13.-15. Jh.* (Istanbul, 1934), pp. 51-53, 177f.

4. Claude Cahen, "Notes pour l'histoire des turcomans d'Asie Mineure au XIIIe siècle," *Journal asiatique* 239 (1951), pp. 339, n. 4, and 342. In Cahen's recent "Quelques mots," which is the best introduction to Şikari, p. 54, there is a brief discussion of the problem.

5. Yunus Emre, *Risalat al-nushiyya ve Divan,* ed. Abdülbaki Gölpinarlı (Istanbul, 1965), pp. xxvii-xxviii. Cahit Öztelli, "Yunus Emre ve Şikari tarihi," *Türk dili* 165 (1965), pp. 618-21.

6. Art. "Karaman-oghulları," in EI^2.

7. I have gathered photographs of all the Şikari manuscripts known to me and hope to prepare a close examination of the text's growth; but as I am neither philologist nor linguist, I cannot promise quick results.

8. I am indebted to Bay Mesud Koman, former director of the Konya Public Library, for an enlightening conversation about the manuscripts of Şikari. The older literature, which is often confusing, includes: Hüseyin Namık, "Histoire des Karamanides," *Körösi Csoma Archiv* 1:5 (1925), pp. 415-17; Fuad Köprülü, "Anadolu beylikleri tarihine ait notlar," *Türkiyat mecmuası* 2 (1927), p. 27, n. 1, and "Anadolu Selçukluları tarihinin yerli kaynakları," *Belleten* 7 (1943), pp. 399-401; articles by Necib Asım in the newspaper *Ikdam,* nos. 8842, 8860, 8885 (I am indebted to Dr. Mahmud Şakiroglu of Ankara University for providing me copies of these issues); M.F. Ugur and M. Koman, eds., *Şikari'nin Karamanogulları tarihi* (Konya, 1946), pp. 1-16 (hereafter SHK). The shorter version is MS TY 646 (formerly 14104), and the Aczi compendium is MS TY 812 (formerly 14105). For their description see Ludwig Forrer, "Handschriften Osmanischer Historiker in Istanbul," *Der Islam* 26:3 (1942), pp. 175-76. My account of the transactions involving Arifi Pasha and Ibrahim Aczi glosses over a difficulty which earlier studies have not tackled. According to the account of Ali Emiri cited below, which I take to be the basis for the later statements by Hüseyin Namık and Fuad Köprülü, the shorter text with the couplet naming Şikari belonged not to Hadimizade Enver but to a certain Osman Efendi, teacher at the middle

school in Larende; Arifi Pasha had it copied by a court clerk, Mustafa Ruhi. Only the longer, anonymous history of Karaman came from Ibrahim Aczi, who copied it from Hadimizade's longer text. Ali Emiri's account, however, cannot stand, for it argues explicity that Hadimizade's one manuscript contained the longer, anonymous version. While it is agreed that Hadimizade had only one manuscript, that manuscript, which still exists and served as the basis for the printed text, contains the shorter version and the couplet identifying Şikari as author. The reconstruction of events I suggest in my text fits the facts as far as the existing manuscripts are concerned, although it does contradict Ali Emiri's description, which, I think, cannot fit the Hadimizade manuscript. Ali Emiri's story came from Rifaat Bey, a friend and former star pupil of Osman Efendi. For what it may imply, the copyist of Ali Emiri's copy of the longer, anonymous history, made from Arifi Pasha's copy, was named Mustafa.

9. See Ali Emiri's open letter in *Ikdam* no. 8876, 1 December 1921. Ali Emiri's Şikari manuscript is now MS T 458 of the Istanbul Millet Kütüphanesi. MS T 457 is Ali Emiri's copy of the Ibrahim Aczi compendium. See *Istanbul Kütüphaneleri tarih ve cografya yazmaları katalogları* 2 (Istanbul, n.d.), p. 126; Forrer, "Handschriften," p. 176.

10. It may be useful to list the known manuscripts of Şikari, most of which have not been studied:
    a. Konya, Milli Kütüphane 4543, formerly Yusuf Aga 27 nr. 175, described in SHK, p. 8. This is Hadimizade's Şikari. The following are copies of this manuscript: Konya, MS in the private collection of Izzet Koyunoğlu; Istanbul Üniversitesi TY 646 (Formerly 14101), Arifi Pasha's copy; there is also a copy of the Konya MS in the library of the Türk Tarih Kurumu, Ankara. See Forrer, "Handschriften," p. 176.
    b. Istanbul Üniversitesi, MS TY 812 (formerly 14105), Arifi Pasha's longer, anonymous history, obtained from Ibrahim Aczi, described in Forrer, p. 175; copied from this MS is Istanbul, Millet Kütüphanesi, Ali Emiri T 457, described by Forrer, "Handschriften," p. 176. As I have grave doubts about the authenticity of this work, I shall not refer to it further in this chapter.
    c. Istanbul, Millet Kütüphanesi, Ali Emiri T 458, copied 1119/1707, described in *Istanbul katalogları*, p. 126.
    d. Istanbul, Belediye Kütüphanesi, MS Muallim Cevdet K 444; 203 pp. in nesih script, numerous marginal notes in rika, with fifteen pages of pencilled notes taped onto the binding at the end.
    e. Los Angeles, University of California, MS copied in 1151/1738-1739 by Mehmed al-Karamani, missing the beginning and lacking some text in the body of the manuscript. I am grateful to Dunning Wilson, Near East librarian at UCLA, for providing me a copy of this text, and to Andreas Tietze for calling my attention to it.
    f. Berlin, MS Or. fol. 3129, 3129a, copied, with notes and a partial translation, at Konya in the 1870s by Consul J.H. Löytved. Described by Barbara Flemming, *Türkische Handschriften*, vol. 1 (Wiesbaden, 1968), no. 1027.

    Once extant manuscripts whose present whereabouts are unclear include:
    a. Bursalı Tahir Bey's Şikari as well as Halil Edhem's partial copy.
    b. A MS owned by Fahri Bilge, director of the Kayseri branch of the Ziraat Bankası.
    c. A MS in the possession of the late Istanbul bookseller Raif Yelkenci. In 1971 Raif Bey, then already a very ill man, kindly told me that he had loaned his manuscript to someone whose name he no longer could recall. The present owner of Raif Bey's manuscripts informs me that he has not come across the Şikari MS, so it is probably now out on permanent loan.

11. "Eğer bilmek istersen bu gubari, ayaklar topragi yani Şikari." SHK, p. 9.

12. Walther Björkman, "Die klassisch-osmanische Literatur," in *Philologiae Turcicae Fundamenta*, vol. 2 (Wiesbaden, 1964), p. 439, following the entry in Şemseddin Sami Fraşeri, *Kamus ül-Alem* (Istanbul, 1891), s.v. "Şikari," and Ali Emiri's *Ikdam* letter.

13. Fuad Köprülü, "Anadolu Selçukluları tarihinin yerli kaynakları," *Belleten* 7:26 (1943), p. 400 no. 1.

14. Mehmed Süreyya, *Sicilli-i Osmani*, s.v. "Şikari."

15. Gölpinarlı, *Risalat*, pp. 27-28, discusses the various candidates. Since the last events Şikari mentions took place in 1517, some eleven years after one of the death dates of Ahmet/Haydar and some sixty-seven before the other, it is difficult to credit him with the authorship of this work.

16. For Şikari, the Seljuk Ala ed-Din is usually the great Ala ed-Din Keykubad I; in fact, Dehhani, a real person, lived and worked during the reign of the less famous and fortunate Ala ed-Din Keykubad III; cf. art. "Dehhani," *EI*[2], and Cahen, "Quelques mots," pp. 54-55.

17. SHK, pp. 8-9.

18. SHK, pp. 1, 7 (in Turkish), 8, 9 (Turkish), 39-40, 49, 54, 80, 206 (Turkish). None of the poetic insertions deals directly with the history of the emirate.

19. Of course, the argument *ex silentio* is always dangerous, especially since so few libraries in Turkey are adequately catalogued. My treatment of Yarıcani differs from that of Cahen, "Quelques mots," p. 54, who notes that Yarıcani's name ceases to enter into Şikari's tale a few years before the irruption of Timur. This could mean that Şikari occasionally mentioned his source until it came to an end. On the other hand, I find the uniformity of tone and matter in the pre- and post-Timur sections compelling. I would suggest that if Yarıcani were a source, he contributed little which Şikari reproduces with any accuracy; but Cahen could well be correct.

Bibliography

A. Sources

Alam ara-yi Shah Esmail. Edited by Asgar Montazer Saheb. Tehran: B.T.N.K., 1971. Persian texts series, no. 43.

Die altosmanischen anonymen Chroniken, in Text und Übersetzung herausgegeben von Dr. Friedrich Giese. Teil I, Text und Variantenverzeichnis. Breslau: Selbstverlag, 1922.

Arif, Mehmed. "Kanunname-i al-i Osman." Published as supplements to fascs. 15-19 of *Tarih-i osmani encümeni mecmuası,* (1912-13), 72 pp.

Arsenius, Patriarch. *Diatheke.* Migne, *Patrologia graeca,* vol. 140. Cols. 947-58.

Aşıkpaşazade. *Die altosmanische Chronik des Asikpasazade.* Edited by Friedrich Giese. Leipzig: Harrassowitz, 1929.

———. *Tevarih-i al-i Osmandan Aşıkpaşazade tarihi.* Edited by Ali Bey. Istanbul: Matbaa-i amire, 1332.

Atsız, Çiftçioğlu Nihal, ed. *Osmanlı tarihleri.* Istanbul: Türkiye yayınevi, 1947.

Barkan, Ömer Lutfi. *XV. ve XVIıncı asırlarda Osmanlı imparatorluğunda zirai ekonominin hukuki ve malı esasları. I, Kanunlar.* Istanbul: Burhaneddin matbaası, 1943.

Beldiceanu, Nicoara. *Les actes des premiers sultans conservés dans les manuscrits turcs de la Bibliothèque Nationale à Paris.* 2 vols. Paris: Mouton, 1960-64.

———. *Code de lois coutumières de Mehmed II.* Wiesbaden: Harrassowitz, 1967.

Beldiceanu, Nicoara, and Irène Beldiceanu-Steinherr. *Recherches sur la province de Qaraman au XVIe siècle.* Leiden: E.J. Brill, 1968.

Berchem, Max van, and Halil Edhem. *Matériaux pour un corpus inscriptionum arabicarum. 3me partie, Asie Mineure.* Cairo: Imprimerie de l'Institut français d'archéologie orientale, 1917. Mémoires publiés par les membres de l'Institut français d'archéologie orientale du Caire, no. 29.

Busbecq, Ogier Ghislain de. *The Turkish Letters of Ogier Ghiselin de Busbecq.* Translated by Edward Seymour Forster. Oxford: Clarendon Press, 1927.

Cahen, Claude. "Ibn Sa'id sur l'Asie Mineure seldjouqide." *Tarih araştırmaları dergisi* 6 (1968), pp. 41-50.

Choniates, Nicetas. *Historia.* Edited by Jean-Louis van Dieten. Berlin: de Gruyter, 1975.

Cinnamus, Joannes. *Epitome rerum.* Edited by A. Meinecke. Bonn: Corpus scriptorum historiae byzantinae, 1836.

Dölger, Franz. *Regesten der Kaiserurkunden des oströmischen Reiches von 565-1453.* Fascs. 1- . Munich: Oldenbourg, 1924- .

Gregoras, Nicephorus. *Byzantina historia.* Edited by L. Schopen. 3 vols. Bonn: Corpus scriptorum historiae byzantinae, 1829-55.

Hammer-Purgstall, Joseph von. *Des Osmanischen Reichs Staatsverfassung und Staatsverwaltung.* 2 vols. Vienna: In der Camesinaschen Buchhandlung, 1815.

Hasan Rumlu. *A Chronicle of the Early Safavis, Being the Ahsanu't-Tawarikh of Hasan-i Rumlu.* Translated by Charles Norman Seddon. Baroda: Oriental Institute, 1934.

Histoire des Seldjoukides d'Asie Mineure par un anonyme. Edited by Feridun Nafiz Uzluk. Ankara: Örnek matbaası, 1952.

Ibn Battuta. *Travels, A.D. 1325-1354.* Translated by H.A.R. Gibb. vol. 2. Cambridge: Cambridge University Press, 1962. Hakluyt Society, 2nd Ser., no. 117.

Istanbul. Başvekalet Arşivi. Tapu ve Tahrir section, Defter no. 32.

______. Tapu ve Tahrir section, Defter no. 33. The material in this defter is also found in Maliyeden Müdevver section, Defter no. 20.

______. Tapu ve Tahrir section, Defter no. 63.

______. Tapu ve Tahrir section, Defter no. 387.

______. Tapu ve Tahrir section, Defter no. 636.

______. Tapu ve Tahrir section, Defter no. 1061.

Juzjani, Minhaj al-Din. *Tabakat-i Nasiri.* Translated by Henry George Raverty. 2 vols. London: Gilbert and Rivington, 1881.

Karaman *kanunnames.* Leiden, Bibliotheek des Rijksuniversiteit, Cod. or. 305.

Kraelitz-Greifenhorst, Friedrich. "Kanunname Sultan Mehmeds des Eroberers." *Mitteilungen zur Osmanischen Geschichte* 1 (1921-22), pp. 13-48.

Loenertz, Raymond-Joseph. "La chronique brève de 1352." *Orientalia christiana periodica* 30 (1964), pp. 39-64.

Mantran, Robert. "Les inscriptions arabes de Brousse." *Bulletin d'études orientales* 14 (1952-54), pp. 87-114.

Moser, Brigitte. *Die Chronik des Ahmed Sinan Celebi, genannt Bihisti.* Munich: Trofenik, 1980. Beiträge zur Kenntnis Südosteuropas und des Nahen Orients, no. 35.

Müneccimbaşı, Ahmed ibn Lutfullah. *Sahaif ül-ahbar.* Translated by Ahmed Nedim. vol. 3. Istanbul: Matbaa-i amire, 1285.

Muntaner, Ramon. *The Chronicle of Muntaner.* Translated by Lady Goodenough. 2 vols. London: Hakluyt Society, 1920-21. Hakluyt Society, 2nd ser., nos. 47, 50.

Neşri. *Ǧihannüma, die altosmanische Chronik des Mevlana Mehemmed Neschri. Band I: Einleitung und Text des Cod. Menzel.* Edited by Franz Taeschner. Leipzig: Harrassowitz, 1951.

Odo of Deuil. *La croisade de Louis VII, roi de France.* Edited by Henri Waquet. Paris: Geuthner, 1949. Documents relatifs à l'histoire des croisades, publiés par l'Académie des inscriptions et belles-lettres, no. 3.

Oschinsky, Dorothea. *Walter of Henley and Other Treatises on Estate Management and Accounting.* Oxford: Oxford University Press, 1971.

Pachymeres, Georgios. *De Michaele et Andronico Paleologis libri tredecim.* Edited by Immanuel Bekker. 2 vols. Bonn: Corpus scriptorum historiae byzantinae, 1835.

Quatremère, Etienne Marc. "Notice de l'ouvrage qui a pour titre: Mesalek alabsar fi memalek alamsar." *Notices et extraits des manuscrits de la bibliothèque du roi* 13 (1838), pp. 151-384.

Les regestes des actes du patriarcat de Constantinople. Vol. I, Les actes des patriarches, fasc. 4: Les regestes de 1208 à 1309, par Vitalien Laurent. Paris: Institut français d'études byzantines, 1971. *Fasc. 5: Les regestes de 1310 à 1376,* par Jean Darrouzès. Paris: Institut français d'études byzantines, 1977.

Ross, E. Denison. "The Early Years of Shah Isma'il, Founder of the Safavi Dynasty." *Journal of the Royal Asiatic Society* (1896), pp. 249-340.

Ruhi. *Ottoman Chronicle.* Berlin, Staatsbibliothek, MS Or. Qu. 821.

Şahin, Sencer. *Katalog der antiken Inschriften des Museums von Iznik (Nikaia).* Bonn: Habelt, 1979. Inschriften griechischer Städte aus Kleinasien, no. 9.

Scutariotes, Theodore. In George Acropolites, *Opera*. Edited by August Heisenberg. 2 vols. Leipzig: Teubner, 1903.

Seif, Theodor. "Der Abschnitt über die Osmanen in Sükrüllah's persischer Universalgeschichte." *Mitteilungen zur Osmanischen Geschichte* 2 (1923-26), pp. 63-128.

Şikari. *Şikari'nin Karaman oğulları tarihi.* Edited by M. Ferid Uğur and M. Mesud Koman. Konya: Yeni kitab basımevi, 1946.

Süreyya. Mehmed. *Sicill-i osmani.* 4 vols. Reprint of Istanbul, 1308-15 edition. Westmead: Gregg, 1971.

Tadhkirat al-Muluk, a Manual of Safavid Administration. Translated by Vladimir Minorsky. London: Luzac, 1943. E.J.W. Gibb Memorial Series, new series no. 16.

Tekin, Talat. *A Grammar of Orkhon Turkic.* Bloomington: Indiana University, 1968. Indiana University Publications, Uralic and Altaic Series, no. 69.

Tuncer, Hadiye. *Osmanlı devleti arazi kanunları.* Ankara: Resimli posta matbaası, 1962. Tarım bakanlığı, mesleki mevzuat serisi, H-7.

———. *Osmanlı imparatorluğunda toprak hukuku, arazi kanunları ve kanun açıklamaları.* Ankara: Gürsoy basımevi, 1962. Tarım bakanlığı, mesleki mevzuat serisi, H-5.

———. *Osmanlı imparatorluğunda toprak kanunları.* Ankara: Güneş matbaacılık, 1965. Tarım bakanlığı, mesleki mevzuat serisi, H-9.

Tursun Bey. *The History of Mehmed the Conqueror by Tursun Beg.* Published by Halil Inalcik and Rhoads Murphey. Minneapolis and Chicago: Bibliotheca Islamica, 1978.

Tveritinova, Anna S. *Kniga zakonov sultana Selim I.* Moscow: Nauka, 1969.

al-Umari. *Al-Umari's Bericht über Kleinasien.* Edited by Franz Taeschner. Leipzig: Harrassowitz, 1929.

Uzunçarşılı, Ismail Hakkı. "Gazi Orhan Bey vakfiyesi." *Belleten* 5 (1941), pp. 277-88.

Yunus Emre. *Risalat al-nushiyya ve divan.* Edited by Abdülbaki Gölpinarlı. Istanbul: Metin, 1965.

B. Studies

Afşin, Zeki, *Konyanın iktisadi bünyesine bir bakış.* Istanbul: Hüsnütabiat basımevi, 1940.

Ahrweiler, Hélène. "Choma-Aggélokastron." *Revue des études byzantines* 24 (1966), pp. 278-83.

———. "L'épitéleia dans le cartulaire de la Lembiotissa." *Byzantion* 24 (1954), pp. 71-93.

———. "L'expérience nicéenne." *Dumbarton Oaks Papers* 29 (1975), pp. 21-40.

———. "Les forteresses construites en Asie Mineure face à l'invasion Seldjoucide." In *Akten des XI. internationalen Byzantinistenkongresses, München, 1958,* pp. 182-89. Munich: Beck, 1960.

———. "L'histoire et la géographie de la région de Smyrne entre les deux occupations turques (1081-1317), particulièrement au XIIIe siècle." *Travaux et mémoires* 1 (1965), pp. 1-204.

———. "La politique agraire des empereurs de Nicée." *Byzantion* 28 (1958), pp. 51-66.

———. "A propos de l'épitéleia." *Byzantion* 25-26 (1955-57), pp. 369-72.

Alderson, Anthony D. *The Structure of the Ottoman Dynasty.* Oxford: Oxford University Press, 1956.

Anderson, J.G.C. "Exploration in Asia Minor during 1898: First Report." *Annual of the British School at Athens* 4 (1897-98), pp. 49-78.

Andrae, Tor. *Mohammed, the Man and His Faith.* New York: Scribner's, 1936.

Angold, Michael. *A Byzantine Government in Exile: Government and Society under the Laskarids of Nicaea (1204-1261).* Oxford: Oxford University Press, 1974.

Anhegger, Robert. "Martoloslar hakkında." *Türkiyat mecmuası* 7-8 (1940-42), pp. 282-320.

Ardant, Gabriel. *Histoire de l'impot.* 2 vols. Paris: Fayard, 1971.

Arnakis, George G. "Byzantium's Anatolian Provinces during the Reign of Michael Palaeologus." In *Actes du XIIe congrès international d'études byzantines, Ochrid 1961,* pp. 37-44. Vol. 2. Belgrade: Naucno delo, 1964.

______. *Hoi protoi Othomanoi.* Athens: Frandjeskakis, 1947. Texte und Forschungen zur byzantinisch-neugriechischen Philologie, no. 41.

Asım, Necib. Articles on Şikari in *Ikdam* [Istanbul], nos. 8842, 8860, 8885 (1921).

Aslanapa, Oktay, ed. *Yüzyıllar boyunca Türk sanatı: ondördüncü yüzyıl.* Istanbul: Milli eğitim bakanlığı, 1977.

Babinger, Franz. *Die Geschichtsschreiber der Osmanen und ihre Werke.* Leipzig: Harrassowitz, 1927.

Bakirer, Ömür, and Suraiya Faroqhi. "Dediği Dede ve tekkeleri." *Belleten* 39 (1975), pp. 447-71.

Barth, Fredrik. "Capital, Investment and the Social Structure of a Pastoral Nomad Group in South Persia." In Raymond W. Firth and B.S. Yamey, eds., *Capital, Savings and Credit in Peasant Societies,* pp. 69-81. Chicago: Aldine, 1964.

______, ed. *Ethnic Groups and Boundaries.* Oslo: Universitetsforlaget, 1969.

______. *Nomads of South Persia.* Oslo: Oslo University Press, 1961.

Bartol'd, Vasilii Vladimirovich. *Turkestan Down to the Mongol Invasion.* 3rd ed. London: Luzac, 1968. E.J.W. Gibb Memorial Series, new series, no. 5.

Bates, Daniel G. "Differential Access to Pasture in a Nomadic Society: the Yörük of Southeastern Turkey." In William Irons and Neville Dyson-Hudson, eds. *Perspectives on Nomadism,* pp. 48-59. Leiden; E.J. Brill, 1972.

______. *Nomads and Farmers: a Study of the Yörük of Southeastern Turkey.* Ann Arbor: Museum of Anthropology, 1973. University of Michigan Museum of Anthropology, Anthropological Papers, no. 52.

______. "The Role of the State in Peasant-Nomad Mutualism." *Anthropological Quarterly* 44 (1971), pp. 109-31.

______. "Shepherd Becomes Farmer." In Peter Benedict, Erol Tümertekin, and Fatma Mansur, eds., *Turkey, Geographical and Social Perspectives,* pp. 92-133. Leiden: E.J. Brill, 1974.

Bawden, C.R. *The Modern History of Mongolia.* New York: Praeger, 1968.

Beck, Lois. "Herd Owners and Hired Shepherds: the Qashqa'i of Iran." *Ethnology* 19 (1980), pp. 327-51.

Beldiceanu, Nicoara. "A propos du code coutumier de Mehmed II et de l'oeuvre juridique d'Ahmed Hersekzade." *Revue des études islamiques* 38 (1970), pp. 163-72.

______. "A propos d'un livre sur les lois pénales ottomanes." *Journal of the Economic and Social History of the Orient* 17 (1974), pp. 206-14.

______. *Le timar dans l'état ottoman.* Wiesbaden: Harrassowitz, 1980.

Beldiceanu-Steinherr, Irène. "La conquête d'Andrinople par les Turcs: la pénétration turque en Thrace et la valeur des chroniques ottomanes." *Travaux et mémoires* 1 (1965), pp. 439-61.

______. "En marge d'un acte concernant le penğyek et les aqınğı." *Revue des études islamiques* 37 (1969), pp. 21-47.

______. *Recherches sur les actes des règnes des sultans Osman, Orkhan et Murad I.* Munich: Societatea academica romana, 1967. Acta historica, no. 7.

______. "Le règne de Selim Ier: tournant dans la vie politique et réligieuse de l'empire ottoman." *Turcica* 6 (1975), pp. 34-48.

______. "Un transfuge qaramanide auprès de la porte ottomane." *Journal of the Economic and Social History of the Orient* 16 (1973), pp. 155-67.

Beldiceanu-Steinherr, Irène, and Nicoara Beldiceanu. "Deux villes de l'Anatolie préottomane: Develi et Qarahisar d'après des documents inédits." *Revue des études islamiques* 39 (1971), pp. 337-95.

______. "Reglement ottoman concernant le recensement (première moitié du XVIe siècle)." *Südostforschungen* 37 (1978), pp. 1-40.

Bilecik il yıllığı, 1967. Istanbul: Son telgraf matbaası, 1968.

Björkman, Walther. "Die klassisch-osmanische Literatur." In Pertev Naili Boratav, ed., *Philologiae Turcicae Fundamenta,* vol. 2, pp. 427-65. Wiesbaden: Franz Steiner, 1964.

Bombaci, Alessio. "The Army of the Saljuqs of Rum." *Istituto orientale di Napoli, Annali* 38 (1978), pp. 343-69.

Bosworth, Clifford Edmund. *The Ghaznavids.* Edinburgh: Edinburgh University Press, 1963.

Bowen, Don R. "Guerilla War in Western Missouri, 1862-1865: Historical Extensions of the Relative Deprivation Hypothesis." *Comparative Studies in Society and History* 19 (1977), pp. 30-51.

Bradburd, Daniel A. "Never Give a Shepherd an Even Break: Class and Labor among the Komachi." *American Ethnologist* 7 (1980), pp. 603-20.

Brosse, Marii Ivanovich. *Histoire de la Géorgie.* 5 vols. St. Petersburg: Imprimerie de l'Académie impériale des sciences, 1849-58.

Broughton, T.R.S. "Roman Asia." In Tenney Frank, ed., *An Economic Survey of Ancient Rome,* vol. 4, pp. 499-918. Baltimore: Johns Hopkins University Press, 1938.

Bryer, Anthony. "A Byzantine Family: the Gabrades, c. 979-c. 1653." *University of Birmingham Historical Journal* 12 (1970), pp. 164-87.

———. "Cultural Relations between East and West in the Twelfth Century." In Derek Baker, ed., *Relations between East and West in the Middle Ages,* pp. 77-94. Edinburgh: Edinburgh University Press, 1973.

Buchwald, Hans. "Lascarid Architecture." *Jahrbuch der Österreichischen Byzantinistik* 28 (1979), pp. 261-96.

Cahen, Claude. "Notes pour l'histoire des turcomans d'Asie Mineure au XIIIe siècle." *Journal asiatique* 239 (1951), pp. 335-54.

———. *Pre-Ottoman Turkey.* London: Sidgwick and Jackson, 1968.

———. "Quelques mots sur Şikari." *Wiener Zeitschrift für die Kunde des Morgenlandes* 70 (1978), pp. 53-64.

Çetintürk, Salahaddin. "Osmanlı imparatorluğunda yürük sınıfı ve hukuki statüleri." *Ankara üniversitesi dil ve tarih-coğrafya fakültesi dergisi* 2 (1943-44), pp. 107-16.

Chapman, Conrad. *Michel Paléologue, restaurateur de l'empire byzantin (1261-1282).* Paris: E. Figuière, 1926.

Charanis, Peter. "A Note on the Population and Cities of the Byzantine Empire in the Thirteenth Century." *The Joshua Starr Memorial Volume,* pp. 135-48. New York: Conference on Jewish Relations, 1953. Jewish Social Studies, Publications, no. 5.

Cohen, Amnon, and Bernard Lewis. *Population and Revenue in the Towns of Palestine in the Sixteenth Century.* Princeton: Princeton University Press, 1978.

Cook, Michael. *Population Pressure in Rural Anatolia, 1450-1600.* Oxford: Oxford University Press, 1972.

David, Geza. "The Age of the Unmarried Male Children in the Tahrir-Defters (Notes on the Coefficient)." *Acta orientalia* 31 (1977), pp. 347-57.

Dernburg, Friedrich. *Auf deutscher Bahn in Kleinasien.* Berlin: Julius Springer, 1892.

Dewdney, John C. *Turkey.* London: Chatto and Windus, 1971.

Diez, Ernst; Oktay Aslanapa, and Mesud Koman. *Karaman devri sanatı.* Istanbul: Doğan kardeş yayınları, 1950. Istanbul üniversitesi, sanat tarihi enstitüsü yayınları, no. 7.

Dilger, Konrad. *Untersuchungen zur Geschichte des Osmanischen Hofzeremoniells im 15. und 16. Jahrhundert.* Munich: Trofenik, 1967. Beiträge zur Kenntnis Südosteuropas und des Nahen Orients, no. 4.

Dyson-Hudson, Neville. "The Study of Nomads." In William Irons and Neville Dyson-Hudson, eds., *Perspectives on Nomadism,* pp. 2-29. Leiden: E.J. Brill, 1972.

Dyson-Hudson, Rada, and Neville. "Nomadic Pastoralism." *Annual Review of Anthropology* 9 (1980), pp. 15-61.

Edhem, Halil. "Karaman oğulları hakkında vesaik-i mahkuke." *Tarih-i osmani encümeni mecmuası* 2:11 (1327), pp. 697-712, 12 (1327), pp. 741-60, 3:13 (1328), pp. 821-36, 14 (1328), pp. 873-81.

Efendiev, Oktaj. "Le role des tribus de langue turque dans la création de l'état safavide." *Turcica* 6 (1975), pp. 24-33.

Ehmann, Dieter. *Bahtiyaren, Persische Bergnomaden im Wandel der Zeit.* Wiesbaden: Reichert, 1975.

Emiri, Ali. Letter on Şikari. *Ikdam* [Istanbul], no. 8876 (1 December 1921).

Erder, Leila. "The Measurement of Preindustrial Population Changes: the Ottoman Empire from the 15th to the 17th Century." *Middle Eastern Studies* 11 (1975), pp. 284-301.

Erdoğan, Muzaffer. *Izahlı Konya bibliyografyası.* Istanbul: Anıl matbaası, 1952.

Erinç, Sırrı, and N. Tunçdilek. "The Agricultural Regions of Turkey." *Geographical Review* 42 (1952), pp. 179-203.

Ettinghausen, Richard. "Arabic Epigraphy: Communication or Symbolic Affirmation." In Dickran K. Kouymjian, ed., *Near Eastern Numismatics, Iconography, Epigraphy and History: Studies in Honor of George C. Miles,* pp. 297-317. Beirut: American University of Beirut Press, 1974.

Evans-Pritchard, E.E. *The Nuer.* Oxford: Clarendon Press, 1940.

______. *The Sanusi of Cyrenaica.* Oxford: Oxford University Press, 1949.

Eyice, Semavi. "Iznikde bir Bizans kilisesi." *Belleten* 13 (1949), pp. 37-51.

Failler, Albert. "Chronologie et composition dans l'histoire de Georges Pachymère." *Revue des études byzantines* 39 (1981), pp. 145-249.

Fisher, Elizabeth. "A Note on Pachymeres' 'De Andronico Palaeologo'." *Byzantion* 40 (1971), pp. 230-35.

Flemming, Barbara. *Türkische Handschriften.* Vol. 1. Wiesbaden: Franz Steiner, 1968. Verzeichnis der orientalischen Handschriften in Deutschland, no. 13.

Fletcher, Joseph, Jr. "Turco-Mongolian Monarchic Tradition in the Ottoman Empire." *Harvard Ukrainian Studies* 3-4 (1979-80), pp. 236-51.

Forrer, Ludwig. "Handschriften Osmanischer Historiker in Istanbul." *Der Islam* 26 (1942), pp. 173-220.

Fortes, Meyer, and E.E. Evans-Pritchard, eds. *African Political Systems.* London: Oxford University Press, 1940.

Foss, Clive. "Archaeology and the Twenty Cities of Byzantine Asia." *American Journal of Archaeology* 81 (1977), pp. 469-86.

______. *Byzantine and Turkish Sardis.* Cambridge: Harvard University Press, 1976.

______. *Ephesus after Antiquity.* Cambridge: Cambridge University Press, 1979.

Frances, E. "La féodalité byzantine et la conquête turque." *Studia et acta orientalia* 4 (1962), pp. 69-90.

Fraşeri, Şemseddin Sami. *Kamus al-alam.* 6 vols. Istanbul: Mihran, 1889-98.

Freilich, Dr., and "Mühendis" Rawlig. *Türkmen aşiretleri.* Istanbul: Kütüphane-i Sevdi, 1334. Aşair ve muhacirin müdüriyet-i umumiyesi neşriyatı, no. 2.

Geanakoplos, Deno J. *The Emperor Michael Palaeologus and the West, 1258-1282.* Cambridge: Harvard University Press, 1959.

Gibb, H.A.R., and Harold Bowen. *Islamic Society and the West.* 2 vols. Oxford: Oxford University Press, 1950.

Giese, Friedrich. *Materialien zur Kenntnis des anatolischen Turkisch, Teil I, Erzählungen und Lieder aus dem Vilajet Qonjah.* Halle: Rudolf Haupt, 1907. Beiträge zum Studien der türkischen Sprache und Literatur, no. 1.

Glassen, Erika. *Die frühen Safawiden nach Qazi Ahmad Qumi.* Freiburg: Klaus Schwarz Verlag, 1970. Islamkundliche Untersuchungen, no. 5.

______. "Schah Isma'il, ein Mahdi der anatolischen Turkmenen?" *Zeitschrift der Deutschen Morgenländischen Gesellschaft* 121 (1971), pp. 61-69.

Gökbilgin, M. Tayyib. *Rumeli'de yürükler, tatarlar ve evlad-ı fatihan.* Istanbul: Osman Yalçın matbaası, 1957. Istanbul üniversitesi, edebiyat fakültesi yayınları, no. 748.

Golf, Richard Arthur. *Die Karakulzucht in ihrem Heimatlande Turkestan.* Berlin: P. Parey, 1933.

Gordon, C.D. *The Age of Attila.* Ann Arbor: University of Michigan Press, 1960.

Göyünç, Nejat. *XVI. yüzyılda Mardin sancağı.* Istanbul: Edebiyat fakültesi basımevi, 1969. Istanbul üniversitesi, edebiyat fakültesi yayınları, no. 1458.

Güngör, Kemal. *Cenubi Anadolu yürüklerinin etno-antropolojik tetkiki.* Ankara: Ideal basımevi, 1941.

Hamilton, William John. *Researches in Asia Minor, Pontus, and Armenia.* 2 vols. London: John Murray, 1842.

Hammer-Purgstall, Joseph von. *Geschichte des Osmanischen Reiches.* Vols. 1-2. Pest: Hartleben, 1827-28.

Hasluck, Frederick William. "Bithynica." *Annual of the British School at Athens* 13 (1906-07), pp. 285-308.

Hendy, Michael F. *Coinage and Money in the Byzantine Empire, 1081-1261.* Washington, D.C.: Dumbarton Oaks, 1969. Dumbarton Oaks Studies, no. 12.

Heyd, Uriel. *Studies in Old Ottoman Criminal Law.* Edited by Victor L. Ménage. Oxford: Clarendon Press, 1973.

Hinz, Walther. "Steuerinschriften aus dem mittelalterlichen Vorderen Orient." *Belleten* 13 (1949), pp. 745-93.

———. "Das Steuerwesen Ostanatoliens im 15. und 16. Jahrhundert." *Zeitschrift der Deutschen Morgenländischen Gesellschaft* 100 (1950), pp. 177-201.

Hjort, Anders, and Gudrun Dahl. *Having Herds.* Stockholm: University of Stockholm, Department of Social Anthropology, 1976.

Hodgson, Marshall G.S. *The Venture of Islam.* 3 vols. Chicago: University of Chicago Press, 1974.

Hogarth, David G. *A Wandering Scholar in the Levant.* London: John Murray, 1896.

Horn, V. "Weideverhältnisse in den Gebieten Vorderasiens." In R. Knapp, ed., *Weide-Wirtschaft in Trockengebieten,* pp. 99-113. Stuttgart: Gustav Fischer, 1965. Giessener Beiträge zur Entwicklungsforschung, 1:1.

Huart, Clement. "Les origines de l'empire ottoman." *Journal des savants* (1917), pp. 157-66.

Hütteroth, Wolf-Dieter. *Bergnomaden und Yaylabauern im mittleren kurdischen Taurus.* Marburg: Selbstverlag des Geographischen Instituts der Universität, 1959. Marburger geographische Schriften, no. 11.

———. *Ländliche Siedlungen im südlichen Inneranatolien in den letzten vierhundert Jahren.* Göttingen: Selbstverlag des Geographischen Instituts der Universität, 1968. Göttinger geographische Abhandlungen, no. 46.

Hütteroth, Wolf-Dieter, and Kamal Abdulfattah. *Historical Geography of Palestine, Transjordan and Southern Syria in the Late Sixteenth Century.* Erlangen: Selbstverlag der Fränkischen geographischen Gesellschaft, 1977. Erlanger geographische Arbeiten, Sonderband 5.

Huntington, Hillard G. "The Rate of Return from the Basseri's Livestock Investment." *Man* 7 (1972), pp. 476-79.

Inalcik, Halil. "Bursa and the Commerce of the Levant." *Journal of the Economic and Social History of the Orient* 3 (1960), pp. 131-47.

———. "L'empire ottoman." *Actes du premier congrès international des études balkaniques et sud-est européennes, Sofia, 1966,* vol. 3, pp. 75-103. Sofia: Editions de l'Académie bulgare des sciences, 1969.

———. *Fatih devri üzerinde tetkikler ve vesikalar.* Ankara: Türk tarih kurumu, 1954.

———. "Osmanlı hukukuna giriş." *Ankara üniversitesi siyasal bilgiler fakültesi dergisi* 13 (1958), pp. 102-26.

———. "Osmanlılarda raiyyet rüsumu." *Belleten* 23 (1959), pp. 575-610.

———. "The Rise of Ottoman Historiography." In Bernard Lewis and P.M. Holt, eds., *Historians of the Middle East,* pp. 152-67. London: Oxford University Press, 1962.

______. "Suleiman the Lawgiver and Ottoman Law." *Archivum Ottomanicum* 1 (1969), pp. 105-38.

Irons, William. "Variation in Political Stratification among the Yomut Turkmen." *Anthropological Quarterly* 44 (1971), pp. 143-56.

______. "Variations in Economic Organization: a Comparison of the Pastoral Yomut and the Basseri." In William Irons and Neville Dyson-Hudson, eds., *Perspectives on Nomadism*, pp. 88-104. Leiden: E.J. Brill, 1972.

______. *The Yomut Turkmen*. Ann Arbor: Museum of Anthropology, 1975. University of Michigan Museum of Anthropology, Anthropological Papers, no. 58.

Istanbul kütüpaneleri tarih-coğrafya yazmaları katalogları. 11 fascs. Istanbul: Maarif matbaası, 1943-62.

Izbırak, Reşat. *Develi ovası ve ekonomik gelişmesi*. Ankara: Türk tarih kurumu basımevi, 1953. Ankara üniversitesi, dil ve tarih-coğrafya fakültesi yayınları, no. 91.

Janin, Raymond. "La Bithynie sous l'empire byzantin." *Echos d'orient* 20 (1921), pp. 168-82, pp. 301-19.

______. "Nicée, étude historique et topographique." *Echos d'orient* 24 (1925), pp. 482-90.

Jung, L. "Böden der Trockengebiete." In R. Knapp, ed., *Weide-Wirtschaft in Trockengebiete*, pp. 51-59. Stuttgart: Gustav Fischer, 1965. Giessener Beiträge zur Entwicklungsforschung, 1:1.

Kaldy-Nagy, Gyula. "Rural and Urban Life in the Age of Sultan Suleiman." *Acta orientalia* 32 (1978), pp. 285-319.

Kappert, Petra. *Die osmanischen Prinzen und ihre Residenz Amasya im 15. und 16. Jahrhundert*. Istanbul: Nederlands Historisch-Archaeologisch Instituut, 1976. Nederlands Historisch-Archaeologisch Instituut Uitgaven, no. 42.

Kinneir, John Macdonald. *Journey through Asia Minor, Armenia, and Koordistan, in the Years 1813 and 1814*. London: John Murray, 1818.

Konyalı, Ibrahim Hakkı. *Abideleri ve kitabeleri ile Karaman tarihi*. Istanbul: Baha matbaası, 1967.

______. *Abideleri ve kitabeleri ile Konya tarihi*. Konya: Yeni kitab basımevi, 1964.

______. *Abideleri ve kitabeleri ile Konya Ereğlisi tarihi*. Istanbul: Fatih matbaası, 1970.

______. *Abideleri ve kitabeleri ile Niğde Aksaray tarihi*. 3 vols. Istanbul: Fatih yayınevi, 1974.

______. *Abideleri ve kitabeleri ile Şerefli Koçhisar tarihi*. Istanbul: Fatih matbaası, 1971.

______. *Nasreddin Hocanın şehri Akşehir*. Istanbul: Nümune matbaası, 1945.

Köprülü, Fuad. "Anadolu beylikleri tarihine ait notlar." *Türkiyat mecmuası* 2 (1927), pp. 1-32.

______. "Anadolu Selçukluları tarihinin yerli kaynakları." *Belleten* 7 (1943), pp. 379-521.

______. *Les origines de l'empire ottoman*. Paris: E. de Boccard, 1935. Etudes orientales, no. 3.

______. "Osmanlı imparatorluğu'nun etnik menşei meselesi." *Belleten* 7 (1943), pp. 219-313.

Koşay, Hamit Z. "Türkiye halkının maddi kültürüne dair araştırmalar, III, hayvancılık." *Türk etnografya dergisi* 3 (1958), pp. 5-59.

Laiou, Angeliki E. *Constantinople and the Latins: the Foreign Policy of Andronicus II, 1282-1326*. Cambridge: Harvard University Press, 1972.

______. *Peasant Society in the Late Byzantine Empire*. Princeton: Princeton University Press, 1977.

______. "The Provisioning of Constantinople during the Winter of 1306-1307." *Byzantion* 37 (1967), pp. 91-113.

______. "Some Observations on Alexios Philanthropenos and Maximos Planoudes." *Byzantine and Modern Greek Studies* 4 (1978), pp. 89-99.

Langer, William. L., and Robert P. Blake. "The Rise of the Otoman Turks and Its Historical Background." *American Historical Review* 37 (1932), pp. 468-505.

Lattimore, Owen. *Studies in Frontier History*. Oxford: Oxford University Press, 1962.

Laurent, Vitalien. "La chronique anonyme cod. Mosquensis gr. 426 et la pénétration turque en Bithynie au début du XIVe siècle." *Revue des études byzantines* 7 (1949), pp. 207-12.

Lennep, Henry J. Van. *Travels in Little-Known Parts of Asia Minor*. 2 vols. London: John Murray, 1870.

Levend, Agah Sırrı. *Türk dilinde gelişme ve sadeleşme evreleri.* Ankara: Türk dil kurumu, 1972.
Lindner, Rudi Paul. "Nomadism, Horses and Huns." *Past and Present* no. 92 (1981), pp. 3-19.
McCarthy, Justin. "Age, Family, and Migration in Nineteenth-Century Black Sea Provinces of the Ottoman Empire." *International Journal of Middle East Studies* 10 (1979), pp. 309-23.
Mellaart, James. "Some Prehistoric Sites in North-Western Anatolia." *Istanbuler Mitteilungen* 6 (1955), pp. 53-88.
Ménage, Victor L. "The Menaqib of Yakhshi Faqih." *Bulletin of the School of Oriental and African Studies* 26 (1963), pp. 50-54.
———. *Neshri's History of the Ottomans.* London: Oxford University Press, 1964.
———. "On the Recensions of Uruj's 'History of the Ottomans'." *Bulletin of the School of Oriental and African Studies* 30 (1967), pp. 314-22.
———. Review of N. Beldiceanu's *Code de lois coutumières. Bulletin of the School of Oriental and African Studies* 32 (1969), pp. 165-67.
———. *A Survey of the Early Ottoman Histories, with Studies on Their Textual Problems and Their Sources.* 2 vols. London: dissertation, 1961.
Minorsky, Vladimir. *Persia in A.D. 1478-1490.* London: Luzac, 1957. Royal Asiatic Society Monographs, no. 26.
Miroğlu, Ismet. *XVI. yüzyılda Bayburt sancağı.* Istanbul: Üçler matbaası, 1975.
Moravcsik, Gyula. *Byzantinoturcica.* 2nd ed. 2 vols. Berlin: Akademie Verlag, 1958. Berliner byzantinistische Arbeiten, nos. 10-11.
Namık, Hüseyin. "Histoire des Karamanides." *Körösi Csoma Archiv* 1 (1921-25), pp. 415-17.
Oral, M. Zeki. "Turgut oğulları." In *IV. Türk tarih kongresi,* pp. 140-158. Ankara: Türk tarih kurumu, 1952.
———. "Turgut oğulları, eserleri-vakfiyeleri." *Vakıflar dergisi* 3 (1956), pp. 31-64.
Orhonlu, Cengiz. *Osmanlı imparatorluğunda aşiretleri iskan teşebbüsü (1691-1696).* Istanbul: Edebiyat fakültesi basımevi, 1963. Istanbul üniversitesi, edebiyat fakültesi yayınları, no. 998.
Öztelli, Cahit. "Yunus Emre ve Şikari tarihi." *Türk dili* 165 (1965), pp. 618-21.
Pastner, Stephen. "Ideological Aspects of Nomad-Sedentary Contact: a Case from Southern Baluchistan." *Anthropological Quarterly* 44 (1971), pp. 173-84.
Pehrson, Robert N. *The Social Organization of the Marri Baluch.* Chicago: Aldine, 1966.
Philippides-Braat, Anna. "La captivité de Palamas chez les Turcs: dossier et commentaire." *Travaux et mémoires* 7 (1979), pp. 109-22.
Planhol. Xavier de. "Geography, Politics and Nomadism in Anatolia." *International Social Science Journal* 11 (1959), pp. 525-31.
Riza, Kazim. *Die türkische Landwirtschaft und ihre wichtigsten Betriebszweige.* Leipzig: dissertation, 1935.
Robert, Louis, *Hellenica.* Vol. 13. Paris: Maisonneuve, 1965.
———. "Un voyage d'Antiphilos de Byzance." *Journal des savants* (1979), pp. 257-94.
Roux, Jean-Paul. *Les traditions des nomades de la Turquie méridionale.* Paris: Maisonneuve, 1970. Bibliothèque archéologique et historique de l'Institut français d'archéologie d'Istanbul, no. 24.
Sahlins, Marshall D. *Tribesmen.* Englewood Cliffs, N.J.: Prentice-Hall, 1968.
Salzman, Philip Carl. "The Proto-State in Iranian Baluchistan." In Ronald Cohen and Elman R. Service, eds., *Origins of the State,* pp. 125-40. Philadelphia: ISHI Press, 1978.
Sanır, Ferruh. *Sultan Dağlarından Sakarya'ya.* Ankara: Ulus basımevi, 1948.
Sawyer, Peter H., and Ian N. Wood, eds. *Early Medieval Kingship.* Leeds: University of Leeds School of History, 1977.
Schneider, Alfons Maria. *Die römischen und byzantinischen Denkmäler von Iznik-Nicaea.* Berlin. Deutsches archäologisches Institut, 1943. Istanbuler Forschungen, no. 16.
Schneider, Alfons Maria, and Walter Karnapp. *Die Stadtmauer von Iznik (Nicaea).* Berlin: Deutsches archäologisches Institut, 1938. Istanbuler Forschungen, no. 9.

Schreiner, Peter. "Zur Geschichte Philadelpheias im 14. Jahrhundert (1293-1390)." *Orientalia christiana periodica* 35 (1969), pp. 375-431

______. *Studien zu den Brachea Chronika.* Munich: Institut für Byzantinistik und neugriechische Philologie der Universität, 1967. Miscellanea byzantina monacensia, no. 6.

Scott-Stevenson, Mary Esme Gwendoline Grogan. *Our Ride through Asia Minor.* London: Chapman and Hall, 1881.

Shinder, Joel. "Early Ottoman Administration in the Wilderness: Some Limits of Comparison." *International Journal of Middle East Studies* 9 (1978), pp. 497-517.

Slicher van Bath, Bernard Hendrik. *The Agrarian History of Western Europe A.D. 500-1850.* London: Edward Arnold, 1963.

Smith, John Masson, Jr. "Mongol and Nomadic Taxation." *Harvard Journal of Asiatic Studies* 30 (1970), pp. 46-85.

______. "Mongol Manpower and Persian Population." *Journal of the Economic and Social History of the Orient* 18 (1975), pp. 271-99.

______. "Turanian Nomadism and Iranian Politics." *Iranian Studies* 11 (1978), pp. 57-81.

Sohrweide, Hanna. "Der Sieg der Safaviden in Persien und seine Rückwirkungen auf die Schiiten Anatoliens im 16. Jahrhundert." *Der Islam* 41 (1965), pp. 95-223.

Sölch, J. "Historisch-geographische Studien über bithynische Siedlungen: Nikomedia, Nikaea, Prusa." *Byzantinische-neugriechische Jahrbücher* 1 (1920), pp. 263-337.

Spooner, Brian. *The Cultural Ecology of Pastoral Nomads.* Reading: Addison-Wesley, 1973.

Spuler, Bertold. *Die Mongolen in Iran.* 3rd ed. Berlin: Akademie Verlag, 1968.

Stotz, Carl L. "The Bursa Region of Turkey." *Geographical Review* 29 (1939), pp. 81-100.

Strzygowski, Josef. *Kleinasien, ein Neuland der Kunstgeschichte.* Leipzig: Hinrichs, 1903.

Sümer, Faruk. "Çukur-Ova tarihine dair araştırmalar." *Tarih araştırmaları dergisi* 1 (1963), pp. 1-108.

______. *Oguzlar,* Ankara: Ankara üniversitesi basımevi, 1967. Ankara üniversitesi, dil ve tarih-coğrafya fakültesi yayınları, no. 170.

______. "Osmanlı devrinde Anadolu'da Kayılar." *Belleten* 12 (1948), pp. 575-615.

Swidler, Nina. "The Development of the Kalat Khanate." In William Irons and Neville Dyson-Hudson, eds., *Perspectives on Nomadism,* pp. 115-21. Leiden: E.J. Brill, 1972.

______. "The Political Context of Brahui Sedentarization." *Ethnology* 12 (1973), pp. 299-314.

Swidler, W.W. "Adaptive Processes Regulating Nomad-Sedentary Interaction in the Middle East." In Cynthia Nelson, ed., *The Desert and the Sown: Nomads in the Wider Society,* pp. 23-41. Berkeley: University of California Institute of International Studies, 1973. University of California Institute of International Studies, Research Series, no. 21.

Sykoutres, I. "Peri to schisma ton arseniaton." *Hellenika* 2 (1929), pp. 267-332, 3 (1930), pp. 15-44.

Taeschner, Franz. "Anatolische Forschungen." *Zeitschrift der Deutschen Morgenländischen Gesellschaft* 82 (1928), pp. 83-118.

______. "Beiträge zur frühosmanischen Epigraphik und Archäologie." *Der Islam* 20 (1932), pp. 109-86, 22 (1935), pp. 69-73.

Tansel, Selahattin. *Sultan II. Bayezit'in siyasi hayatı.* Istanbul: Milli eğitim basımevi, 1966.

Tekindağ, M.C. Şehabeddin. "II. Bayezid devrinde Çukur-Ova'da nüfuz mücadelesi." *Belleten* 31 (1967), pp. 345-73.

______. "Son Osmanlı-Karaman münasebetleri hakkında araştırmalar." *Tarih dergisi* 17-18 (1962-63), pp. 43-76.

Thierry, Nicole. "L'art monumental byzantin en Asie Mineure du XIe siècle au XIVe." *Dumbarton Oaks Papers* 29 (1975), pp. 73-111.

Tinnefeld, Franz. "Pachymeres und Philes als Zeugen für ein frühes Unternehmen gegen die Osmanen." *Byzantinische Zeitschrift* 64 (1971), pp. 46-54.

Tomaschek, Wilhelm. "Zur historischen Topographie von Kleinasien im Mittelalter." Akademie der Wissenschaften, Wien. Philosophisch-historische Classe, *Sitzungsberichten,* 124:8 (1891).

Treu, M. "Manuel Holobolos." *Byzantinische Zeitschrift* 5 (1896), pp. 538-59.

Troitskij, I.E. *Arsenij i arsenity.* Reprint edition. London: Variorum, 1973.

Tsakyroglou, Michael G. *Peri giouroukon, ethnologike melete.* Athens: n.p., 1891.

Turan, Osman. *Selçuklular zamanında Türkiye.* Istanbul: Istanbul matbaası, 1971.

Turan, Şerafettin. *Kanuni'nin oğlu Şehzade Bayezid vak'ası.* Ankara: Türk tarih kurumu basımevi, 1961. Ankara üniversitesi, dil ve tarih-coğrafya fakültesi yayınları, no. 80.

Üçer, Sırrı, and M. Mesud koman. *Konya ili köy ve yer adları üzerinde bir deneme.* Konya: Yeni kitab basımevi, 1945.

Ünver, A. Süheyl. "Eski Mısırda, Islam dünyasında ve bizde tahnit maddeleri hakkında." In *Fuad Köprülü armağanı,* pp. 581-87. Istanbul: Osman Yalçın matbaası, 1953.

Uzunçarşılı, Ismail Hakkı. *Osmanlı devleti teşkilatına medhal.* Ankara: Türk tarih kurumu, 1941.

———. *Osmanlı tarihi.* Vol. 2. Ankara: Türk tarih kurumu, 1964.

Vita-Finzi, Claudio. *Archaeological Sites in Their Setting.* London: Thames and Hudson, 1978.

Vreeland, Herbert Harold. *Mongol Community and Kinship Structure.* 2nd ed. New Haven: Human Relations Area Files, 1957.

Vryonis, Speros, Jr. "The Byzantine Legacy and Ottoman Forms." *Dumbarton Oaks Papers* 23-24 (1969-70), pp. 251-308.

———. *The Decline of Medieval Hellenism in Asia Minor and the Process of Islamization from the Eleventh through the Fifteenth Century.* Berkeley: University of California Press, 1971.

———. "Evidence on Human Sacrifice among the Early Ottoman Turks." *Journal of Asian History* 5 (1971), pp. 140-46.

Waechter, Albert. *Der Verfall des Griechentums in Kleinasien im XIV. Jahrhundert.* Leipzig: Teubner, 1902.

Wallace-Hadrill, J.M. *Early Germanic Kingship in England and on the Continent.* Oxford: Oxford University Press, 1971.

Watt, W. Montgomery. "Islamic Conceptions of the Holy War." In Thomas Patrick Murphy, ed., *The Holy War,* pp. 141-56. Columbus: Ohio State University Press, 1976.

Wenzel, Hermann. *Forschungen in Inneranatolien, I. Aufbau und Formen der Lykaonischen Steppe.* Kiel: n.p., 1935. Schriften des Geographischen Instituts der Universität Kiel, 5:1.

———. *Forschungen in Inneranatolien, II. Die Steppe als Lebensraum.* Kiel: n.p., 1937. Schriften des Geographischen Instituts der Universität Kiel, 7:3.

———. *Sultan-Dagh und Akschehir-Ova.* Kiel: Geographische Institut der Universität, 1932. Schriften des Geographischen Instituts der Universität Kiel, no. 1.

Wittek, Paul. *Das Fürstentum Mentesche.* Istanbul: Universum, 1934. Istanbuler Mitteilungen, no. 2.

———. *The Rise of the Ottoman Empire.* London: Luzac, 1938. Royal Asiatic Society Monographs, 23.

———. "Der Stammbaum der Osmanen." *Der Islam* 14 (1925), pp. 94-100.

———. "Türkentum und Islam, I." *Archiv für Sozial wissenschaft und Sozialpolitik* 59 (1928), pp. 489-525.

———. "Von der byzantinischen zur türkischen Toponymie." *Byzantion* 10 (1935), pp. 11-64.

Woods, John E. *The Aqquyunlu: Clan, Confederation, Empire.* Minneapolis and Chicago: Bibliotheca Islamica, 1976.

Zachariadou, Elizabeth. "Observations on Some Turcica of Pachymeres." *Revue des études byzantines* 36 (1978), pp. 261-67.

Index

CPSIA information can be obtained
at www.ICGtesting.com
Printed in the USA
LVHW010456180723
752701LV00003B/403